THE COMING AMERICAN REVOLUTION

THE MACMILLAN COMPANY
NEW YORK · BOSTON · CHICAGO · DALLAS
ATLANTA · SAN FRANCISCO

MACMILLAN & CO., Limited
LONDON · BOMBAY · CALCUTTA
MELBOURNE

THE MACMILLAN COMPANY
OF CANADA, Limited
TORONTO

THE
COMING AMERICAN
REVOLUTION

BY

GEORGE SOULE

Author of "A Planned Society" and "The Useful Art of Economics"

NEW YORK
THE MACMILLAN COMPANY
1934

SET UP BY BROWN BROTHERS LINOTYPERS
PRINTED IN THE UNITED STATES OF AMERICA
BY THE FERRIS PRINTING COMPANY

TO

ISOBEL WALKER SOULE

THE author gratefully acknowledges permission from *The New Republic* and *Harper's Magazine* to incorporate in this book various passages from articles which originally appeared in their pages.

CONTENTS

PART I

THE NATURE OF REVOLUTION

	PAGE
1. THE PRESENT AS HISTORY	3
2. THE TRIAL PATTERN	4
3. WHAT REVOLUTION IS NOT	11
4. VIOLENCE AND REVOLUTION	13
5. REVOLUTION IS NOT SUDDEN	16
6. THE RÔLE OF THE MOB	19
7. THE PURITAN REVOLUTION	22
8. THE FIRST AMERICAN REVOLUTION	30
9. THE FRENCH REVOLUTION	45
10. THE RUSSIAN REVOLUTION	53
11. WHAT REVOLUTION IS	66

PART II

CHANGES UNDER THE SURFACE

1. MACHINES AND PROCESSES	75
2. PEOPLE AND THEIR OCCUPATIONS	94
3. BUSINESS UNITS AND OWNERS	107
4. THE RIGIDITY OF DEBT	119
5. OTHER INTERNAL RIGIDITIES	131
6. THE RIGIDITIES OF FOREIGN TRADE	136
7. THE SIZE OF THE COMMUNITY	146
8. THE SUM OF THE CHANGES	146

PART III

THE CRISIS OF THE THIRTIES

                                                    PAGE
1. THE EBBING TIDE   153
2. THE HOOVER RESISTANCE   158
3. THE SECOND PHASE OF HOOVER PLANNING   171
4. FERMENTATION   183
5. THE NEW DEAL IS DEALT   203
6. THE NEW DEAL IS PLAYED   221

PART IV

THE COMING REVOLUTION

1. WHAT KIND OF PREDICTION?   265
2. PLANNING FOR PROFITS   267
3. PLANNING FOR THE MASSES   278
4. SOCIALISM, COMMUNISM, OR FASCISM?   283
5. DOES THE PATTERN FIT?   296

   SELECTED BIBLIOGRAPHY   305

   INDEX   309

PART I

THE NATURE OF REVOLUTION

BECAUSE history always deals with the past, most persons, during long periods at least, do not regard the present as a historical process. Change stopped dead in the last paragraph of the textbooks. You can read of wars and revolutions, of heroes and traitors, of outlandish fashions now forgotten, of the rise and fall of men, families, classes, nations, races. But now everything is permanent and sensible at last. Society, which has lived through such a vast turbulence, so much marvelous transformation, has become fixed. Anyone who stirs the brew of human habits is a dangerous enemy. This mood especially characterizes a people which has founded its political ideas on a previous revolution. To win that revolution and preserve it in its infancy, one had to regard it as the achievement of complete felicity, one was obliged to enshrine its leaders and rubricate its doctrines. To think of new change thereafter seems disloyal to the old. Thus the Americans and the French have long been the most conservative of peoples. Doubtless the Russians will soon become so.

But there are periods when people become conscious that deep changes are taking place. Events tumble over one another; a bewildering array of new ideas is advanced; old ideas which have been in disrepute are revived. The bent toward fixity is supplanted by the bent

3

toward adventure. Confusion and uncertainty, a turmoil of hopes and fears floods the land like a spring freshet. This present is a time of conscious history-making. What does it all mean? It would be interesting to know. We watch the stream, fascinated. Our interest is deeper than aloof curiosity. More and more of us are caught up in the current. We must learn how to steer our craft. Now, when the historical process is working so visibly and relentlessly, we need the advice of cartographers who can draw the pattern of the present and extend it into the future.

We are unfortunate because no scholar can do this, at least with any pretense to certainty. Yet every period of change has its guesses and predictions, its charts of unknown waters. These projections seem fantastic, but they are usually founded on some truth. They profoundly influence action. Columbus, when he blundered upon a new continent, expected to find India. But he did rightly believe that the world was round, and that belief sent him on his way. It led to its own logical fulfillment through the partially ignorant but informed action of brave men. If any basic generalizations can be fixed now, they will help us to act, even though the precise goal of the action may be unforeseen. The cartographers of the new society have been busy. It is worth while to compare their designs, and, if we can, to improve their pictures of the unknown into which at last we are consciously making our way.

2. THE TRIAL PATTERN

If we are to arrange events so that we may derive a meaning and direction from them, it is well to have a trial pattern in which to group them. How do they best fit together? If we can see an imaginary picture, showing how they might fit, we can then test it by assembling the known parts. At any rate this will be an interesting way to tell the story of the present. For it is like the way in which historians tell the story of the past. They know, for instance, that the American Revolution, reaching its crisis in 1776, separated the colonies from England and created a new nation. They apply this pattern to the actions of years before and after, and thus fit them together into a connected account. The pattern is known as the American Revolution. We do not yet know exactly what the crisis of our own period will be, or what will be the outcome, or what name future historians will give it. But let us make a bold guess, to serve as a hypothesis. Let us call it a revolution—the coming American Revolution.

Our hint for this name comes from contemporaries themselves. During the last year of the Hoover administration, when the depression reached an all-time low, there was much talk of a coming revolution. Some feared it, a few hoped for it. After Franklin D. Roosevelt's accession to office, the "hundred days" of the special session of Congress, with the activities begun in fulfillment of the legislation it passed, were frequently called a revolution. Those who feared a revolution under Hoover, and those who thought they observed it under Roosevelt, were really talking about quite different things. The first group were thinking about mobs, riots, barricades, confiscations, executions, a triumphant proletariat. The second group were thinking about sudden changes in the way of managing affairs. These are only two of the many kinds of ideas which people associate with revolution. The word itself is so vague, indeed, that it can be of little use to us unless it is more carefully defined. What sort of thing can we have in mind when we ask if a revolutionary process is now working in the United States?

It is obvious now to all, as it was to some at the time, that the kind of revolution expected by many under Hoover was not really imminent. If you wanted to hear discussions of the future revolution in the United States, you had to go to Park Avenue and Wall Street, or to the gatherings of young literary men. Well-fed people anxiously inquired when you thought the revolution was coming. They admitted in a large way that profits must be abolished and that some form of Communism might be desirable. In the next breath they might express doubt whether the Democrats could muster enough votes to defeat Mr. Hoover for reëlection, or they might oppose moderate reforms like unemployment insurance. But searching for actual flesh-and-blood revolutionary proletarians was a thankless task. Most of those who really suffered from the depression were, according to the best-informed reports, simply stricken dumb by it. Like the Republican administration, they were awaiting nothing more drastic than the return of prosperity.

The strange inertia of those who would have benefited most by a revolution and, therefore, it was supposed, would create it, was a subject for frequent remark. When an economist heard that the son of a prominent banker had become a Communist he replied that he would be more impressed if the son of a prominent workman had become a Communist. As a matter of fact, if one could believe the reports of the party membership drives in the

Daily Worker, converts were numbered by dozens or at most hundreds rather than by thousands or hundreds of thousands. There were a few strikes and riots, to be sure, but why were there not more? The unemployed numbered more than ten million.

A man in close touch with workers' movements of all sorts received a telephone call from the chairman of a committee engaged in raising money for unemployment relief. "Our funds are running low," said this gentleman, "and we are having difficulty in collecting more. I think it would help if a good scare were thrown into our contributors. They don't realize how desperate the situation is. Can't we have a bread riot?"

"Well, I'll see what I can do by consulting my Communist friends."

"Oh, that won't do at all," was the reply. "Everybody expects the Communists to riot, with or without cause. What we need is an unmistakable expression of resentment and desperation, a real mass movement."

"In that case, I'm afraid I can't help you. The masses are in a desperate condition all right, but unfortunately there is no sign that they feel the slightest resentment. They just sit at home and blame prohibition."

Later months brought more violence. But even bread riots do not necessarily mean revolution. People may smash windows because they are hungry without wanting a governmental overturn or knowing how to bring it about. As far back as the 1870's, mobs of unemployed men looted shops and burned railroad stations; in fact, they frightened substantial citizens so much that the movement to build armories and recruit state militia was set under way. For the first time in the history of this country, the idea was born that troops might be necessary as a protection for wealth against a propertyless class. But we did not come within hailing distance of a revolution, and the passing of the crisis left scarcely a trace of any organized radical movement.

The most solid recent gains of the revolutionary faith took place among the intellectuals. So marked was the drift of writers toward the left that it was discussed at length in the critical reviews. These persons, who are, with few exceptions, of middle-class origin and training, identified themselves emotionally with the worker. Not, however, with the American worker as he actually is and thinks in the great average, but as he ought to be and ought to think, according to revolutionary theory. The worker, in this sense, is not a concrete or representative person, but an abstraction, a Platonic ideal. The workers might not be conscious of the class struggle, but that made no difference to these intellectuals; the class struggle was there just the same, and the workers were unconscious of it only because their minds had been poisoned by bourgeois ideology. Given the right leadership and education, they would respond. This intellectual zeal sometimes laid itself open to ridicule. An ardent young college instructor, a recent convert, who, so far as is known, never was dependent on the wages of daily labor for his sustenance, yet wrote that an argument by another in behalf of a labor cause could not be sincere because the author of the argument was a "bourgeois intellectual." An ironic letter to a literary column revealed the practical dilemma of these revolutionaries. They had justifiably made up their minds, the letter stated, that capitalists could not be relied upon to change the existing order. The measures proposed by the moderate reformers who did not contemplate a revolution were, therefore, unworthy of support. It was also obvious that labor was not prepared to revolt. Why, then, did not the writers form a party of their own to fight both capital and labor?

It will be recalled that at the beginning of the previous decade there was also an avid interest in revolution and labor. Except among a few intellectuals, however, this interest evaporated with the coming of prosperity and the disappearance of any immediate hope, not merely for a revolution, but even for a moderate movement of protest. Most of the younger intellectuals during the years of prosperity were not interested in social and economic questions at all. They were concerned about Freudian psychology and about exotic literary movements which were as remote from the common man as the abstruse calculations of astronomers. It seems to be a far-cry from Proust and Joyce to the proletariat. One wondered what would happen to the recent enthusiasm if the collapse of capitalism upon which the fashionable revolutionary faith was built did not occur. If business revival took place, would not the literary intellectuals veer off again to some new, non-proletarian sensation? These reflections suggested that the state of mind of the intelligentsia was itself a cyclical phenomenon. In addition to the curves of car-loadings and steel tonnage with which the economists measure the progress of the business cycle, we ought to have curves of the wordage of revolutionary sentiments in print.

It would be easy thus to dismiss the whole subject with a superior smirk, to join the humorous writers of the respectable press in kidding the parlor-pinks. But that is not either a just or a sound conclusion from these observations. The revolt of the intellectuals has a more valid meaning than it would have if one accepted all their phrases and assumptions at face value. Of course they are not proletarians, and cannot become proletarians. The revolution to which they looked forward has not yet occurred. But the mistake may not lie in the intellectuals' sense of the needs of modern society or its main drift. The mistake may reside in their beliefs as to the exact course which revolution is to take, and in their timing of the process. I believe that, in one sense of the word, we are veritably in the midst—though nowhere near the end—of a great social revolution. But a hardboiled look at the facts indicates that the prevalent popular beliefs about what a revolution is and how it comes about were naïve and unscientific.

These popular beliefs—held, apparently, both by the literary radicals and by the Park Avenue conservatives —may be briefly summarized as follows:

1. Capitalism will soon come to an end by a final collapse.
2. A revolution begins and ends in a violent overturn of political government.
3. Nothing is essentially changed, or can be changed, before this overturn; after it a brand-new order is suddenly set up.
4. The revolution is brought about by rioting mobs who overrun the capital and loot and massacre; there are barricades in the streets, and the air is noisy with gunfire.
5. The riots and mobs result from the discontent of an oppressed class, whose misery is so profound that it is driven to revolt. Actual starvation is the usual motive for revolution.

3. WHAT REVOLUTION IS NOT

Every one of these beliefs about revolution is almost completely unfounded. A mental picture of revolution based only on these assumptions is sure to be misleading.

First let us examine the collapse of capitalism. This is a vague term. Precisely what is meant by it? The closing of banks? The inability to get money with which to buy goods? Wholesale bankruptcies and defaults? Vanishing of capital values through the shrinking of trade and the disappearance of profits? Widespread unemployment? Starvation? There is not one of these phenomena which has not occurred in previous depressions. In previous crises banks were closed for days and nobody could get a check cashed. We have had numerous financial panics in which, for a time, no new money at all was invested, and the rates for even collateral loans rose to prohibitive heights. Failures, shrinkage of trade, unemployment—these are the common marks of hard times. Our unsystematic system always fails to work when we have a crisis. Perhaps the difference is one of degree. The system may not be in danger when the curve of economic activity sinks 20 per cent or 30 per cent. But perhaps at, say, a decline of 47 per cent it will pitch over into the abyss. In order to make the argument conclusive, let us imagine the drop of the curve to be 100 per cent. All businesses shut down, all railroads stop running, all banks are closed. All stocks and bonds, all deeds to real estate become worthless. Everybody is unemployed, nobody has a cent of income. What would happen?

What would happen would depend, not wholly on exterior conditions, but also upon what was in people's minds. If they were still imbued with habits of trading, of individualistic competition, of accumulation, they would immediately start to rebuild capitalism. The man with an extra suit of clothes but no food would try to trade what he had for what he lacked. All previous notions of the values of property and labor being swept away, bargaining would start all over again on the basis of absolute necessity. In other words, a new balance of prices would arise. Those who had the most necessary commodities could command the most in exchange for them. Production and employment would start. Accumulation of wealth would begin anew. Vigilance committees would safeguard property against robbers. Soon barter, being too clumsy, would give way to the use of a commonly known and valuable article as a means of exchange —in other words, money. Men of property who were trusted to pay their debts would issue notes. Thus credit would expand. Little by little capitalism would be created all over again. For capitalism is not a complete and rigid system, invented and consciously applied; it is the natural behavior of trading, competitive, acquisitive men, which grows and is elaborated with time.

If, on the other hand, enough energetic leaders had developed ideas and habits of coöperation, of placing the common welfare ahead of the individual, and if the collapse and prospective rebuilding of capitalism involved so much suffering that large bodies of people were willing to follow these socially minded persons, another system might be set up. The stores of material, the factories, and land could be taken over for the community, private ownership of capital could be forbidden, and everybody could be set to work making goods to be distributed more or less equally.

Capitalism *did* collapse, but it did not come to a sudden end. It collapsed in the fall of 1929. It has collapsed many times before—1921, 1893, 1873, for instance. The point is that a collapse of capitalism does not necessarily lead to a revolutionary change. The revolution depends on what is in men's minds and habits. Capitalism fails, in some degree, every time we have a depression. It is rebuilt every time we come out of one. The whole building does not crash down in dust and splinters, to be sure, but parts of the roof give way, walls sag and crumble, foundations rot. Whether we replace them or abandon the old structure and erect a new building depends on something more profound than the chronic unworkability of individualism in production and distribution. Kreugers may commit suicide, railroad companies may go into receivership, banks may close. But that does not mean that new Kreugers, new railroad companies, and new banks may not eventually take their places, and carry on in essentially the same way.

4. VIOLENCE AND REVOLUTION

The second assumption about revolution—that it is a violent overturn of political government—does not accurately describe the sort of social revolution we have in mind.

In the first years of the nineteenth century there came in Great Britain a period of storm and stress universally called the Industrial Revolution. It brought immense changes in methods of production in the kind of articles made, in the way people lived. It was marked by restlessness, sporadic violence, and political agitation. It involved suffering and eventually resulted in enhanced popular welfare. It was not consummated without shifts of political power—though it was by no means a complete social overturn. There is some justification for calling by the name of revolution the alteration in human affairs which accompanied the introduction of steam power machinery, and the factory system. This became eventually a world-wide revolution—(the greatest revolutions usually spread from one country to another). Yet, in England as well as in some other countries, this change went on without any forcible capture of governmental power by a new set of rulers.

Karl Marx, the prophet of Communism, wrote during the latter part of this period. He expected a complete abolition of capitalism and a final victory of the working class to occur within a few years. He predicted that this change would not be accomplished without civil violence —in most countries. But in England, where he lived while the striking changes of the Industrial Revolution were taking place, and where reforms were eventually made without the overturn of the existing structure of government, he thought it barely possible that even the proletarian revolution might be brought off without resort to arms. Thus, not only did the process usually called the Industrial Revolution proceed without the victory of illegal political force, but its predicted culmination in a society ruled by the working class was thought, by the leading advocate of such an overturn, to be conceivable through constitutional political methods. The very fact that he discussed this possibility—even though he believed it unlikely—proves that the essence of an important revolution is not merely violent rebellion. This use of the word is too narrow. The Industrial Revolution has not really ended yet. Its end is not likely to come without more changes of power and more violence than have yet occurred. But violent rebellion is certainly not the whole of it.

Not only can a revolution occur without a sudden seizure of power, but violent seizure of power can occur without a true revolution. According to the newspaper on my desk as I write, a "revolution" has just succeeded in Cuba. President Machado has been driven from office, mobs have been surging through the streets, a hated police executive has been assassinated. But the correspondent goes on to say that the economic situation of Cuba has not been changed. The new government has the selfsame problems to solve which the old one bungled. The social revolution in Cuba is still to come. No new class has gained ascendancy. Politicians who profess to believe in liberal democracy supplanted politicians who believed in, or at least practiced, dictatorship and arbitrary oppression. This may be fortunate, but it does not mark an epoch. Similar seizures of power have occurred almost every year in some Central or South American countries, in Asia, in Europe. Sometimes it is the dictator who throws out the democrat. Sometimes one dictator succeeds another. Often the difference between the victor and the vanquished is not so genuine as it was in Cuba in August, 1933. Tweedledum may expel Tweedledee. This is commonly called "revolution," but really it is only a primitive substitute for an election. A sudden change of government is not properly a revolution just because it is accomplished by violence. It may be a palace revolution, or a coup d'état, or even a successful insurrection, but alone it is not the sort of thing which Karl Marx was talking about, or the sort of thing we mean when we discuss the Industrial Revolution, or the sort of thing to which people refer when they speak of revolution in the United States to-day.

Most of the great revolutions of modern times were, it is true, punctuated by violent seizures of power. This occurred in the Puritan Revolution of Seventeenth Century England, in the American, French and Russian Revolutions. There were even successive seizures of power in each one of these revolutions except ours; in Russia the Tsar was followed by the Provisional Government, by Kerensky, by the Bolsheviks. It would be naïve not to expect some such thing in the course of a social revolution; but it is not the distinguishing mark of the affair. Violence is likely to break out at various stages of the process, and to signalize the victory of the new order. But in any case the violence is but a symptom of a far deeper readjustment.

5. REVOLUTION IS NOT SUDDEN

If it is true that the essence of social revolution is not the forcible seizure of power, it follows that the changes made by revolution are not merely sudden changes accompanying such an overturn. Those who think that nothing can be essentially altered before a coup d'état, and that immediately after it everything will be brand-new, are amusing themselves with fairy tales. It is as if we should be awakened some night by a terrific crash, and on looking out the window to see what had happened, should be informed that capitalism had collapsed. And as if in the morning we should see a brave new socialist world, every tree, factory and house labeled, "made in Russia."

A true revolution takes many years, even generations, in the making. At a given stage of the growth of human habits a certain type of social and political organization exists to give them form. But habits go on changing. New wants are felt; new devices are invented to meet them. The technique of production and exchange grows by a process of collective accretion. Property rights change form. Religions and social ideas develop. Ways of individual and group behavior are altered. New ambitions are felt, new solidarities coalesce. In the course of events the old forms of authority become ill adapted to the existing situation. This fact is recognized at first by only a few. The old traditions are sanctioned by custom. Some persons are direct beneficiaries of the old forms; they do their best to uphold them. The masses remain loyal to these forms by habit; they will break away only with the utmost reluctance and after many miserable experiences. Lyford P. Edwards, who wrote "The Natural History of Revolution," after an attempt to examine scientifically many revolutionary periods, believes that it usually takes at least three generations of intense disillusionment to undermine traditional loyalties. Eventually, however, change of some sort must be made in the forms of authority, to register and organize the new social situation which is actually coming into being. A new sort of government is then set up, usually amid uncertainty and turmoil. This is the critical moment which is popularly called revolution. Actually, however it is not the cause of the change but the result. It does not create the new society out of a void, but creates the form into which the elements of the new society, already in existence, may fall. And when this is done, the revolution is not over. It has to defend itself against reaction. When the revolutionary government is attacked, after it comes into being, there frequently occurs a revolutionary or civil war. Then the new government has to complete and perfect the change, making many blunders and backward steps in its course. Eventually the cycle is completed and a new cycle of change is begun.

The state of affairs in which a given order of society becomes ill adapted to social reality is not the exclusive characteristic of any one kind of government. People sometimes loosely identify oppression with autocracy, or feudalism, or dictatorship, or capitalism. But each of these systems, under the circumstances proper to it, has its reason for being in the greatest feasible welfare and security of the more important parts of the community. It becomes oppressive and due for destruction only when the circumstances have made it inappropriate.

There is no more fallacious trick of speech than that which opposes revolution to evolution, and argues that we can choose as a means of progress the one or the other. Revolution, in a better sense, is merely a name for a single cycle in the long evolutionary process of human society. It represents the turn of the wheel from one form of temporary social stability to another form. Revolution is a part of evolution, and would be impossible without it. Nor can we, socially, evolve without revolving. At least no people has ever yet done so. Advocates of violent revolution sometimes make fun of those who stress the importance of minor adjustments, on the ground that these moderates are basing their faith on an absurdly automatic "inevitability of gradualness." If the proponents of minor and continued changes suppose that by this means they can avoid all danger of sudden social overturn, they deserve the ridicule of the extremists. Nevertheless the extremists are equally ridiculous if they rest their hopes solely on the inevitability of suddenness, without understanding the significance of the alterations which take place between crises. There can be no revolution without evolution, and no evolution without revolution, in its larger sense. Both are inevitable, just because change is inevitable.

To say this is not, of course, to say that the will and the intelligence have no part to play in the process. It is not to raise the old and insoluble (because false) antithesis between free will and determinism. The direction and the nature of change are both greatly influenced by what people do. What man cannot do is to command history to stand still; and as long as he cannot do that, he must be prepared to cope with the pulsations and rhythms of change.

6. THE RÔLE OF THE MOB

If all this is true, bloody riots in the streets cannot and do not bring about the principal alterations which we mean by revolution. Nor can it be the whole truth that revolutionary rioters are brought to their desperate acts mainly by increasing misery, which grows deeper and deeper until the people rebel from very starvation. There are, of course, riots in revolutions. But there are riots when no revolution occurs. And even during revolutionary crises it is not the riots which do the main part of the work. The more dramatic and popular stories of revolutions, like those of Carlyle, Dickens, or even Taine, have misled us on this score. But read Edwards' "Natural History of Revolution," an objective study by a sociologist, or Trotsky's "History of the Russian Revolution," a masterly picture by a participant, and you will see how superficial the popular view is. At the risk of seeming dogmatic, we can lay down certain rough principles in regard to the relationship between mobs and revolutions, which may seem more reasonable when we come to examine specific periods of history.

1. The old régime never is in danger from the popular violence which attacks it from without until it has been weakened from within. Mobs have little part in this internal process.
2. When the people are in their most desperate and miserable condition, they are often least inclined to revolt, for then they are hopeless. They usually are ignorant of the real cause of their miseries, and have no leadership or poor leadership. Only after their position is somewhat improved and they have sensed the possibility of change, do they revolt effectively against oppression and injustice. What touches off insurrection is hope, not lack of it, rising confidence, not bleak suffering.
3. When a shift in power actually occurs, it is usually begun, not with a seizure of power by outsiders, but with reforms by insiders. These reforms are the cracks in the dam which invite the flood. They are caused, not by sudden violence, but by the irresistible pressure of events.
4. Those newcomers who seize authority at the end of a successful revolution are not chance members of an insensate mob, but highly intelligent men with solid organi-

zations back of them, men confident of their own ideas and abilities.

5. Revolutionary mobs themselves, when effective, are well organized and know precisely what they are doing. There is of course "spontaneous" fervor behind them, but no revolution can be brought about by passion alone. The transfer of power itself is often quick and comparatively painless, because the old régime has been so weakened and has lost so much of its self-confidence that it vanishes almost without resistance. Its most trusted supporters abandon it. The new rulers step into a void. The function of the "mob" is not to create disturbance but to occupy the foci of power.

6. The most serious revolutionary violence—and there often is a great deal of it—occurs *after* the new régime has seized power, and must defend itself against reaction in civil or foreign war. Even the domestic "terror" usually occurs some time after the seizure of power itself. This is not mob violence, but organized and purposeful violence.

Far more important in the total revolutionary process than blind rebellion of the mob is the shift of ideas, traditions, loyalties, which precedes the uprising. This shift is led by intellectuals. They publicize the injustices and corruption of the old régime, ridicule its infirmities, attack the system of thought which gives it its sanctions. They cause the old régime to lose its confidence, its aura of sanctity. Their imaginations foreshadow a new and better system. They lead the reforms which are forerunners of greater change. They supply the slogans for popular revolt. This activity by intellectuals usually covers a long period of time. It is confused and sporadic. Most of those engaged in it are not, consciously, revolutionary plotters. Many profess loyalty to the old régime and implore it to live up to its better possibilities, even to the very last moment. The intellectuals are divided among themselves. But the ferment of ideas to which they give voice in a revolutionary period is the necessary accompaniment of change, and one of its most certain harbingers. For when a régime is stable and immune against overturn, the artists, writers and philosophers, whose sensitive antennæ feel most truly whatever is in the surrounding atmosphere, are occupied in celebrating, adorning and justifying the existing order.

There have been learned but futile debates as to whether the ideas of intellectuals are the cause or merely the sign of revolution. They are both. Disembodied ideas, with no counterpart in the social life of the time, get nowhere. Mental formulæ which do not seem to work out in life as it is lived are ignored. On the other hand, no social ferment can progress without mental formulations appropriate to it. The intellectuals always exhibit violent disagreements with one another. They are unable to foresee in detail what is going to happen and why and when. When only a few vagrants among them are disaffected, drastic change is still far off. But when those who are disaffected rapidly gain influence, when the fashion is to be critical of what exists, when those creative spirits who do try to accommodate themselves to the ruling order become stale, artificial, and shallow, the slow fire of revolution is almost certainly burning.

7. THE PURITAN REVOLUTION

If a social revolution is not the sudden collapse of an old régime, the mere violent overturn of political government, changing everything at once, and brought about by rioting mobs who are driven to insurrection at the deepest point in the curve of their misery and oppression, what is it? How does it come about? Can we recognize its approach, and predict, however crudely, its successive stages? Perhaps a brief examination of former revolutions will help us to see the pattern in its broadest outlines.

The first important revolution in modern history was that which is usually called the Puritan Revolution in England. From its beginning to its end, it occupied the greater part of the seventeenth century, and included the beheading of Charles I in 1649, the Commonwealth and dictatorship of Cromwell, the restoration, and the final end of absolutism by the overthrow of James II in 1688. It was a period of immense agitation and unrest, punctuated by governmental changes and civil war. The old way of writing the history of this period is to tell it as a struggle of religious faith, of war and rebellion, of dynasties and democracy, of Roundhead against Cavalier. Later historians have seen that these are only the surface aspect of what was going on. The conflict of religious ideas was indeed important, but it was important not so much because of the abstract significance of these ideas as because they represented the mechanism of attack and defense between economic and social classes who were struggling for power. Since religion had been of overwhelming authority in its sway over men's minds and action, it was natural for the mental side of the struggle to be cast at first in a religious mold. To establish the legitimacy of one's aspirations in the material world, it was then necessary to provide religious sanctions for them. The process of doing this was not conscious hypoc-

risy; far from it. The religious slogans were repeated
with real fervor; countless men and women were ready
to die for them. If it had not been for the translation of
the Bible into English and the welter of religious dogmas
which arose therefrom, the so-called Protestant revolt
might for a time have been repressed. Nevertheless the
affair was far more than a struggle between the freedom
of the individual conscience and the authoritarian church.
These doctrines symbolized the struggle between a rising
economic class on one side and the alliance of church,
king and hereditary nobility on the other. It signalized
the sprouting of capitalism out of the muck of a decaying
feudalism.

Two groups had been growing more powerful for many
years before the open conflict. These were the merchants
and the landed gentry, which together formed the basis
of what was eventually to become the capitalistic middle
class. As discovery in the fifteenth and sixteenth centuries opened up lands across the Atlantic, and sea-borne
traffic began to accumulate profits for the merchants and
traders, these occupations grew rapidly both in numbers
and prestige. England was one of the first countries to
show signs of becoming a "nation of shopkeepers." Partly
because of her geographical position, and partly because
of her relative youth as a powerful nation, this development took place more rapidly there than in France and
Spain, where the conquest of the new world was exploited
more for the benefit of the ruling dynasties and the
church.

The profits of trade in England almost immediately
gave rise to merchant capitalism in a form which has
characterized capitalism ever since—the chartered com-

pany, or corporation, which sets out on profit-making enterprise with the combined capital contributed by share-
holders. The London Company, created in 1606 to settle
and exploit Virginia, raised the money necessary to
finance its adventure not mainly from earls and bishops
but from other classes as well; it was advertised from the
pulpit, and the appeal for funds combined the claims of
religion, patriotism and profit. The business boom which
accompanied the expansion to the new world enriched
the merchants and enlarged their class.

Meanwhile the landed gentry not only sought profit by
colonial investment, but broadened their base at home.
During the sixteenth century a change in a purely economic condition gave rise to far-reaching social consequences. The woolen industry expanded. This made
sheep-growing profitable. There had been, before this,
trading for profit in grain and other crops, but the feudal
era had been one in which agricultural products were used
mainly in sustaining the life of the locality. The great
estates, owned by the crown, the church or the princes,
were largely self-contained economies, worked originally
by serfs bound to the land. Most of these serfs had been
freed and had become tenants. There was also a class of
free yeomen, owning their own farms and possessing common lands, largely used for pasture. But when it became possible to sell wool for profit, there arose a land-
hunger for sheep pastures. The common lands were
enclosed by the powerful, and many small farmers were
deprived of their use. Landlords changed grain fields into
pastures and drove the tenants off. Vast estates of monas-
teries were seized by secular owners.

The dispossessed peasants and the ruined yeomen became one of the most miserable and oppressed classes in history. At times they seethed with discontent. But it is worth noting that they did not then successfully revolt in their own interest, nor did they constitute the impetus of the coming revolution. An oppressed class can suffer the most outrageous treatment without upsetting the settled order of society, unless that class is already close to power, and destined at the time for a rise. The backbone of the Puritan rebellion was formed by the landed gentry who were made richer and more aggressive by the enclosures, the eviction of peasants and the seizure of church lands. The Cromwells, Hampdens and Pyms all belonged to this class.

In one sense, however, the unfortunate victims of oppression did contribute, through no will of their own, to the fattening of those who were to win the revolution. Seeking a means to eat, they became artisans and laborers who worked both for the expanding number of employers at home and enlisted as emigrants under the companies which needed settlers abroad. The rank and file of the English emigrants to America was largely composed of those who had been dispossessed from English agriculture. And, eventually, those economic exiles who did not seek their daily bread across the water composed a large part of the armies which fought in England. Without these laborers, colonists and soldiers, the Cromwells, Hampdens and Pyms would have had neither the material nor the human resources to overthrow the Stuarts and despoil the church.

There was a long period in which the landlords and merchant classes who were eventually to win the revolution gathered strength before there was any overt rebellion at all, or any sign of danger to the monarchy. The old order was gradually decaying, the new one gradually growing. This was the stage of revolution which is usually called "evolution." But it was perhaps the most substantial part of the revolution; when the new order finally cracked the shell of the old and emerged as the dominant political power, it was merely registering and formalizing the change which had already, in large part, taken place.

The Puritan Revolution, aside from its clothing of religious words, is now recognized as a struggle of the rising middle classes—with some allies from the princes—to acquire lands, to free themselves from the tithes, fees, laws and jurisdiction of the clergy so that they could accumulate capital, trade freely and exploit the chances for profit in the newly born capitalist world, and, for the same purpose, to be rid of crown monopolies and manifold governmental restrictions on business. It eventually established the sovereignty of Parliament as a representative—not of the whole people by any means—but of those who had the franchise, mainly the merchants and landed gentry.

This was not a quick, simple and logical process. In summarizing it as we have done here, cross currents and complications have been overlooked which volumes are required to detail. One observation, however, cannot be overlooked, in addition to the conclusion that the revolution was the slow rise of the middle class to dominance. The split caused by the conflict of power began very near the top of society. Gradually it extended toward the bottom. A faction which had been in the opposition to established authority and had won its battle, was in turn forced to defend itself against another more popular and hitherto less powerful faction, one which had been allied with it.

This process was marked by frequent reversals. As the power of various groups and classes was laid on the scales, the pointer wavered back and forth, though always tending somewhat more to the left. It finally came to rest at the mark which indicated the true balance of power among the classes. This mark was not so far to the left as the pointer had for a time swung—it largely excluded the interests of the dispossessed artisans and peasants. Let us see briefly how the pointer wavered.

Henry VIII himself set the fashion for despoiling the church and limiting its authority by subjecting it to the state. A quarrel between the mighty thus began the breach in the old order.

Under Elizabeth there were mutterings of discontent. During the reign of James I the House of Commons in plain language declared the rights of the merchants and landed gentry. Thus the struggle was already on. (In the King James version of the Bible the monarch himself authorized a translation which gave the literate direct access to divine revelation and thus added to the ferment of religious discussion and the weakening of clerical authority.)

Charles I introduced a reaction back to personal government, defying Parliament. This was ended by the Civil War and the execution of Charles in 1649. As a result of this war, the dominance of Parliament—a Protestant but not yet dissenting Parliament—was established.

Soon, however, Parliament had a rebellion on its hands. Cromwell and his forces purged it of the more conservative members, and with the authority of the remaining "rump," established a dictatorship which aimed at democracy two hundred years ahead of its time.

Then another faction, still further to the left, raised its head—the "levellers"—partisans of the more plebeian elements in the community, the propertyless artisans and peasants. But they were not yet ready even for a temporary rise to power; Cromwell ruthlessly suppressed them.

After Cromwell's death, the pointer swung back to the right with the restoration of the Stuarts. James II tried to pretend that nothing had happened. But the historic time for absolute rule had passed. In 1688 he was overthrown and the supremacy of Parliament permanently established. The House of Lords was packed with peers from the newly dominant forces, so that it could not veto the change. The revolution of the middle classes was accomplished; the pointer came to rest—for a time.

Another comment must be made to complete the picture. During all these years, the agitation of the intellectuals in reformulating ideas, in attacking the old order, was incessant. There was a confused and discordant outcry of protesting voices—of pamphlets, books, sermons, speeches. At first it was mainly religious; later it assumed a more political cast. Historians of thought have pointed out how the assertion of the claims of the individual conscience was the logical foundation of the material liberty sought by merchants and capitalists to trade and accumulate individual wealth. They have shown how various strains in Protestantism—for instance, the doctrine of predestination in Calvinism—seemed to establish divine sanction for the gains and power of individuals who succeeded as business men, how they aided in the struggle against the Catholic disapproval of interest on capital—or, as it was called, usury. Corruption, moral and material, of the Church, was exposed and ridiculed. The supposedly loose moral standards of the restoration and its monarch gave fervor to the revolt against them. Many of the charges were doubtless false, as revolutionary charges frequently are, but they satisfied the emotional needs of the partisans.

In the works of John Locke, the revolution of 1688 found its philosophical sanction. His doctrines of the separation of powers, of natural rights—including the right of property—were just what the newly dominant class needed to establish its legitimacy. It was from Locke that the American revolutionists later derived many of their ideas.

This intellectual ferment, this manifold and apparently spontaneous attack on established ways of thinking and on established authorities is never absent in a revolutionary period. It is at once a portent and a weapon of the rising classes.

8. THE FIRST AMERICAN REVOLUTION

From England the course of revolution took its way across the Atlantic; the American Revolution was largely a continuation and completion, on this side of the water, of the revolution which had occurred a century earlier in the mother country.[1] It was complicated by the tendency to nationalism which was a natural outcome of the growth of capitalism. This aspect of it is what has survived mainly in our tradition; schoolbooks speak of it as

[1] For the sources of this chapter, I am deeply indebted to Charles and Mary Beard's "The Rise of American Civilization."

the attainment of liberty from England, as the birth of a new nation. It was that, of course, but in a deeper aspect it was a social revolution, the rebellion of a new middle class, both against the dominance of the Crown and against the now older middle class of England which controlled the government and attempted to exploit the new land for its own benefit. No two revolutions are exactly alike; differences in time and geography introduce many variations in them. Nevertheless we can see in the pattern of the American Revolution many of the same designs as in the English.

The settlement of North America was largely the work of capitalistic trading companies. We have mentioned the London Company which in 1606 was chartered to exploit Virginia. The Dutch West India Company opened up New York—then New Netherlands. Even the Pilgrims who, when looking for Virginia, landed first on Cape Cod and then at Plymouth, sailed under a corporate charter. The Massachusetts Bay Company, which settled Boston, rescued and annexed them. Georgia, though founded as an asylum for poor debtors, was settled under a charter from the king to trustees, like the other companies.

Almost from the beginning there arose a struggle between the actual settlers and those at home who expected to profit from their work and their hardships. The effort of the London Company in Virginia, for instance, to retain ownership of the land was soon abandoned; tenants would not cultivate and develop it profitably so long as they did not regard it as their own. A landowning class was built up on this side of the water—composed of officers with their great estates and of small freeholders.

But the land had to be paid for, and paying was not easy. The London Company sent over governor after governor, in the attempt to deal with the stiff-necked colonists, and many of them adopted severe measures, without much lasting success. In the course of these struggles the House of Burgesses was set up—the first approach to a democratic assembly. In 1624 the charter of the company was annulled and the colony, by order of James I, became a royal province. But the trouble did not cease.

In Carolina a similar contest went on. The colonial assembly began to issue fiat money to relieve the debtors of quit-rents. The proprietors—Stuart loyalists—vetoed the measure, partly under the influence of British merchants. The assembly thereupon deposed the governor— a genuinely revolutionary act. The owners in despair then sold out to the Crown, but the struggle between American debtors and British creditors went on under the royal governors. In New Jersey and Pennsylvania also—even in Pennsylvania under the well-intentioned Quaker, William Penn—there raged bitter conflicts over quit-rents and inflation of the currency at the expense of the creditors. This was a debtor country at the very beginning, and it remained so for centuries, since after the land was bought many kinds of manufactures had to be imported. The necessity to pay debt had its repercussions on every other issue—such as taxation, currency policy, trade restrictions. It also had its personal effect even upon the richest strata of American society, upon men who became leaders of the Revolution. On the very eve of that conflict southern gentlemen especially were deeply in debt to London merchants.

The landowners, both large and small, thus were struggling to rise, and in the beginning found their way opposed by the propertied interests of the old country, just as these in turn were rising against king and church. Before long other capitalist occupations added their strength to the movement. Navigation, commerce and fishing grew, and industry sprang up—textiles, wood-working, iron. These new trades met all kinds of restrictive legislation and regulation installed at the behest of British merchants and manufacturers who looked upon this country as a market and did not relish competition from their customers. The struggle to develop native industry played a large part in the revolt of the northern colonies, especially of New England.

Here the land question had been of less urgency; the Pilgrims soon bought out the English stockholders in the company which financed them, while in the case of the Massachusetts Bay Company, the owners themselves came to this country. They came with the intention of setting up the same kind of manorial feudalism, with its balance between large estates and a class of small freeholders, which was coming into ascendancy in England. The nature of the soil and climate, however, was unfavorable to the crops which were suited to large-scale agriculture in the South—tobacco and cotton—and so in the North the small freeholder and the small farm came to predominate. The energies of the newly born capitalist class quickly turned to shipping, trading and manufacture. The constant push to the westward and the settlement of new regions also strengthened the small freehold farmers.

At first the restrictive English laws helped the colonial capitalists; the navigation acts, the first of which was passed in 1651, limited the commerce of English subjects to English ships, and since the vessels of the colonists flew the English flag, they profited by the legislation. The trade laws were more irksome, however; they were intended to force the colonists to trade exclusively with England, and thus fell afoul of a good deal of profitable commerce with France, Spain, Holland and their dependencies. A direct conflict of interest arose over the long series of laws which forbade manufacture in the colonies. Woolen goods in 1699 formed one-third of England's exports, when a law was passed against the fabrication of wool in America. Other restrictions were directed against hat factories and iron and steel foundries.

In 1690 there was set up in London the Board of Trade and Economy to supervise colonial affairs, and this was very active in handling the grievances of English merchants and manufacturers who were being injured, or thought they were being injured, by the business activities of the colonists. When colonial legislatures passed acts in pursuance of local purposes which were distasteful to the economic powers in England, the King in Council, acting as an appellate tribunal, could nullify them. There was, of course, continual conflict between the legislatures and the royal governors about such things as taxation, patronage, and trade. The governor was, in effect, the colonial manager sent out by English capitalism to safeguard its interests; he not only did that but in many cases, like distant commercial agents from time immemorial, took advantage of his position to line his pockets, assert privileges, collect perquisites, and sustain a machine of supporters and hangers-on.

In the North as well as in the South the colonial debtors were in conflict with the English creditors. Here the issue was not so much the payment for land, even at the beginning, but rather payment for English manufactures and repayment of English credits. The colonists complained, in effect: "Whatever we have to buy, you force us to buy from you. You compel us to buy many necessities which we could make for ourselves, because you forbid us to manufacture them. We are thus in continual debt to you. All our money is drained out of the country; we have not enough to supply our needs or develop our industrial life. Therefore we must print our own money, and we must relieve debtors in other ways, as by cancellation of debts and bankruptcy proceedings." The English responded with laws safeguarding creditors. As in our own day, the debtors favored inflation, the creditors frowned upon it. In 1751 a law was passed forbidding the issuance of paper money in New England. Later it was extended to the other colonies.

It is easy to see why the rising middle class in America came into collision with the newly risen middle class in the home country. One could therefore jump to the conclusion that the colonists early foresaw the necessity of independence, that they gained nothing, and could gain nothing, until they established their own political power by a revolutionary war. This is the sort of conclusion present-day advocates of violent revolution—as well as opponents of it—frequently express concerning the oppressed classes of our own day. But this conclusion is directly contrary to the facts. Nothing could be more important in the study of the nature of revolution than to recognize its falsity.

During the century or more of struggle which preceded the Revolutionary War, most of the colonists had no thought of complete independence, or of fighting a war against England to get it. Almost every complaint was accompanied by a protestation of loyalty to the sovereign. A movement agitating for independence would have been outcast, until the very end of the conflict. It was too foreign to the customary and accepted molds of thought. Rather, the colonists acted to gain their ends within the established order, to justify their purposes by reference to principles accepted by those who were their oppressors. Occasionally they behaved as if they were independent—but without acknowledging, even to themselves, that they were doing so. Even at the very end, the prevailing doctrine was that they were rebelling against an unreasonable monarch rather than against English rule conceived as a democracy. The revolution of English democracy itself against absolutism furnished their precedent and justification. (In fact, of course, Parliament played fully as large a rôle as did George III and his predecessors in supporting the measures which drove the colonists to revolt.)

And during this century of conflict within the forms of legitimacy, the colonists actually succeeded in their main purposes. Colonial capitalism grew and established itself in trade and manufacture. Debtors did escape much of their burden. Many laws were successfully flouted. Colonial legislatures grew and extended their powers. During the war with France, merchants traded with the enemy. Occasionally, unpopular laws were repealed or restrictive measures withdrawn. Toward the latter end of the long period of discord, boycotts by the colonists forced abandonment of hated measures—as in the case of the stamp tax.

John Hancock and others who eventually led the rebellion, and who were denounced by the British as "smugglers" because they had evaded the trade and tariff laws, were representatives of a large class of highly respected citizens, whose disobedience of English decrees had become not only a matter of course, but also a symbol of patriotic spirit. To evade these laws was even less a crime in popular opinion than to buy liquor during the recent period of the Eighteenth Amendment. On the eve of the Revolution, the colonial assemblies had almost everything their own way and the royal governors were in despair.

The main objects of the Revolution were in fact gained during the long period of evolution which preceded the open warfare. They were gained under the ægis of constitutionality. The American middle class actually rose and actually established its economic power before 1776. As in the revolution of England, the rise of the new rulers of society was well under way before the overturn of government, and their rise was not a matter of sudden change, but of gradual piece-by-piece encroachment against opposition. There was, of course, an immense and long-continued disturbance, a great deal of oppression, and of resistance to oppression. There was a multitude of illegal acts. But the revolution had in essence succeeded before an open crisis led to war.

In another way the colonists had consolidated their power before the break with the mother country. They had learned how to conduct war and had begun to coöperate with each other. They had learned this in the process of dealing with more immediately hostile forces, before their way was clear to take on the last opponent. Benjamin Franklin drew a plan of union for a colonial conference to prepare for the war with the French and their Indian allies; this conference was held in Albany in 1754. In the course of the French and Indian War the foundations were laid for the political and military conduct of campaigns on a continental scale.

Why, then, if the colonial middle class had already established itself and was ready to defend its position, did the Revolutionary War occur? Here, again, is an important principle concerning the nature of revolutions. Organized violence was precipitated by an effort of the former master class to regain a status which it had in fact lost. It looked upon this status as its legitimate right. It did not hesitate to use force in order to establish this legal right, and expected that a show of firmness would quickly suppress resistance. Its fatal mistake was the failure to recognize the revolution which had already occurred. The colonists now had their own ideas of right, their own status to protect, their own power with which to protect it. The show of force appeared to them in the guise of aggression, and they refused to retreat before it. They were at the end confronted with a sharp alternative—organized warfare or *loss of substantial gains already established*. This is the kind of crisis in which a revolutionary choice is consciously made. Under circumstances like these arises the main violence of a revolution. Violence is almost never resorted to by revolutionists in order to *make* the revolution, but rather in order to *defend* it against reaction, once it is made. Let us see how this logic worked out in our own revolution.

The final prelude to the Declaration of Independence was crowded with events, but lasted only a few years. During the conflict with France, there had occurred the usual war prosperity, accompanied by the usual budgetary inflation. At the end of the war the British public debt amounted to the figure, large for those times, of $140,-000,000. Deflation and depression followed, as it invariably does after war and inflation. There arose, as the night succeeds the day, an intensified competition for markets, an embittered struggle between debtors and creditors, and a furious controversy about taxation. The British government—Parliament no less than George III, and the Whig members no less than the Tories—authorized measures taken in the interest of British merchants, creditors and taxpayers. Grenville attempted to enforce the existing laws. He forbade the colonists to engage in fur trading in the Crown lands just won from the French. A blow was struck at the West Indian trade of New England. The list of imports which the Americans must send exclusively to England was enlarged. It was at this time that Parliament forbade the issuance of paper money by all colonial legislatures. The Stamp Act was passed to help pay for the war which, the British argued, had been fought largely in behalf of the colonists themselves.

Apparently the British had not the slightest anticipation of the furious opposition these measures would arouse. This sort of thing had been enacted or decreed for a hundred years or so, and was regarded as perfectly just and legitimate. But, weighing down on the depression and deflation on the western shores of the Atlantic, the action seemed intolerable. The result was the forming of secret revolutionary organizations like the Sons of

Liberty, the rousing of mobs which rioted and burned, the Stamp Act Congress of 1765 in New York, and a colonial boycott of British goods. Startled, the government gave way and repealed the Stamp Act. As usual, after a surrender of this sort, the colonists expressed loyalty to the king. But the appeasement was short-lived.

In 1767 new duties were imposed, the proceeds from which were to be devoted to the expenses of the colonies. Surely nothing could be more reasonable! But so inflamed had the crisis become that even slight irritations produced disproportionate outcries. Every controversy became a matter of principle. The home government, in order to make sure that the duties would be collected, specified that this function was to be performed by officers of the Crown. But so general was the "smuggling" that search and seizure had to be resorted to. And the hated "writs of assistance" had to be evoked. The effort to get revenue came to resemble less the ordinary peaceful process of tax collection than the levies of an invading army upon a hostile people.

There followed the usual array of inflammatory incidents. In the "Boston Massacre," red-coats fired on a crowd of unruly boys. The Tea Act of 1773, creating a monopoly of retail trade for the great East India Company, threatened the profits of local merchants—and the Boston Tea Party followed, in which young whites in Indian war paint and feathers threw the tea from recently arrived ships into the harbor. The British government, its authority challenged in dozens of ways, believed that now or never was the time to be firm. It replied by sealing the Port of Boston, revoking its charter, forbidding town meetings except when permitted by the governor, ordering that trials for murder be held in England, and quartering troops on the population. The reaction was now being supported by frank war measures to suppress the "rebels." Lexington and Concord showed that the rebels were not thus to be intimidated. It was not long before the Continental Congresses, arising on the basis of the Committees of Correspondence which had been active in the work of uniting the leaders of the several colonies in their common cause, passed from the stage of petitions setting forth grievances while declaring loyalty, to the stage of declaring independence and raising an army to defend it.

As in the case of the English Revolution, we cannot overlook the part played by the intellectuals. For many years, agitation had aroused and helped to unite the colonists. Preachers thundered from the pulpit, not only about theological matters but about political, for their prestige in the early days of protestantism was tremendous, and, in the beginning, secular matters were as truly their domain as were religious ones. Another profession soon arose, however, to share their influence—the law. Lawyers were numerous among the educated classes, and were elected in large numbers to the colonial assemblies, where their debates advanced the self-consciousness of the rising colonial merchants and freeholders, and their ingenuity went far to establish the political gains of the new capitalists. Finally, the press joined the growing agitation, and was most potent of all. Literacy was general before the revolution; its result was accurately foreseen by an early governor of Virginia, who wrote in 1671: "I thank God we have no free schools nor printing; and I hope we shall not have these hundred years. For learning has brought disobedience and heresy and sects into the world; and printing has divulged them and libels against the government. God keep us from both." No colony was without its journal, some of them had far-flung circulations and many were exchanged with other editors. For a time they were carried free by the post. The more daring of these papers began, about the middle of the eighteenth century, to ridicule the agents of the Crown, to fulminate against injustices. The climax of this agitation was Thomas Paine's eloquent pamphlet, "Common Sense," which, appearing in 1776, called for complete independence, and had a sale of 100,000 copies. The colonial agitators of course found plenty of material for the set of revolutionary principles which they were establishing in the literature of the English revolution itself.

Another important element in the Revolutionary population cannot be left out of account. Though the forefront of the movement was composed of landholders, merchants, manufacturers, the rank and file consisted of small farmers, poor debtors, artisans, laborers. American society was far from democratic. It is true that the Pilgrims who settled Plymouth were, in the main, lowly people accustomed to sustain themselves with the work of their own hands. But this was almost the only colonial group who did not try to reproduce on this continent the class stratification which existed in England. In the North, the Winthrops, Endicotts and Eatons came from the same source as the Cromwells, Hampdens and Pyms—they were country gentlemen, opposed to the absolutism of church and king, it is true, but representatives of a dominant owning class. In the South, the large estate owners constituted the apex of society from the beginning. Beneath the big landowners were the yeomen, or small farmers. And at the bottom were the laborers, many of whom had started as indentured servants, who could become free only by working and paying for their freedom. It is true that the flexible conditions and almost unlimited land in the new country made it easier to rise from one class to another, but the class distinctions themselves remained.

John Locke himself, the great apostle of the middle-class revolution, drew a constitution for the proprietors of Carolina, according to which the owners were to reserve one-fifth of the land for themselves, another large fraction was to be held by the aristocracy and tilled by serfs, and the remainder sold to small freeholders. He wished to avoid a "numerous democracy"—he distrusted the lower classes. This scheme did not wholly work; white serfdom was not adapted to the new country. But black slavery was. And in almost no colony did the qualified electorate include the lower classes. The turbulent assemblies were elected by those who had property qualifications, which were not completely abolished until after the Revolution. When a Boston bricklayer was made Justice of the Peace in 1759, he was attacked because of his social origin, and defended himself not by arguing that bricklayers ought to be allowed to hold office, but by denying that he was a bricklayer.

The plight of the laborers and artisans was often desperate; like their counterparts in the English revolution they underwent far more hardships and were more bitterly oppressed than those who formed the spearhead of the revolution itself. They composed the mobs who

looted and burned in the cities, disturbing the very merchants in whose behalf the agitation against England was
being carried on. They worked in the shops and mills,
they fought in Washington's army. They drew little distinction between the cause of the propertied middle class
and their own. Yet the mere fact that they were oppressed
did not mean that they revolted in their own behalf and
won supremacy. This was really the revolution of a class
above them, already numerous and powerful.

When the Constitutional Convention met, it was composed of the very same sort of persons who in England
had composed the Parliament against whose enactments
the colonists had rebelled, and these persons were just
as careful to protect their own property and safeguard
the debts owed to them as their English counterparts had
been. Of course there was Jefferson as well as Adams;
the delegates were by no means of one mind, and the internal struggle was not easily compromised. Under the
preceding Confederation, the pointer had swung further
to the left, but the balance of social forces was not such
as to keep it there; the "people" did not yet form a
stable and homogeneous class capable of governing a state.
Somewhat later, when reverberations of the French Revolution were heard on this side of the Atlantic, and Thomas
Paine, irreconcilable radical, wrote his "Rights of Man,"
there was another upsurge of a purer democracy, but it
could not establish itself. The doctrines of liberty were
securely appropriated, during the formative period of
the young republic, by the American propertied classes.
The point to be noted is not simply that the first American Revolution was a conquest of power by the middle
class, but, what is even more important in a study of the

nature of revolutions, that the class which established its power did not do so because it was the most deeply oppressed but rather because it was already well on the way to supremacy. Economic and political circumstances had smoothed the way for its march to power.

9. THE FRENCH REVOLUTION

From America the middle-class revolution traveled back across the Atlantic Ocean to France, a nation in which the absolute supremacy of the king, supported by the nobility and the church, had been longer and more firmly established than in England. Nevertheless the traders, manufacturers and capitalists had been gaining economic status for years. The growth of trade, the raising of crops for sale and the spread of commercial manufacture were undermining feudalism and local self-containment there as inevitably as elsewhere. These forces took longer to burst through the crust of custom, but when they did so, they followed a course which, though exhibiting surface differences from the English and American Revolutions, had recognizably similar basic characteristics and finally settled down into essentially the same pattern.

Oppression of the peasants and of the rising business community had been going on for more than a century, without consequences other than occasional outbreaks, easily put down. Neither side was, on the whole, acutely conscious of it. The government of Louis IX, called Saint Louis, was actually far worse than that of Louis XVI. The Bourbon monarchy in the seventeenth century began to create discontent by the expulsion of the Huguenots, by costly wars, by the expensive court, by heavy and inequitable taxation. But it was long before unrest began to identify the monarchy and feudalism as the enemy. Meanwhile the oppressed classes were gaining strength. Tradesmen and professional men were becoming richer. By 1789 the French peasants had risen far above their lowest state of misery; they were, on the whole, better off than peasants in other parts of Europe who had no thought or hope of change.

After many years of unrest, repression, agitation, and polemic, the monarchy and the nobility, corrupt and inefficient as they were, began to be undermined by divisions and by loss of faith in themselves. They cracked from within. They failed to defend their traditions and their privileges with vigor and faith. They seemed to sense the approach of death. There were plots against the throne among the upper circles; it has long been suspected that many of the pamphlets attacking the extravagance and character of Marie Antoinette were paid for by other members of the ruling family. Many nobles had become infected by the writings of Voltaire, Rousseau and the Encyclopædists; these enemies of the old order had been popular in fashionable salons. When Louis was informed of the fall of the Bastille—which never would have fallen if it had been competently defended by loyal troops—and was told that this was not a rebellion but a revolution, he believed it. He was a student of English history, and is thought to have inclined to the conclusion that Charles I would have kept his head if he had been willing to make concessions.

These states of mind were not mere imaginary vagaries which in themselves affected the course of history; rather they were indications of the true condition of affairs.

How did it happen that Louis summoned the Estates General which made the beginning of the change in the established order? There was an immediate crisis which profoundly upset the nation. Finances were in a bad way. The wars with England had been ruinously expensive. A business depression ensued. Something had to be done. The business community and financial structure of French life had become so important that their distress was the distress of the state itself. Necker, the Swiss financier, was called in by Louis to help straighten things out. Like financiers from that day to this, he placed great emphasis on business confidence. What could restore confidence and enlist support for the necessary financial reforms? Only a representative assembly, and one which should represent, not merely the nobility and the church, but the Third Estate as well—that is, the business men. Necker advised calling it, and Louis acted on the advice. Historical development had made it necessary for this class to be called to power, and it was called by the absolutist himself. Revolution began by reform from above—reform necessitated by the powerlessness of the old régime, under the circumstances, to deal with the situation.

And so for a time the Revolution proceeded by the alternate granting of concessions from above and the demand for more concessions from below. There were, of course, even at the beginning, mob outbreaks and demonstrations, but these were not the forces that wore away the power of the king. Confidence and popular sentiment gathered about the rising classes because they in fact had the keys of the situation in their hands. The king could not effectively defend his royal prerogatives because there was no point in doing so, and many of those upon whom he would have had to depend for support knew it. Power evaporated in his region and was condensed and precipitated the realm of the bourgeoisie.

For a long time after the Revolution began the king still lived, and lip-service was paid to his authority. For a long time there was little violence. Changes were accomplished within the forms of law; Louis himself consented to a Constitution. The hitherto disfranchised classes gained actually all the power they wanted by these means; they held the royal family in Paris as a hostage, as a symbol of their authority. Not until after the attempted escape, not until the people had become convinced that the revolution, now accomplished, was endangered by plots of the royal family which would lead to the destruction of the new government through foreign invasion, did the reign of terror come and revolutionary violence break out. Here as elsewhere, the revolutionary rise to power proceeded at first as a result of irrepressible social forces and by a series of steps rather than by bloody rebellion. And violence came to defend the revolution rather than to make it.

The progress of the revolution was, of course, far from an orderly and systematic process. The moderates who first came to power succumbed to the arguments of those who wished to restore prosperity and national solvency by inflating the currency. The issuance of assignats, which were supposed to be secured by the value of the lands taken over by the state, at first brought a needed stimulation to business. Mindful of previous experiments with inflation—that under John Law, for instance—the assembly at first strictly limited the amount of the issues.

But, in view of the success which attended them, the temptation to make further and continually larger issues in order to fill the gap between expenses and revenues, caused by the failure to collect sufficient taxes, was too great to be resisted. The result was that which various nations have experienced since that time, when huge governmental expenditures are financed by an indefinitely expansible medium of exchange. Prices soared. Hoarding of commodities began. A speculative class arose and made enormous paper profits. Though money existed in larger quantities than ever, there was a shortage of it in relation to prices. This caused an irrepressible demand for more, thus driving upward the spiral of inflation. Bread became scarce and high in price, relative to the incomes of the populace. The bread riots came after the revolution was well under way. They were caused, not by the oppression and heartlessness of the old régime, not by heavy taxation, but by the difficulties and mistakes of the moderate revolutionists who first assumed power. The inflation crisis, occurring as an incident of the revolution itself, reënforced the rising tide of hostility against the King and brought power to the Terrorists. They not only put to death members of the nobility but shopkeepers and others whom in present-day language we should call inflation profiteers.

One faction after another drove its predecessor out of the government. Moderates gave way to the hundred percenters. For a time it looked as if the Paris populace itself would rule. But though the proletariat had been far more bitterly oppressed before the revolution began than persons of more substantial means, it was not yet close enough to a secure economic status—it was not essential enough in the scheme of affairs—so that it could remain on top. The pointer of the social scales for a time wavered far to the left, in the desperate effort of the people to get food, stamp out profiteering, and exterminate their old enemies, but it eventually came to rest in a state where capitalism was free to grow.

But it was neither the more ignorant of the French peasants nor the riff-raff of the cities who, at the apex of the revolutionary curve, overthrew the monarchy, extirpated the nobility, and renounced the Church. Picturesque descriptions of the "sans-cullotes," together with the ritualistic language of the revolutionaries themselves, are deceptive on this score.

The Jacobins who used the break in the walls to carry through the change to its bitter end were a compactly organized minority who for a time controlled both the national assembly and most of the local governments. They partly led and partly coerced the more inert majority. But they were not sans-culottes in the literal sense; they had excellent breeches, and many pairs of them. A scholarly study by Clarence Crane Brinton—"The Jacobins"—shows that dues of the Jacobin clubs would be roughly equivalent to fifty to eighty dollars a year at present. People belonged to them who would now belong to golf clubs. Such membership records as are available reveal that about 60 per cent of the members were bourgeois (many of these being upper middle-class and professional men); 25 to 30 per cent were working class, and the small remainder peasants. Jacobins were almost never poor enough to be exempt from taxes; on the contrary, their tax payments were higher than those of the average male citizens by 50 per cent or more. They bought many of the confiscated estates. They were not hot-headed youths, but hot-headed men with an average age of over 40, and for the most part residents of their towns rather than drifters. Though in the later stages of their power they became slightly more proletarian in color, these substantial citizens, representative not of failure but of success, many of them the best educated in the nation, were those who beheaded the king, carried on the Reign of Terror, closed the churches, and established the Republican institutions and the "natural liberties" which, in spite of subsequent reactions, have survived in France.

It is significant, when we consider what part is played by the ferment of ideas in a revolution, that the Jacobin clubs were the lineal descendants of the literary societies which had been formed to discuss the theories of Rousseau. A symptom of approaching change which has not been absent in any revolutionary era is the disaffection of the intellectuals. This begins early in the process; it grows as unrest develops; eventually the more influential writers and teachers have shifted their loyalties from the existing order, if not to a new class, at least to a new range of social ideas. In a normally functioning régime it is the job of the intellectuals to pass on the sanctioned tradition, to enrich, embroider, and develop them, to celebrate existing faith. They connect the future with the past. But when their leaders begin to feel ill at ease, to strike out in new directions, it is a sign that the old order is moribund. The classic example is, of course, that of the French Encyclopædists. Few of these men were avowed revolutionaries; nearly all professed loyalty to the monarchy. Nevertheless, they brought in the era of "enlightenment," the new ideas of liberty and equality on which the revolutionaries fed.

During the crises of the revolution itself, the press was active as never before in history. Pamphlets streamed from the printing establishments and were circulated by the hundred thousand. Journals sprang up over night. What before had been dignified literary and philosophical argument now became, in the heat of the times, conscious propaganda. Some of the most disreputable of this propaganda—though by no means the least effective —was bought and paid for by interested parties, and contained deliberate and monstrous lies. But the best of it, like the best speeches and writings of the English and American revolutionaries, exemplifies the finest political literature ever created.

An observation germane to our present purpose is that in none of these revolutions, in which the ideas of intellectuals played such a large part, was the more important revolutionary literature of a conspiratorial nature. It was not vigorously controlled by a central agency and disciplined by a single purpose. The flood of thought could not have been dammed by suppression of a single source. The revolutionary writers, though a certain broad tendency is discernible in them, disagreed with one another on current issues. It was the manifold activity and freedom of thought rather than the imposition of a single logical will, which did the work of breaking down the old sanctions, exposing and ridiculing the personifications of old centers of power, building the new concepts of government. Vigorous controversy among agitators is a sign, not of weakness among the forces destined to build a new society, but of burgeoning life.

10. THE RUSSIAN REVOLUTION

The history of the nineteenth century in Europe—yes, even in the United States—might be strung on the thread of revolution. Or perhaps we should say on two revolutionary threads. One was the continuance of the rise of the business owning class, as it wore away the power of feudalism, of kings and nobles and church. This rise, punctuated by the reaction against it by the old order, was the principal driving force in the building of new national states such as Germany and Italy, in the revolutionary movements of 1848 in Europe, and of the Civil War of 1860 in the United States (which was a contest between the manufacturing capitalists and freeholding farmers of the North on one side, and the feudalistic slave-holding landed aristocracy of the South on the other). The other thread was the rise of the growing working class in the face of the new owning classes—a proletariat whose forerunners were already distinguishable in English and American Revolutions, and which for a time had exercised some power in the French Revolution through the organization of the Paris factions. This new class became stronger, more distinct and more conscious of its separate aims all through the century; it was a discernible force everywhere in Europe in the crisis of 1848; it was especially prominent in the Chartist Movement in England, and in the political reforms which accompanied the industrial revolution there. It came to the surface again in France for a brief period after the war of 1870, in the Paris Commune. The politics of the latter part of the nineteenth century and the first decade of the twentieth were deeply influenced by the growth of socialist and labor movements in every important European country.

The times were looked upon by many as a prelude to a new kind of revolution which would signalize the rise of the working classes to power and would replace bourgeois capitalism with socialism. This development was interrupted by the World War, a war which temporarily shattered socialist movements as badly as it did capitalism. Near the end of it, however, occurred the great revolution of our own times, the first successful seizure of power by the working class. We cannot end this brief examination of the nature of revolution without a few comments on the overturn in Russia. Perhaps the false impressions now prevalent regarding revolution are based on a misunderstanding of what happened in Russia in 1917 as much as on anything else.

Russia's revolution was a paradox; it seemed like a biological sport. Why did a proletarian revolution occur first of all in one of the most industrially backward nations of the world, a nation which had not yet had its liberal revolution against an absolute Tsar, the hereditary feudalism of a noble class and the state church? Least of all did the orthodox followers of Karl Marx expect the immediate rise of a socialist state here, because they believed Marx had taught that capitalism must come to its full flower and exhaust its possibilities before it could be replaced by a higher order. Certain doctrinaire socialist scholars, like Kautsky, rejected the Bolshevist revolution after it had occurred, predicted its failure and argued that it was contrary to the logic of history. The Russian Revolution stands as a warning against a too rigid interpretation of historical processes, against the danger of mechanical prediction on the basis of historical parallels.

Nevertheless this leap-frog performance, like other biological sports, has a reasonable explanation, once we understand the real nature of what occurred. And, when properly understood as it can now be understood in retrospect, it does confirm most of the conclusions concerning the nature of revolution, drawn from other revolutionary periods.

In its first stages, the Russian Revolution obviously ran true to form. There had been for centuries sporadic agrarian uprisings. The serfs had been freed in 1860, and since then the peasants had been struggling for more land and higher status. Moderate land reforms had been introduced, and by the outbreak of the War, the peasants, while still far from satisfied, had risen considerably. And, although capitalist industry had not developed nearly as much as in western Europe, nevertheless there was a liberal and professional class in the cities which looked forward to a constitutional democratic régime. Revolutionary literature, much of it disguised on account of the censorship, had been published and read for decades. You can find in Dostoevsky—himself a writer of reactionary tendency—glimpses of numerous revolutionary sects and factions which seem even more confused and incapable of action than those which exist now in the United States. In 1905, after the disastrous war with Japan, there occurred a popular insurrection, ruthlessly put down by loyal troops, but resulting in the establishment of the Duma as a national assembly with a quasi-constitutional status, and in other reforms. There developed within and outside Russia that general lack of confidence in its ruling classes and system of government, that rise of new elements toward power, which is customarily a prelude to revolution.

The World War intensified these tendencies. At first all elements were swept off their feet in a tide of patriotism. But soon there came terrible defeats. The dynasty was revealed as hopelessly incompetent. The Tsar, the Tsarina and their circle were preys to superstition; they substituted petty favoritism for statesmanlike government. The Tsarina, with her German connections, was suspected of betraying the national cause. Divisions and factions arose within the court circles themselves. Palace revolutions were discussed. In an effort to furnish the materials for a better conduct of hostilities and to introduce some order into affairs, liberal and industrial circles formed the Union of Cities and the Zemstvos Union; the coöperatives gained status. These extra-governmental institutions took over large economic functions.

When at length the populace rose early in 1917 —almost without leadership on the part of the professional revolutionaries—the old régime vanished with scarcely a struggle, and because of its own weakness. The soldiers in St. Petersburg (now Leningrad) and Moscow would not put down the strikes, attempt seriously to clear the streets, or defend the public buildings, but went over to the people. The Commandant reported that he had no reliable troops. Even the police succumbed. The Tsar, who had left to visit the front, could not get back to the capital; the railway-men would not take his train through. In a last-minute attempt to keep some prestige for the old régime, the Tsar was persuaded by his advisers to abdicate in favor of another member of the royal family, but it was too late. People simply would not obey any tsar. The truth was once more exemplified that no régime, however absolute its formal power, however fortified it may be with guns and bayonets, can rule indefinitely if it cannot retain the confidence of the rank and file.

Thus the actual destruction of the old régime occurred in the usual way—a long period of discontent and agitation, the granting of reform from above, the rise of new classes, the loss of confidence in the rulers, their cracking from within, and, in a crisis, the eventual disappearance of their power, almost without violence. At this stage there was nothing new or unexpected to students of history, about the course of the revolution.

It was natural to suppose also that the inheritors of power would be moderates who would establish a constitutional democracy under which agrarian reform would take place by distributing the feudal estates, and industrial capitalism would proceed develop in the usual way as it had done in England, France, the United States and Germany. The Constitutional Democrats, the party of business men, whose leader, Miliukoff, was for a time Premier, supposed this to be true, and so did the dominant opinion in the rest of the world. The Allies immediately proceeded to recognize the Provisional government, and to count upon it for more effective continuation of the war. Even the leaders of the victorious workers, soldiers and peasants, as represented in the Leningrad soviet, many of whom were theoretically socialists of one brand or another, acted on this formula. They handed power over to the Provisional government during the crisis, though retaining the right of veto or criticism. At some future time there would be a Constituent Assembly elected by popular vote, and after the new Constitution was adopted and the new government was set up, the socialists would fight out their differences with the capitalists by the constitutional methods familiar in the Western countries. Anything like a socialist revolution was still thought to be a long way off. The immediate struggles of the soviet and its leaders were for reforms like the eight-hour working day.

Even the most conventionally minded of the revolutionists should have been prepared by history for a temporary swing of the pointer to the left. No social revolution has occurred in such a neat and orderly fashion that the moderates who first assume power retain it without at least some challenge from more dissatisfied and more extreme elements. The accession, first of the fiery Kerensky, and then even of some faction like the Bolsheviks, might have been foreseen as probable by anyone familiar with former revolutions. What was less to be expected was that the pointer would not swing back again, that the center of gravity of the social and economic forces could remain where the Bolsheviks pushed it.

Failure to understand that the extreme program really did embody a stable balance of forces, that it was not merely a conspiratorial coup d'état, put over on the majority by force and deceit, for years stood in the way of the acceptance of the Bolshevik revolution by world opinion, even by some socialist opinion, though the socialists were not blinded by prejudice in favor of capitalism. Yet the truth is that the October revolution was a more genuine popular movement than the February one, and that the government which it overthrew vanished just as surely through its own incompetence and lack of basis in popular consent as did that of the Tsar. There was little bloodshed or violence when the Soviets assumed power, under Bolshevik leadership. How and why this happened has been explained in masterly fashion by Trotsky in his "History of the Russian Revolution"—the first objective and extended account of a revolution ever written by one of its chief participants, a participant who was at the same time a scholar well acquainted with history and with revolutionary theory.

The capitalist classes did not form a really dominant group in Russia at the time of the Revolution. Their growth had been in part hampered by the old régime. The most important element of their weakness was the absence of as numerous a body of small business men as existed in countries of older capitalist development like the United States, France or Great Britain. When capitalism began to grow in earlier decades, the typical capitalist was the small trader, the small manufacturer. Large corporations and the dominance of finance-capital did not arrive until a later stage; it rose on top of an already numerous petty-bourgeoisie. But in Russia, when modern industrialism began, the world had already reached the stage of the large enterprise and of great accumulations of finance capital. Capital for establishment of new business in Russia came largely, not from domestic accumulations, but from abroad. It came in large blocks, and it established concerns comparatively big at the start. Thus Russia leapt over the period of the dominant small enterprise, of its gradual growth or combination into larger units. Trotsky quotes some interesting figures showing how much larger the average manufacturing establishment was in Russia before the Revolution than in Western industrial nations. There were probably just as big

single establishments in these countries, but there were
also many more small ones, which held down the average.
Thus the Russian capitalists were not so numerous relative to the population as in other nations.

A second weakness at this particular time was that the
Russian business men were in reality economic and political agents of the foreign capital invested in their enterprises. The millions of workers and peasants in the army,
as well as those still at home in the factories and fields,
were heartily sick, not merely of the inefficient conduct
of the War, but of war itself. After the overthrow of the
Tsar, they wanted to get away from the mud, the vermin
and the horror of the front. They wanted above all to get
home and enjoy the fruits of their victory over the old
régime. Peasants were in a hurry to claim the land which
they understood would now at last be theirs. But the
Provisional government was so closely tied to the Allies
by economic bonds that its first purpose was not to bring
the internal reforms wanted by the people but to continue
and win the war. To the rank and file, nothing seemed to
be changed by the Revolution. The people had thrown
out the Tsar—but to what end? The only tangible benefits they received were promises of elections at some
future time. The Bolsheviks told the people that if they
wanted peace and land they would have to take these
things for themselves by throwing out the Provisional
government. And it was not long before the people acted
on their advice.

The Provisional government could not even regiment
economic life for the more efficient prosecution of the
War with any real effect. Lenin, in a pamphlet before
the October uprising, challenged the government to

take the necessary action by a more rigorous organization of banking and industry in the public interest. But
this was the sort of thing which business men are reluctant to do, even in time of crisis. What cracked under
the pressure of war was not simply an autocratic political
machine, but the industrial and economic machine which
is the prime necessity for the conduct of modern hostilities. Primitive as it was, it could not support millions
of men in the field, at least without a much higher degree
of efficiency than was possible under the existing stage of
capitalism. To the cries for peace and land was added an
insistent cry for bread.

The chance of liberal capitalism in Russia thus came
too late; history had swept beyond it. In order to have
established itself so firmly that it could have survived
this crisis it would have had to begin earlier when it could
grow in smaller and more numerous units, it would have
had to rest more on native capital, it would have had to
become strong enough to supply the war against an
efficient capitalist enemy.

Opposed to the weakness of the capitalist class, and its
inability to cope with existing situations, was the relative
strength of the industrial proletariat. The industrial
working class was not, to be sure, numerous relative to
the peasant population. But it was numerous relative to
the business community, and it was highly concentrated
in industrial centers, where large establishments pre-
dominated. The lateness of capitalist growth made it
necessary that a large proletariat should come into being
at the very beginning. Without its consent, no revolutionary government could prosecute the war or even live.

Added to this concentration of potential power was a

consciousness of actual power. Trotsky shows the rising curve of strikes before the Revolution of 1905, followed by a period of proletarian quiescence, and then again a rising curve of strikes from 1914 to 1917. Though he does not say so, this is evidence similar to that found in other countries, showing that modern war, with its insistent demand for production, strengthens the economic position of the workers and makes it easier for them to win advances. It virtually eliminates unemployment and creates a labor shortage. At the same time it creates budgetary and speculative inflation. Rising prices, which follow the urgent demand for more products, a demand financed through credit expansion, supply the impetus to strike. The cost of living soars faster than wages, short-ages of goods are painfully evident on every hand. The worker sees that there is no one to take his place and that his bargaining power is increased; he is driven by his hardship to act; and at the same time he is stung by the contrast of the overabundance in the hands of war profiteers. A habit of collective action had strengthened the Russian proletariat before the Revolution. Even the overthrow of the old régime in February was accomplished by the St. Petersburg and Moscow masses. And the only real power exercised by the Provisional government itself was exercised by grace of the Soviets which directly represented the people. The Bolshevik cry of "All power to the Soviets" was merely a slogan urging the assemblies representative of the masses—assemblies which were not a Bolshevik invention but which already existed—to take over formally and wield the power which they actually held, instead of delegating it to others.

Add to these facts the fact of overwhelming importance

—that the armies were now popular armies and that in them the workers and peasants themselves were armed— and you have the final reason why no class or group to which the workers and peasants were not content to remain in subservience could hold power in the flux of revolution.

It was of course possible to conceive that the peasants, being in an overwhelming numerical majority, would finally dominate the revolution. This might turn out to be an agrarian revolution simply, rather than a socialist one. But at the time of the establishment of the Soviet government there was no visible split between the peasants and the industrial workers; they both sought the same ends. The Bolsheviks were the only leaders who expressed the immediate wants of the peasants—peace and land. And after the peace of Brest-Litovsk was signed and the peasants had gone home, they were scattered and occupied with consolidating their victory. The subsequent Civil War, in defense of the revolution against the reactionaries with their foreign allies, threatened the gains of the peasants as obviously as those of the workers, and kept them united.

It was not until after the victorious Bolshevik government began vigorously to create a socialist economy that any real split occurred between the city and country. Even then the peasants were divided among themselves and were in no position to control the direction of affairs, although for a time the sabotage by the expropriated kulaks gravely endangered the food supply of the new state. But, on the whole, the success of the proletarian revolution in Russia was no historical vagary; the pointer of power finally came to rest in accordance with the real balance of social forces; the industrial proletariat was, in the circumstances, the strongest of the various classes which might have ruled. It had already risen to potential dominance before it seized the state. It seized the state not by a bloody rebellion against a master class, but simply by exercising power which it already had gained. The really serious violence, as in other revolutions, came at a later stage. The "terror" followed the attempted assassination of Lenin and the fear that internal enemies could not be conciliated. The Civil War was fought in defense of rule already achieved.

The Russian Revolution also furnished a prime example of the important part played by intellectuals in the development of social forces. The ferment of revolutionary theory, of agitation and of literature, which began in Russia years before the final overturn and burst forth with feverish intensity at the end is too well known to require comment. But the part played by the Bolshevik leaders themselves, and especially by Lenin, is particularly striking. When he arrived in Russia from exile, after the first stage of the Revolutionary crisis, few revolutionaries themselves were conscious of the direction in which affairs were drifting; only a few were not amazed by the extreme character of his proposals. A popular conception of Lenin is that of a demagogue, who by skillful agitation led the crowd and assumed personal power. But the facts, as revealed in his speeches and the accounts of contemporaries, are quite otherwise. His incisive analysis of fundamentals, his keen and logical foresight, his inflexible will, his mastery of economic and social theory, enabled him to see what was happening more clearly than others, and he gave to events the form which history had prepared for them. He first by sheer logic converted his own party—at that time a small minority in the Soviets—to what he saw was the required line of action. He then galvanized it into a group intellectually prepared to assume leadership. The party, by virtue of its correct strategy, gained the confidence of the Soviets and eventually of the masses in the factories and the army. When the time for the revolutionary act arrived, the movement was well prepared, and the "mob" had most capable leaders, who knew exactly what their objectives were and exactly how they were to be achieved. After the accession of power there began the long and difficult task of defending the revolution and building, by successive stages, a socialist state.

Though the Russian Revolution thus fundamentally follows the revolutionary pattern, in spite of its surface variations from previous revolutions, it cannot be regarded as an exact precedent for future proletarian revolutions in other countries with different geographical situations, in different stages of economic development, and with different balances of social and economic power. Just as crude historical parallels blinded many to the actual situation which gave rise to the successful Bolshevik revolution in Russia, so this historical parallel is misleading if applied literally to countries like Germany, England or the United States. Future revolutions in these countries will doubtless comply in a broad sense with the basic requirements of revolutionary development, but they will not occur in exactly the same way and in the same succession of stages as the Russian. One great difference— to name only one—is that in these other countries capitalist industrialism has had a much longer and fuller course of growth. Marx did not anticipate that the first proletarian state would have to build most of its industry *after* it took power; he thought that capitalism would first exhaust all its possibilities and that the workers would take over a highly developed industrial plant. Lenin at first believed that, on account of the primitive stage of Russian industry, the Russian Revolution itself could not survive unless it was soon followed by a world revolution. These mistakes even of the greatest minds warn us that revolutionists of to-day, whose attention is concentrated on what happened in Russia, are likely to make mistakes about what will happen elsewhere. While history repeats itself, it does not repeat by rote. Like the composer of a great symphony, it returns to old themes, but they are always interwoven anew, in different keys and tempos. It is necessary to make a re-application of the underlying principles if we are to have the slightest chance of apprehending, even vaguely and uncertainly, what is likely to happen in the United States.

II. WHAT REVOLUTION IS

We began by noting what a social revolution is not; now we may be able to outline more definitely what it is. What is the pattern that we may apply, as a test, to present events?

First, there must be basic changes in ways of conducting affairs—changes often brought by new mechanical or economic techniques. Such changes in past revolutions have been the spread of wool cultivation and the discovery of new markets for wool fabrics, the development of manufacture for sale and of foreign trade, the growth of capitalist enterprise, the settlement of new areas, the introduction of mechanical power and the factory system, and—as in Russia—the rapid beginning of large-scale factory production. Such changes arise, as it were, spontaneously. They are not planned; their results are not foreseen. They occur within the framework of the old order. But their consequences are momentous.

The main consequence is a new alignment of social classes. Some classes grow numerically; others shrink. Some classes achieve greater power and status, others lose power. Sharper class divisions arise; some benefit at the expense of others. Oppression comes, not as conscious and recognized cruelty or injustice, but as a natural result of a class division in which those who suffer misery protest or rebel against specific evils, while those who hold power under the old régime strive to retain their prerogatives and their status against "disturbing elements." At the beginning neither oppressors nor oppressed understand the true situation. The mere existence of oppression is no sign that a revolutionary period is approaching a crisis in which the oppressed will seize power. The ruling classes will for a long time sternly and effectively suppress any sporadic discontent. The masses will for a long time remain loyal to the old régime. When the oppressed are in their most miserable and hopeless situation they are not likely to put up a strong opposition. Not until a class has achieved potential power and has gained confidence in itself does it recognize a class enemy or does its activity assume a revolutionary aspect. Arrival at this stage usually takes many decades. During the development of the class struggle there are cycles of tension—periods of outbreak followed by periods of quiescence—and there are occasional foretastes of the future crisis as the friction caused by the rise of the new classes within the narrow bounds of an outworn system throws off heat.

As the unseen and unrecognized revolution takes form, the world of ideas ferments. Evils of the old order are attacked. Its religious or philosophical sanctions are undermined, its values are transformed. Satire exposes the absurdity of the position of the old rulers, it reveals the corruption of individuals. This intellectual activity gradually destroys both the popular loyalty to the old régime and, to a large extent, its faith in itself. The intellectuals also throw out new dogmas, which in time, and to influential groups of people, come to seem more genuine and reliable than the old. In devious and confused ways this intellectual ferment makes people conscious of what is going on. It creates the mental apparatus which is necessary as a tool to bring a new society out of the old.

As the revolutionary period progresses, divisions appear within the old régime, it begins to weaken and disintegrate. Reforms are made which strengthen the rising classes without satisfying them. Programs of reform are often supported by moderates as an alternative to revolution and are attacked by revolutionists because they are believed to offer false hope to the oppressed. But in reality reforms are often a prelude to revolution. It makes little difference whether these reforms are voluntarily granted from above or wrested by demands from below. It makes little difference in the end whether the old régime is compliant or stiff-necked. Charles and Nicholas were convinced absolutists who would not yield an inch; Louis was a reasonable man who consciously gave way to pressure: all three were swept away. It is possible to conceive of a revolution occurring without violence if one can imagine that the old régime will sur-render, without resistance, to a sufficiently complete change, but it is impossible to conceive of avoiding per-manently the revolutionary change itself, when history is ripe for it, by temporizing and by compromise. A reform sufficient to avoid revolution would be a reform equivalent to revolution.

At length there arrives a revolutionary crisis which can be recognized by two main characteristics. First, the old ruling classes are unable, because of their own weakness under the circumstances, to carry on successfully. They face a problem insoluble by the old social order. They fail in a miserable and spectacular way, thus losing con-fidence in themselves—except for a few die-hards—and forfeiting the loyalty of the people. Second, the rising classes have already achieved substantial power, which they need only to consolidate and exercise in order to supersede the old rulers. Both elements are necessary for the revolutionary mixture—failure of an old régime bodes nothing unless there is a new one to take its place, while nobody can throw out rulers who are successful in their governing. When a rising and confident class confronts a failing and weak one in a crisis, the formal shift in power takes place—often without violence, or with very little of it.

Those leaders who first exercise power in a revolution-ary crisis are usually moderates, who want to make a minimum of change. They are almost inevitably chal-lenged by others who want to make more drastic changes. There is a shift, or a series of shifts, from right to left and sometimes back again, in the group holding suprem-acy until something like a stable balance of social forces is reached. It is rare indeed that those who begin a revolution end it; but without their preparatory work, the final leaders could not rise. For the people themselves frequently do not understand at the beginning how far it is necessary to go. The hopes raised by the moderates must first be tested; it is necessary for the moderates to fail in order that the more extreme may obtain popular support.

Revolutionary violence of importance occurs when those who have been thrust from power strive to regain it. It comes in defense of a revolution which has been made, or virtually made. Reigns of terror, civil war, revolutionary war, are conducted not to bring about revolution, but to preserve it. It is therefore silly to discuss whether or not one is "in favor" of a violent revolution. If a revolution is destined to succeed, it will usually succeed at the beginning with less violence than is exercised every year in a country like the United States in suppressing strikers and lynching Negroes. It will succeed because many people want it, and are ready to obey the new authorities. After it has taken place, the choice as to whether there will be violence will rest with the enemies of the revolution.

Sometimes revolutionary violence ends temporarily in the victory of reaction. The old régime may assume power again for a while. Or, if the extremists do not represent a stable balance of social forces, they may lose permanently. Revolutionary periods are often punctuated by victories of the reactionaries. This is especially true when the rising classes have not yet gained sufficient status to keep power, or when the immediate crisis confronting the old régime disappears for a time. But no reactionary régime can hold power indefinitely when basic conditions have made it necessary that great social changes take place. The civil war and the restoration in England did not prevent the final victory of Parliament. Nor did the long succession of changes in the French régime, from Napoleon on, prevent the rise of liberal capitalism in France. One should never mistake the eddies of history for the main current.

PART II

CHANGES UNDER THE SURFACE

1. MACHINES AND PROCESSES

ANYONE looking for the source of the kind of changes in ways of living and working in the United States that might lead to revolution must begin with technology. It is from new machines, new sources and applications of power, new techniques of the organization of human effort, that disturbances to customary institutions most obviously stem.

Just as our recent ancestors were amazed by Watts' steam engine, by the spinning jenny and the cotton gin, by the locomotive and the side-wheel steamer, so we are fascinated by belt-conveyors, mechanical stokers, high-tension electric transmission, or innumerable instances of special-purpose automatic machinery such as that described by the Department of Labor for making electric lamp bulbs, a "highspeed unit lamp-assembly machine in five sections, for (1) stem making, (2) stem inserting, (3) filament mounting, (4) sealing the mount in the bulb and exhausting the air, and (5) attaching the base." As a result of this and similar processes, the productivity of labor in the bulb industry increased by four and one-third times between 1920 and 1931. An encyclopædia could be filled with the known changes in the technique of production in recent years, while many of the important inventions are unknown, being closely guarded trade secrets.

The early inventions, which gave rise to the factory system and caused the turbulence of the period known historically as the industrial revolution, are not different in general character from those which have come into use ever since. In reality the industrial revolution has been a continual process, the end of which has not yet arrived. But that does not mean that its social and political accompaniments will continue to follow the same outlines as in the nineteenth century, that there are no new or more serious problems to worry about. Invention is a cumulative process. In the beginning it depended on the genius of a few individuals; its impingement on the general life was sporadic. Now it is institutionalized; its scientific basis is continually being broadened and perfected; research into new ways of doing things is regularly carried on; new processes are developed not by occasional ingenuity but by the contributions of many persons, who refine and improve in detail after detail. Whereas, in the beginning, factory centers were islands in a sea of a more ancient and stable culture, now we are all directly dependent on the industrial complex and the trade and finance which has flourished about it, while technology itself has extended its régime to agriculture, fishing and forestry. The same *kind* of thing may happen now as a result of the introduction of new processes as happened in 1834, but it happens faster, with greater force, and with wider incidence on the whole of our life.

Various attempts have been made to measure the overall growth of production in the United States. The results of these attempts are called "indexes of physical production" as distinguished from measurements which take money values into consideration. According to one of the best of these indexes, the Day-Persons, total pro-

duction has grown at an average rate of 3.7 per cent a
year between 1870 and 1930; according to another, the
Warren-Pearson, it has grown at an average rate of 3.8
per cent. Meanwhile the population has grown at the
slower average rate of 1.9 per cent. If these indexes do
not overestimate the growth of production, they indicate
that our industrial plant has been creating more and
more material riches per capita of the population, at a
rate which, compounded as it is, means a very rapid
change. This growth of activity extends throughout
most occupations—it is found in agriculture, mining, construction and trade as well as in manufacture. Only in
fisheries and forestry has the growth of production been
smaller than the growth of population. Growth has been
most rapid in mining and manufacture.

As Arthur F. Burns points out in his recent study,
"Production Trends in the United States Since 1870," [1]
these indexes are by no means accurate measurements of
physical production; in most respects they underestimate
rather than overestimate the growth of the "utilities"
received by the consumers of the goods produced. The
nature of production changes continually: old industries
decline and new ones spring up, and the long-term indexes
give greater weight to the old industries which are declining, less to the new which are expanding. They seldom
include service industries, which have grown more rapidly
than those engaged in making and distributing material
goods. They do not take adequate account of secondary
production—that is, the refinement and fabrication of
primary products like steel and coal, or of by-products.
Nor do they take into consideration improvements in

[1] National Bureau of Economic Research.

quality—for instance the improvement in automobiles which has increased the mileage, riding comfort and economy to be expected from 1,000 cars to-day as compared with 1,000 cars in 1917. In the index of production, 1,000 automobiles in one year count just as heavily as 1,000 fifteen years later.

Recent commentators of the Technocratic school have observed that these production indexes show a declining percentage of increase as time goes on. By application of mathematical analysis they have predicted that the curve would gradually turn over and production would begin to decrease. But the underlying data are not a sufficiently good support for the mathematical methods applied to them. They are not the kind of exact data derived from laboratory measurements, with which the engineering analysts are familiar. Dr. Burns shows quite clearly that there is no sufficient proof that the rate of increase in total production has been slackening; indeed there is a distinct possibility that it has been accelerated, on the average. (This statement, of course, overlooks the admitted decrease during the recent and former depressions, and applies merely to the average rate over a considerable period of years.)

So far, we have been considering total production only, and in relation to the total population. The crude observation to be drawn from the facts is that here we have an industrial system basically conditioned by a rapid increase in production. In some way the population must receive and use every year more goods than it received and used the year before, and it must keep this up year after year for a long period, if the system is to operate with any degree of smoothness. If at any time and for any reason, the population cannot absorb more goods, you have a collision between the irresistible pressure of a growing technical capacity and the barrier of stationary or falling consumption. The collision is made sharper as the rate of potential production increases and as the rate of population growth falls. In no previous social system of history was there so rapid an increase in goods produced; at most times, the increase was so slow as not to be taken into account at all.

When we take into consideration the production of separate industrial groups, and the working forces engaged in them rather than the whole population, the figures are even more impressive. In manufacturing, it is estimated by Professor Frederick C. Mills that the output per wage-earner grew 43 per cent between 1919 and 1929, or at the rate of 3.8 per cent a year. This compares with a growth of 1.7 per cent a year for the fifteen-year period 1899-1914—in other words, the rate of productivity more than doubled in manufacture. The rate of growth of output per wage-earner is considerably faster than the rate of growth of output per inhabitant. Striking increases occurred also in railways, mining, agriculture and other occupations. And even higher rates of growth are obtained when output is compared, not with number of wage-earners, but with man-hours worked. It is the output per man-hour that is the true measure of productive efficiency. What all this means, in general, is that fewer men, working fewer hours, could every year turn out more goods for every inhabitant. There are many indications that in the period immediately preceding the depression this increase in productive efficiency went on at a more rapid rate than before and during the War.

During the depression, beginning in 1929, according to Professor Mills' estimates, the rate of production per man-hour jumped even more rapidly. This most recent leap is not to be taken as a sign that such a pace of advance will continue. It customarily requires fewer man-hours to produce a given quantity of goods during a depression because the less efficient factories and machines are stopped and the less efficient workers are laid off. Nevertheless the level of efficiency attained during the depression is not likely to be lost. As Dr. Mills says, "Records of manufacturing production reveal no decline of consequence in the productivity of labor at any time within the last forty years. The increase has been somewhat irregular, but continuous. The gains brought by adversity are maintained in subsequent periods." The Mills index shows that, on the average, one man who, by working one hour, could produce 100 units of output in 1927, could produce 120 units in 1932. A growth of one-fifth in five years! The chances are that in 1937 he will not be able to produce 144 articles, but he will certainly not produce less than 120.

Rapid as the growth of total production and of output per man-hour has been, it is nowhere near so rapid as it might have been. Nobody can say definitely how much more rapid, but informed opinion is almost unanimous that the potential limit is high. A committee formed by President Butler of Columbia University sent a detailed questionnaire to leading engineers and executives in numerous industries, to sound them out on this point. To the question, "What per cent of increase could be effected by the industry reported if equipment and management were brought up to the level of the best current standard?" the estimate of the engineers was 90.1 per cent and of the executives 84.4 per cent. The same question concerning "all industries" rather than the "industry reported" brought an estimate by the engineers of 77.6 per cent. This means that without any new inventions, but simply by the universal application of the best-known existing methods, industry could increase the products made in every year by three-quarters. And this increase would be counted, not from the depression level of total output, but from the highest preceding one.

Of course invention will not stop short. Before the less progressive establishments have adopted the best methods now known, the more progressive ones will have adopted new and better methods. The pyramiding of invention will create a possibility of growth in production much greater than that now estimated on the basis of present technical knowledge.

Just as important as the growth in total production is the shifting character of production. All industries do not grow continuously and at the same rate. An industry customarily grows very fast at the beginning, reaches a peak, and then begins to decline. It is at length jostled out of its place by a new industry competing with its products. Whaling disappeared before petroleum. Iron rails gave place to steel, carriages and harness yielded to automobiles. Even older industries which do not disappear, but remain essential, grow much less rapidly than newer ones. Agriculture grows more slowly than manufacture, steel less than aluminum. Rapid technical change increases the necessity for this shifting of our productive energies and resources. The more rapid is the growth of production in general, the more unstable are particular industries. It is to be expected that when total output is rising at its most rapid rate, many industries will be declining; the increase in output occurs most markedly in new industries.

As technique reaches higher stages, this internal instability of industry is accentuated. The wants for elementary necessities—such as simple food and clothing—are relatively well satisfied at lower levels of production, at least on the part of those who have money enough to buy them. New wants of consumers with extra money are more likely to be for semi-luxury goods in which style or fashion is important, or for mechanical contraptions which may soon be superseded by improvements, or for durable goods like automobiles and houses, which are not consumed quickly. There is a steady demand for standard, basic necessities which are consumed from day to day. Their sale fluctuates little. But in the case of luxury goods in which style is important, the curve of growth and decline is likely to be much sharper and to run its course more quickly. The same is true of new popular inventions which are not basic necessities—such as radio instruments. There are more possibilities of choice before the consumer, as the kinds of things for sale become more numerous.

In the case of the more important durable consumers' goods like automobiles and houses, two major circumstances combine to increase instability of production. One is that the sale of these goods rests to a great extent on credit extended for a year or more; and credit is expanded in good times more than cash incomes, and in bad times is contracted more. The other is that these durable goods may be made to serve for a long period without replacement when times are hard. You cannot postpone the purchase of food for more than a day or two, but you can postpone the purchase of a new car for four or five years, and of a new house for a lifetime. The result is that relatively slight increases or decreases in the earnings of purchasers will cause large increases or decreases in the sales of durable consumers' goods. This element of instability becomes of far greater importance as technique advances and a larger proportion of the nation's productive resources is devoted to making durable consumers' goods.

Still another element of increased instability is the fact that as higher stages of productive technique are reached, a larger part of our industry is occupied in making durable capital goods—machinery, industrial and commercial buildings, railroad cars, locomotives and rails, ships, trucks, and the like. New inventions cause shifts from one type of machinery and building to another, even from one type of heavy industry to another—as from railroads to trucks. Large and expensive aggregates of equipment may become antiquated in a few years; the rate of obsolescence constantly increases. Furthermore, the output of industries making durable capital goods fluctuates far more widely between prosperity and depression than that of industries making perishable necessities for individual consumers.

Professor Frederick Mills' figures show that, if we take a base line at the production level of 1927, output of goods entering into capital equipment increased 19 per cent to the peak in 1929, and then in 1932 dropped 64 per cent below the 1927 mark, while consumption goods increased 11 per cent to 1929 and in 1932 dropped 31 per cent below 1927. Or, throwing capital goods and consumers' goods together, and dividing them rather according to their durability, Dr. Mills finds the following changes in production between 1927, 1929 and 1932:

Durable goods—in 1929 rose 19 per cent above 1927, in 1932 dropped 66 per cent below.
Semi-durable goods—rose 6 per cent, dropped 25 per cent.
Non-durable goods—rose 11 per cent, dropped 11 per cent.

Professor J. M. Clark has pointed out, in his study of "Strategic Factors in Business Cycles" [1] that it does not take an actual reduction in the sale of goods to consumers to bring about a reduction in the demand for new machines and other equipment required to make those goods. A mere slackening in the *rate of growth* of sales to consumers may cause an actual decline in production of capital goods. The same principle applies to construction and to durable consumers' goods. This is because, in all these things, there is a large stock always on hand. Much of the new production is not to replace this stock as it wears out, but to add to it. If, then, the existing stock is increased in a given year only half as fast as the year before, the production of the new units necessary to increase it will be cut in two.

A good illustration of the comparative instability of an industry making durable goods is automobiles. The number of cars actually in use did not decrease from 1929 to 1930, but the number of new cars manufactured dropped sharply. By 1932, the number of car registrations had dropped a little over 9 per cent from the 1929 level; while

[1] National Bureau of Economic Research.

the production of new cars had dropped nearly 75 per cent.

A generation ago there was no industry making durable consumers' goods comparable in importance to the motor industry. There were some industries of the sort, and sharp fluctuations in their output occurred, but they did not affect so many wage-earners or so many material manufacturers, or so many workers in mines and forests, or so many farmers.

As this summary of machine improvement, of growing production and of rapidly shifting production has been followed, the reader has undoubtedly been thinking of the effect on employment. "Technological unemployment" has disturbed many in recent years. The phrase is perhaps unfortunate, for it has been interpreted in too narrow a sense, both by those who argue that it is important and by those who argue that it is not. Let us look at the subject a little more broadly, and let us make some necessary distinctions, in arriving at an answer.

The crude way of regarding the subject is easily disposed of by economists. If you maintain that as machines and processes are introduced which can turn out more goods with less labor, there must be a constantly growing number of unemployed, you can be refuted both by theory and by figures. The theory states that your proposition overlooks the nearly inexhaustible demands of consumers for goods and of workers for leisure. As more goods can be produced with less labor, the cost of producing those goods declines, and consequently the price can be lowered. Or, if the price is not cut, the wages of the workers and the profits of the owners can be increased. Either way, people have the power to buy more goods. The demand for goods thus increases, and as many or more persons are employed in producing them as before the improvements in process were made. Or the benefit of the improvements can be registered in shorter hours for those engaged in production.

The answer by resort to figures points out that a much larger number of persons is employed in industry now than a century ago, or fifty years ago, or thirty years ago, before many of the improvements were known. Even a larger proportion of the population is so employed. Also, hours of work are considerably shorter. Thus the improvements have resulted, not in a steadily growing number of unemployed, but in a higher standard of living and in shorter hours of work. The statisticians also prove that in certain industries where the most rapid improvements have been made, such as the making of automobiles, there was a growth of the number employed rather than a decline—at least before the recent depression. The most serious unemployment occurred in obsolete industries, the demand for whose products was declining, or in backward ones where mechanical advance was less rapid.

Certainly, if we reduce the problem to its simplest terms, the machine alone cannot be blamed for unemployment. Take the most extreme conceivable case. Suppose some gigantic intellect should invent a great series of wear-proof machines, occupying a single factory, which could turn out in a single day all the goods of every kind that the whole population could use for a whole year. And suppose that these machines were so nearly automatic that no labor was required to run them except that of one attendant. One man-day per year would therefore

suffice to satisfy everybody's wants. The results would be
(1) that everybody could have all the goods he needed or
thought he needed, and (2) that everybody could have
complete leisure—except one man, who would have to
work but one day a year. In other words, there could be
a material utopia.

It is obvious that the main problem arises, not from
the mere existence of the machine, but from the way the
goods are distributed. In this case, the goods would have
to be given away, because nobody could earn by work
anything with which to buy them, except the one attendant. If, on the other hand, the factory in question were
privately owned, and if its product belonged to the owner
until somebody else bought it, everybody but the owner
and the one workman would be "unemployed" and would
starve, because nobody else could earn or buy anything.
Even the workman would probably starve, for the factory
would not have to be operated more than a few seconds at
the outside to make everything the owner could use.

In the real world the difficulty arises, therefore, not
from the machine, but from the distribution of the product. Pushing the economists' theory a step further, it is
easy to see that if, when improvements are made, prices
are not lowered, wages are not increased, and hours are
not reduced, the sole immediate gain will go to the owners.
The same is true to a limited extent if prices are lowered,
wages increased and hours reduced, but not rapidly
enough to compensate for the reduction of costs due to
the improvements of process. The question then becomes
what the owners will do with their profits. If they buy
all of the increased output, no unemployment theoretically
results.

But at this point the theory becomes more intricate, and economists begin to dispute among themselves. Complexity arises because of the different kinds of goods that are customarily bought with capital owners' profits. A much larger fraction of profits is devoted to saving and hence to investment in new capital goods than is saved and invested out of the incomes of wage-earners. Therefore, if, when mechanical improvements are made, we increase profits, instead of increasing wages or reducing prices, we tend to increase new investment, and new purchases of capital goods, rather than increasing purchases of consumers' goods. And among consumers' goods themselves, we increase purchases of those kinds which are bought by more wealthy people, such as furs, jewels, yachts and expensive cars, rather than the less expensive goods turned out by mass production.

Now, of course, people are employed in making capital goods and expensive luxuries just as well as in making necessities for the poor. So it is argued by conservative economists that even a large growth of profits at the expense of wage-incomes does not lead to unemployment. But others argue that instability is eventually caused by "over-saving." It is true, according to this theory, that while the new capital goods are being made, employment may be large. But most of these goods are themselves designed, in a modern economy, to make things for the masses rather than just for the rich. You therefore cannot keep piling them up indefinitely unless the purchasing power of wage-earners grows with some close relationship to the growth of new productive capacity. There will, otherwise, come a time when industry is seen to be "over-equipped" in relation to popular purchasing power, and in consequence there will cease to be profitable channels of new investment, the demand for new capital goods will suddenly fall off, and unemployment will sharply increase, especially in the heavy industries.

In this connection we must remember that it is not necessary for the demand for consumers' goods actually to decline in order to cause a slump in the industries making new buildings and machinery designed to produce and distribute these goods. A mere slackening of the growth of purchases of consumers' goods will eventually cause a depression in the capital-goods industries. This in turn will affect employment and industry in general. The figures showing the relatively sharp rise and fall of the capital-goods industries are consistent with this theory of "over-saving."

There are many variants of the theory that trouble is caused when the benefit of improvements is not passed on quickly enough to wage-earners and other low-income consumers, but is devoted rather to an increase of profits and a growth of new investment. All, however, unite on the point that disturbances and unemployment are caused by the fact—admitted now by everyone who is not blind to figures—that the growth of new productive capacity is extremely irregular and spasmodic in character. This is the way in which new machines most clearly affect employment.

Technological unemployment thus becomes transmuted into *cyclical* or *crisis* unemployment. We have, not a steadily growing reservoir of unemployed, but one which increases in depressions and declines in revivals. And this fluctuation is due, not to the mere introduction of machines, but to the impact of the introduction of machines upon our system of prices and incomes. Whatever difficulty arises from this source naturally is more acute as technological advance is speeded up and as the importance of the industries making capital goods increases.

So much for generalities covering unemployment as a whole. But there are more detailed considerations which are of undoubted importance. We have noted that while the output of some industries increases, the output of others declines. What happens when technological advance occurs in declining industries, or in industries the demand for whose product is not growing rapidly? Take bituminous coal as an example. The demand for soft coal does not grow very much. It is not what economists call "elastic." Lower the price of coal as much as you like, and still not much more coal will be used. Therefore improvements in the process of mining coal, though they are passed on to the consumer in lower prices, will not result in much larger output. Rather, they throw miners out of work. Due to overexpansion of the industry and technical advance, there are to-day probably 200,000 ex-miners who will never be able to work in a coal mine again. These particular men are, in the true sense of the word, technologically unemployed. Now it might be that at the same time other industries are employing more men—as they did before the depression. This growth might match the drop in the employment of miners, so that on the average it will not appear that unemployment has increased. Nevertheless, even during prosperity, there are pools of unemployment like this throughout the country, in specific industries and specific localities, partly caused by technical advance. Perhaps some of these men will learn other occupations and will eventually find new jobs. But not all. And those who do will have difficulty in learning new trades and in fitting themselves into our economy in some other place.

In theory, this is a problem of *shifting* employment, or, as it is technically called, of increasing the mobility of labor. But, since it is an undoubted fact that labor is and must remain slow and imperfect in mobility, rapid technical advance is bound to increase unemployment of this sort. The more rapid the advance, the more will certain industries decline, the more will improved processes in these industries throw men out of work, the more numerous will be the isolated pools of unemployment, and the more shifting will be necessary. The existence of such unemployment is damaging to the markets for all industries, not to speak of its damage to the persons concerned and to the social structure. When industrial crises occur, they are greatly aggravated by the existence of this type of unemployment.

Another instance of the same sort is farming. Technical advance occurs in agriculture as elsewhere. There are tractors, combines, better types of seed, improvements in live stock. But the market for agricultural products as a whole is not capable of rapid growth. Much has been said during the depression concerning the absurdity of talking of agricultural surpluses while so many people are starving or undernourished. This is true; yet the fact remains that the number of calories which can be absorbed by the purely physical bodies of a definitely limited number of people is not capable of indefinite expansion, even if they could all buy all the food they wanted. Shifts from less luxurious to more luxurious types of food can of course take place. But, with all allowances for deficiencies in popular purchasing power, the basic physical facts are reflected in the statistics which show that agricultural output grows much more slowly over a period of years in relation to the population than does manufacturing. As a consequence, sufficiently rapid technical improvement drives people out of agriculture, even in times of relative prosperity for the city consumers.

It drove out 800,000 agricultural workers in the United States between 1919 and 1927, according to the U. S. Bureau of Labor Statistics. If the farm output had not grown at all during this period, increased efficiency would have driven out 2,530,000 workers. But, since farming is not only an occupation but a way of life, farmers stick to the soil as a rule until they lose their land. And, since it is highly competitive, prices fall easily as productive efficiency grows. The resulting low level of agricultural prices, in relation to other prices, has brought difficult problems. It has diminished the farmers' purchasing power for industrial products. Thus unemployment in the cities is partly the result of technological improvement on the farms. That is, it is a result of the combination of this development with the other equally important development that the prices of manufactured products *did not* fall as rapidly as technical improvement in factories would have made possible.

A general observation emerges from this highly condensed examination of the results of widespread and intensified technical advance. In every direction, the advance requires rapid readjustment to the new situations it creates, if it is not to cause serious trouble. As production increases, the wants and the purchasing power of the population in general must increase. Our buying and living habits must change. There must be easy and rapid readjustments of prices and incomes. There is an intensified necessity for the mobility of labor and capital among industries—from the declining industries to the growing ones. We have developed an industrial complex in which there is an insistent requirement for greater flexibility. No such requirement was felt when modes of production and consumption persisted with little change from generation to generation. Even later, when great technical changes began to be introduced, they touched such relatively small areas and limited numbers of people that the necessity for flexibility was not so all-pervasive. But now nearly everyone and every occupation is involved. We *must* have flexibility permitting easy readjustment to changing conditions, or at least methods of compensating for the lack of flexibility where it cannot be attained. Our system must be such that it can bend easily and quickly, if it is not to break under the strain.

The car of modern technical progress needs balanced design, sensitive springs and shock absorbers, low-pressure tires. A vehicle equipped to do a hundred miles an hour requires more careful engineering than an ox-cart. Its parts must be measured with a micrometer instead of a foot-rule; it must be weighed and tested for strain in all its parts. Yet here is the paradox. In many ways, as we shall see, this greater need for calculated resiliency and balance has developed alongside an increasing rigidity in our economic structure. Adjustments, instead of becoming easier, have become more difficult. This fact is one that portends the end of twentieth-century capitalism. This is an internal contradiction which shows that the old régime has begun to outlive the day of its usefulness and power.

2. PEOPLE AND THEIR OCCUPATIONS

For several centuries the land occupied by the people of the United States has gradually been filling up. Successive waves of immigrants came in to seek opportunity. Each new wave helped to increase the riches of those who had come before, by working for the previous settlers in farm or in factory, by providing new markets for the growing amount of products, by adding value, through denser occupation, to land. Increase of population through an excess of births over deaths was also rapid; these immigrants from human fertility helped to carry on their shoulders the economic growth of the nation. The population increased from about 2,500,000 in 1776 to 122,775,046 in 1930.

In recent years the rate of increase of the population has been slowing down. Until 1860 the increase per decade hovered about 35 per cent. Then it began to fall, and has fallen ever since—with a few minor reversals, being only a little over 15 per cent in recent decades. The result is that the numerical growth, instead of proceeding in geometrical advance, has been flattening out. A sharp decline both in the rate of increase and in the numbers added to the population is already in sight for the decade ending in 1940. In 1931 only 875,000 persons were added to a population of 122,000,000. Experts predict that long before the end of the present century the population will probably stop growing entirely and may even begin to decrease. Certainly the chances are that the growth of numbers will be so small as not to have the same effect on our economic order as it had in the past century. One estimate is that the population will reach its high point at about 146,000,000 in 1970.

Immigration has sharply declined, first on account of the War, then on account of quota restriction, and finally also on account of the fact that in recent years there were few opportunities to attract immigrants. No jobs were waiting in the factories, while farmers already on the land could scarcely make a living. This was in part due to the depression which affected nearly all nations and which may prove to be temporary. But there are more permanent tendencies which lessen opportunity for the immigrant. The rate of increased production per man-hour was so great even during prosperity that mechanized industries did not, on the whole, demand large new quotas of labor. Unskilled manual labor was in many directions supplanted by machines, as anyone who watches sewer construction or road work can testify. And such immigrants as might have gone directly into farming—for many years a small proportion of the total —have recently found all the good land occupied and producing a surplus.

As Turner pointed out some years ago, the frontier has disappeared. The valuable natural resources have, for the most part, been appropriated. This is not to say that there are not enough resources still in reserve to support in comparative affluence a much larger population than we have. But individuals low in the income scale can no longer go out and wrest their fortunes from nature by pioneering. This safety-value of escape from economic pressure in older sections is closed not only to immigrants

from Europe but to migrants within this country. Again
and again in American history, the discontent of city
workers and of farmers in developed regions was relieved
by opening up new areas for settlement. That can never
happen now.

The cry of the democratic spirit in past generations
was almost always phrased in a demand for greater opportunity for advancement through individual enterprise
and private ownership. This tradition persisted because
the opportunity was in fact there. The tradition is still
powerful, but the facts which gave it validity have almost
vanished. It is a prime example of one of those rules of
life which attracts loyalty because for a long period it
works, but which eventually becomes hollow because the
material conditions underlying it imperceptibly change.

Between 1920 and 1930, for the first time in many
years, the current of internal migration was reversed. It
flowed from farm to city instead of from city to farm.
The urban population grew in this decade by 14,600,000
while the farm population declined by at least 1,200,000.
Population in the country but not on farms grew only
3,600,000. The rural population, which in 1900 was 60
per cent of the total, fell to 44 per cent of the total in
1930. The principal growth of population occurred in
the industrial states of Michigan, New Jersey, North Carolina and New York. People became more concentrated
in cities. In 1930, 17 per cent of the people lived in cities
of over 500,000, and 12.6 per cent in cities between
100,000 and 500,000. Thus nearly one-third of the population dwelt in the big cities. Almost 18 per cent more
lived in cities of 10,000 to 100,000. Many of these smaller
municipalities are in metropolitan areas, or are "satellite

cities" of larger centers of population. Population increased twice as rapidly in the small satellite cities as in
cities of equal size in rural areas. Even the rural population in the neighborhood of large cities increased 57 per
cent, as compared with a growth of only 6 per cent in the
rural population elsewhere.

We hear a great deal today of the "decentralization"
of city population. But this spreading of people means
merely that they are spreading from the more congested
areas of big cities to other parts of the metropolitan
region. Near cities of over 250,000, the satellites grew
more rapidly than the planetary city itself, in the last
decade.

In so far as we still have a frontier, it consists in any
advancement of opportunity which may be offered by
metropolitan regions to those dwelling in the backwoods.
But this opportunity is of a different character from the
old one. You do not rumble down Broadway or Main
Street in a covered wagon, stake out a claim, and build
yourself a house of logs or sod. You become a wage-
earner in an automobile factory or a textile mill, or a
clerk in a store or wholesale house, or a mechanic in a
garage. The conditions of advancement are the conditions imposed by modern industry and commerce. You
may come—as many did come after 1920—not to seek
your fortune, bι merely in a desperate attempt to gain
a livelihood denied you in the country because two of
your brothers were enough, with the tractor and the
combine, to help run the old farm, and there was little
prospect of success in buying other land in the neighborhood, even supposing you could raise the money.

During the depression the stream of migration turned

back again toward the country, but it was a hopeless and belated sort of pioneering. Jobless persons with relatives on farms went back where they could at least find food and shelter; the farmers thus paid a large part of the national dole by supporting many of industry's temporarily unwanted machine-tenders. Shacks sprang up, not in virgin forests and rich prairies, but on waste and cut-over land, on inferior soil, where it might be possible to raise a crop of corn or two among the stumps before moving on. This pitiful ghost of the old pioneering spirit haunted the sadly altered scenes of its earlier triumphs. Thousands of men and women went to the mountains to pan gold dust from the streams, not in hope of striking it rich and founding a fortune, but for the dollar or two a day which they could not find anywhere else. In earlier days surplus workers in the city could escape to the farm; later, surplus workers on the farms trudged to the cities; now there were surpluses in both places at once and there was no escape for either except backward to an earlier and more primitive culture. After the Empire State Building, the best we could do was to revive the log cabin.

In addition to these shifts in the geographical distribution of people, there have been important shifts in their occupations. Of course the relative number of farmers has declined as the city population increased. Of the gainfully occupied, 52.8 per cent were farmers in 1870, only 21.3 per cent in 1930. Those occupied in manufacturing and mechanical industries became more numerous from 1870 to 1920. But here began an important shift in the callings of city persons themselves. There were actually fewer persons engaged in manufacturing in 1930 than in 1920. Productivity per worker had so greatly increased that in spite of the larger output, fewer workers were needed. The factory and mechanical workers were 30.5 per cent of the total in 1920, 28.6 per cent in 1930. (Even so, there were considerably more factory workers than farmers.) Those engaged in trade and transportation became slowly more numerous throughout the entire half-century, being 20.7 per cent in 1930. The sharpest increases occurred in clerical and professional services. Domestic and personal services remained almost stationary. As mechanical civilization advances, the groups which grow most rapidly are those in the "white collar" class. Together they formed in 1930 nearly 15 per cent of the population.

In 1870 about 75 per cent of the gainfully employed were engaged in producing physical goods on farms and in factories, in mining and building. In 1930 only 50 per cent were engaged as literally productive workers. The rest were busy distributing the goods, teaching, keeping books, working in government offices or banks, and in general performing services which do not involve physical production.

We should not mistake this growth of white-collar workers for a growth of small tradesmen or independent business men—a class usually called, in revolutionary terminology, the petty bourgeoisie. Quite the contrary. In the trade industries, for instance, the employees—salespeople and store clerks—have grown in numbers much more rapidly than retail dealers, and are now the largest group. Very rapid increase is observed, in these and other industries, among shipping and office clerks, bookkeepers and accountants, and stenographers. Telephone

and telegraph operators, elevator operators, janitors, jour-
neymen barbers and hairdressers have all increased
markedly.

Among professional groups we see a rapid increase of
teachers and an even more sharp advance of technical
engineers and electricians, of draftsmen, of librarians, of
chemists and metallurgists, of authors. Trained nurses
have also become much more numerous. But there is a
distinctly slower growth of independent professional men
of the older types such as doctors, lawyers and clergymen.
It is noteworthy that those groups which have increased
most rapidly are important in the operation of a highly
advanced technical society, and have immense potential
power. Their specific skills are essential and central: how
should we operate our machines or train any one else to
do so without teachers, engineers, chemists and metallurgists? From these groups also (including the authors)
come the intellectuals—the natural leaders of the rapidly
growing and essential white-collar classes, if not, indeed
of large sections of farm and factory workers.

One very important distinction is that between the employers and the employees. The chance to own and manage a business is what the American industrialist or politician is usually thinking of when he talks about "opportunity" or "private enterprise," or "individual initiative."
How many, as a matter of fact, can exercise this initiative? How characteristic of the lives of the total population is the pursuit of independent business enterprise?
No exact figures exist, but an estimate, quoted by Ralph
G. Hurlin and Meredith B. Givens in "Recent Social
Trends" is that only 10 per cent of the gainfully occupied
are owners of independent business in the literal sense,

and that from 60 to 75 per cent of these are farmers, many of whom do not employ anybody. Most of the remainder—but 3 to 4 per cent of all the working population—are retailers; in 1930 there were 1,703,000 of them. The number of independent business proprietors is declining in relation to the total population. If you do not already own a business and want to engage in private enterprise, your choice is virtually limited nowadays to buying a farm or starting a retail shop in competition with the chain stores, or setting up still another filling station or garage or beauty shop on still another corner. You have little chance of starting a factory unless you already have a lot of money—and even then the opportunity is dubious. Not a very inspiring outlook! The bulk of our enterprise to-day is carried on by corporations which are managed not by their owners but by salaried employees.

What are the main consequences of the declining growth of total population and its shifts among regions and occupations?

First and most important, the tide of population no longer rises rapidly, floating business up with it. It is no longer so easy to "grow up with the country." Does productive capacity expand? The addition of mouths to feed and of bodies to clothe is not rapid enough to occupy surplus capacity. Speculators in land or natural resources can no longer, as a whole, count on increasing density of population to bring value to their property. If the extra goods which technology is teaching us to produce in ever larger quantities are to be sold, the existing persons must have growing purchasing power; nature no longer solves the problem by providing new persons in abundance. This fact is of particular significance to the farmers, who produce food staples, and to producers of other standard necessities, the demand for which among a given number of persons cannot greatly increase. An element of rigidity has been added to demand.

Second, as population growth declines, the proportion of persons under the age of 20 decreases in relation to those over 20. There will be a rise in the proportion of those between 20 and 45, who are of the most effective working age. More persons to employ—will there be more jobs for them? Unemployment will constantly be a graver problem on this account unless the consumption of goods by all is increased. The proportion of those between 45 and 64 will be enlarged by one-quarter in the next twenty years, and of those over 65 by one-half. More persons with settled habits, making change more difficult, as change becomes more necessary. Fewer superannuated persons leaving opportunities vacant for maturing youth, especially in the newly important white-collar and professional occupations, in which the limit of effective working age is much higher than in manual labor.

The decline of immigration means that there will be fewer aliens to exploit, fewer to fill subservient positions, satisfied to do so because their opportunity in the new country is greater than in the old. Large groups of workers can no longer be looked upon complacently as an inferior class because they are "ignorant foreigners." If we are to have a class stratification, the various classes must be composed more and more of persons having a common cultural heritage and language. No group can rise on the shoulders of vast numbers of recent arrivals.

Thus, unequal economic status and privileges will be more sharply challenged. Working-class movements will no longer be partitioned between "Americans" and "hunkies."

Opportunity to rise by individual private enterprise is limited by the disappearance of the frontier, the shrinkage of agriculture, the decreasing importance of small business in the city. Achievement by the individual means, more and more, advancement as an employee or attainment of professional eminence; it can be gained less and less by the accumulation of wealth as an independent business man. The great majority of persons will be working in groups, and for somebody else—this somebody else being in most cases an impersonal corporation rather than a personal employer.

A country dominated for many years by the habits and ideals of rural life and the small town has become definitely urban. Even the farm is being urbanized: more farmers are close to cities; machine technology stretches out to revolutionize farm work; the radio, the talkies, the magazines, the automobile, the nationally advertised and distributed products all combine to citify the way of thought and of life on the farm. The farmer is in debt to city insurance companies and banks or to federal finance institutions rather than to local small capitalists, at least to a far greater extent than in previous generations. And he is far more dependent on city agencies for marketing his produce; the era of individual selling to individual consumers is long past. Essential as the farmer is as a source of food supply and other raw materials, and as a consumer of city products, his traditional individualism and conservatism no longer can set the tone of the national culture. Even more, the individualism of the small business man in the rural town is a fast-declining influence. If metropolitan regions stimulate group action and more highly integrated organization, this tendency will govern the life of the nation. The power of the city's example has stimulated vigorous group action and organization even among farmers.

We have, it is true, a new tendency of decentralization from the more congested centers to neighboring small cities and suburban rural regions. But people seek the country for pleasant and healthful life, for recreation, rather than as a dependable means of making a living. Megalopolis can pile too many skyscrapers at its center and breed too many slums in its crowded areas for health, comfort or efficiency. But when relief comes, it comes by moving industry and dwellings to the land, by a spread of city culture, not by a return to ruralism except as a means of play and rest.

The shifts of population not only have brought more rigidity to the old type of individualist economy, they have resulted in the rise of some classes and the decline of others.

As the industrial workers have become more numerous, they have also become more important to the nation's life. Few families could live at all without the product of factories and power plants; none could live with any comfort or ease. All but a scattering of farms are dependent on the purchases of city workers in order to sell their output. This situation of course did not exist a century ago, it was by no means so widespread fifty years or thirty years ago.

Now that industrial and machine workers have begun

to be less numerous in relation to the total population, their importance and potential power is by no means decreased; quite the contrary. We are all more than ever dependent on continual and efficient operation of the machinery which, in combination with other factors, has tended to decrease the number of machine workers. A single worker tending or repairing a machine which can turn out as much product as twenty-five workers could formerly make has the importance of those twenty-five. Since the industrial working class has not decreased anywhere nearly in proportion to the increase of machine productivity, it has, as a whole, a greatly heightened weight in the social scales. Without its tacit consent and collaboration—even if it be an enforced collaboration—our society could not live a week. And without its welfare and efficiency, without a capacity on its part to buy increasing amounts of products, the owners of the machinery and the executives of industries themselves cannot in the long run prosper.

At the same time another type of city employee has arisen to share in fuller measure the importance of industrial workers proper. The clerks, the bookkeepers, the salesmen, the government employees and all the other white-collar workers are essential to the distribution, the complex details of management and integration, without which the products of the field and the machine cannot be produced and exchanged. In the economic sense, they are as truly producers as those who make physical articles. Without the kind of work they do, the far-flung national productive plant, with its diversified specialization, could not operate at all. They are bound to grow more numerous as machine production becomes more highly developed, as its output is elaborated and its market is widened. And, as they become more numerous, their purchasing power is more necessary for the consumption of the products made and services rendered.

Most striking of all is the rise of a class which was almost unknown when the industrial revolution was young. This class is composed of what we may call the productive professions. Early economists used to dilate on the contributions of the employer—the original small enterpriser—with his ingenuity, his development of new processes, his combination of, and oversight over the factors of production. They were right; he was at the time perhaps the most important personage in the industrial picture. But as technique advanced and as enterprises grew larger, the productive functions of this personal employer have largely been delegated to professionally trained employees. The chemist, the metallurgist, the mechanical engineer, the worker in the research laboratory, the skilled cost accountant, the specialist in management, the psychologist and biologist—yes, even the applied economist—now constitute the brains of industry. It is they who furnish the material of great changes, who keep the wheels running—when they run. Without this class the owners, the big executives, the workers and the farmers would all alike be helpless. If it should disappear, our whole industrial plant would rust and rot away, unless others could be educated to take their places.

Closely allied to them are the teachers, the higher government employees, and the experts in economic, social and political problems, whose heads are beginning to appear above the horizon in government itself as well as in industry. And we must not overlook the authors and artists and the rest of those called loosely "intellectuals." The intelligentsia are often scoffed at by the philistines, but their influence over the rising and crucial class of brain workers—even supposing it extended no further— is so great that it is beginning to count in the national life to an extent undreamed of even a decade ago. The intellectuals have always been important because they have reflected, defined and altered the minds of other classes; they are now important also in their own right.

As the city workers in factory and office, the members of productive professions and the intellectuals expand in numbers and rise in potential power, the small-town business man, banker and lawyer decline, the individual owner and manager of small business in the city gradually loses out. And, as we shall see in the next section, even the "owner" of big business is deprived of both functions and power; he is rapidly becoming a vermiform appendix in the industrial organism.

3. BUSINESS UNITS AND OWNERS

Are our factories becoming larger? Is the big concern pushing out the little one? Is it destined to dominate the scene? People who do not think so have a good deal to say about the superior efficiency of a small or medium-sized plant. They point out that the relatively small establishments still greatly outnumber the large ones. Those on the other side of the argument will reply that while this is true, the comparatively few big factories employ more wage-earners altogether than the little ones. As far back as 1923, Willard Thorp found that while only 4 per cent of the factories employed more than 250 workers each, this 4 per cent accounted for more than half the industrial wage-earners.

But these questions are really not so crucial as they seem. How big a given factory ought to be depends on the technique of the process and the nature of the market for that particular product. A factory may turn out a large value of product and dominate its competitive field and yet, if it is highly mechanized, it may employ relatively few people. On the other hand, a cotton or rayon mill employing thousands of hands because so much labor is needed for the kinds of work done, may be one of a large number of competitors for a big market. A large plant in one sort of industry would be a small one in another. There is undoubtedly, at any given stage of technique, an optimum size of plant for any particular kind of production, and this size may well be short of gigantic in many industries. But what we are most interested in is ownership and control, rather than the physical size of particular plants. A lot of small plants may be part of a big aggregate. Would you say that the important thing about a chain store system is the size of its individual branches, rather than the whole combination? A giant corporation may, in a process where small units of production are most efficient, utilize small factories and decentralize their administration, while keeping control over their major policies.

When we concentrate on the factor of ownership and control, forgetting the size of the individual units of production and distribution, there is no question whatever that big business is dominant and is becoming more so. An incomplete record of mergers in manufacturing and mining by Willard Thorp shows that between 1919 and

1930, 8,003 separate concerns in manufacturing and mining disappeared as separate entities either by merger or acquisition. In public utilities, 4,329 concerns disappeared up to 1928, while 1,793 banking mergers occurred in this period. In merchandising, too, the concentration increased. By 1929 chain stores sold 27 per cent of the food, 19 per cent of the drugs, 30 per cent of the tobacco, 93 per cent of the varieties (of the 5- and 10-cent sort), 27 per cent of the apparel, 14 per cent of the department store and dry goods merchandise, 26 per cent of the general merchandise, 14 per cent of the furniture and 15 per cent of the musical instruments. Even the independents, who are more numerous than their share of the business would indicate, began to organize voluntary or "coöperative" chains in large numbers. In public utilities the holding company has been used to centralize profits and control to an enormous extent. In 1930, according to James C. Bonbright and Gardiner C. Means, ten groups of holding companies controlled 72 per cent of the electric business and sixteen controlled 42 per cent of the gas business.

The change brought over the whole face of industry by this tendency has been colossal, especially if we take into consideration not only the combinations of one sort or another but the recent growth of concerns which were already large. Mr. Means has calculated that the 200 largest business corporations (excluding banks, insurance companies and the like) though they represented less than one per cent of the total number of corporations, had at the end of 1929 nearly half the corporate wealth of the country. This was 38 per cent of all the business wealth, if we include also unincorporated business in the total, and it was about 20 per cent of the total national wealth. The growth of these big concerns had been two to three times as rapid as the growth of the lesser ones. If their relative rapidity of increases were maintained at the same rate, by 1950 the 200 biggest corporations would own four-fifths of the corporate wealth and about half the total wealth of the nation.

Adam Smith published "The Wealth of Nations" in 1776, and the Constitution of the United States was adopted not long thereafter. On Adam Smith's precepts are based most of the traditional economic ideas concerning the operation of the capitalist system, the functions of private enterprise and competition. Yet, when he wrote, so rare was the corporation and so limited was the domain of big units of business that he thought the corporate form was not well adapted to any sort of enterprise except routine operations of the utmost public necessity, such as canals, banks and the like. This is an indication of the change which has come over the world since capitalism first began to flower. We really have no idea what Adam Smith would have thought of a system in which so much of business enterprise was in the hands, not of small, competing, personally managed businesses, but of gigantic aggregations. Even John Stuart Mill, a much later representative of the classical school, looked askance on large corporations.

When Smith and Mill wrote, it never occurred to them that ownership and management could be or would be separated from one another. The owner risked his capital, and this was a spur to careful management on his part. The profits were in large degree a reward for his shrewdness in selecting a field of enterprise and for his ability in management. But it is far otherwise with the great modern corporation. Much of its capital is likely to be raised by bond issues, which technically are loans with a fixed return, no possibility of capital appreciation, and no powers of control unless the corporation defaults. The owners of this capital are completely separated from control. The owners of the concern itself are, technically, the stockholders. They are supposed to take the place of the old owner-manager. They do indeed assume much of the speculative risk and often get profits if the concern is profitable. But they exercise almost no real management or even control over management. Most of them are widely scattered and know nothing whatever about the business. They cannot even exercise to any purpose their legal right to vote for directors—when they are not deprived of this right by such new devices as non-voting stock. Berle and Means show that of the 200 largest corporations, only ten are actually controlled by owners of a majority of the stock outstanding, and these ten represent but two per cent of the total assets. All the others are controlled by small groups of minority stockholders, by various legal devices, or by the salaried executives themselves.

But there is a still further concentration of control. Each of these large corporations is not itself a totally independent unit, competing freely with all the others in its field and separate from those in other industries. Quite the contrary. A study by K. W. Stillman reveals in some detail the generally known fact that there is much duplication among the memberships of their boards of directors, and among their boards and those of the great banks and insurance companies. He listed the directors of the biggest business corporations—those with assets of over $500,000,000 each. There were forty-three of these companies. He also listed the directors of twelve large banking houses and three big insurance companies. He found that 298 directorships in the giant businesses, plus 117 directorships in the financial houses, were held by 166 individual men. At the end of 1931 these 166 men were legally responsible for assets of $46,000,000,000—over half the wealth of the 200 corporations studied by Berle and Means. They were in charge of 28 per cent of our total corporate wealth and 22 per cent of all business wealth. The Chase National Bank alone controlled fifty-four votes on the boards of twenty-seven of these corporations, which had combined assets of $25,000,000,000. J. P. Morgan and Company had twenty-six directors on thirteen of the boards, the Bankers' Trust Company twenty-nine directors on eighteen boards. And so on.

Out of the forty-three largest corporations, only one, the Ford Motor Company, was managed by those who own a majority of the stock. This is the only one which in any degree corresponds to the unit of business that was typical at the time when Adam Smith wrote—and of course it is tremendously larger than anything he imagined. In fourteen others, control is in the hands of small groups of minority stockholders. Management itself controls fifteen, while a combination of management and minority ownership or other legal strategem controls the rest.

When we talk about "business enterprise" in the United States to-day, therefore, and use the words in the sense of those who own and manage business—the capitalist class—we are really talking about a situation somewhat as follows. There are over 122,000,000 persons in the country, and of these, 48,000,000 usually work for a living. Of the 48,000,000, perhaps 3 to 4 per cent are owners of small independent businesses, and most of these are proprietors of retail shops and other establishments which are rapidly losing ground to big corporate business. Who owns the corporations? Corporations have had recently about 18,000,000 stockholders listed on their records—but there are not 18,000,000 separate stockholders or anywhere near it, since many persons hold shares in more than one company. One can only guess how many persons actually own stock, but a liberal estimate would be four to five million or but one-tenth of the gainfully occupied. The vast majority of these "owners" of industry have no share in business enterprise except a chance at the profits and losses. They have little more relationship to it than the bettors at a race-track have to the owning and racing of horses. They are sharply divided both in respect to the amount of their stake, and even, in many cases, in the direction of their real interest, from those who actually run big industry. Of this we shall see more subsequently. The minorities in whom stock control is concentrated, together with the active directors and managers of the bulk of corporate business, do not number more than a few thousand persons. Less than 200 men are active in the top control of the big business and banking concerns which are the real center of our system. On what they do or don't do the welfare of 48,000,000 others and their families depends. There is a gulf between such a régime and the régime that was prevalent or even conceived of when our traditional economic ideas were formulated and when our form of government was adopted, which is far wider than the gulf between modern capitalism and communism.

This situation is full of meaning in regard to the class structure of our society. Whatever government of industry is exercised by private enterprise is largely in the hands of a small class, entrance into which is barred to the average farmer, wage-earner, or professional man. But it has another, equally important aspect. Under the kind of control exercised over them by private capitalists, these large business corporations tend to make serious trouble in the operation of the capitalist system itself. They set up rigid barriers against which the pressure of technical change, which demands flexibility, is constantly pushing.

Suppose a technical improvement is introduced which makes possible more production with less labor. If it is introduced in an industry which still corresponds to a primitive capitalism because its units of production are numerous and are owned by individuals who compete freely with one another, the result is a prompt increase in output. The enlargement of supply reduces prices. The consumers of the products benefit. If the product in question is one which can be used in larger quantities by a given population, the producers also should lose little in the end because while they sell at a lower price, their sales are increased.

But large corporations which introduce technical improvements are not forced, as a rule, to lower prices so quickly. They want to retain for themselves the gain which results from the reduction in cost.

If the corporation has a monopoly of its product, it certainly will not reduce prices rapidly. But even if there is no absolute or formal monopoly, competition among a few large firms is quite different from competition among many small ones. They can more readily reach an agreement, tacit or otherwise, to divide the field or maintain minimum prices or engage in a hundred-and-one other practices which tend to keep prices up. Or, without any agreement, one concern will hesitate to start a price war, knowing that a reduction on its part will lead to a further reduction by others. Competition in these cases does not operate promptly to pass on gains from increased efficiency to consumers and wage-earners. This leads to an immediate increase in profits, which stimulates additional investment in the industry, a resulting growth in productive capacity, and an eventual lack of balance between the productive ability of the industry and the demand for its products at the prices charged.

An industry of big units, with an enormous capital structure, may give every appearance of prosperity while it is growing rapidly. It may sell increasing quantities even though it does not reduce prices anywhere nearly as rapidly as costs of production are cut. But when its growth curve begins to flatten out or turn down, it gets into serious difficulties. Necessary readjustments are not easily made. A big concern in a declining industry hangs on until the last gasp, whereas a little one would be compelled to give way more quickly. When the big concern finally does crash, it affects more people more suddenly.

All these maladjustments are concealed in a period of general prosperity. The full current covers the reefs and shoals. But when business recession comes, what has gone up so easily sticks on the way down. Let us see what happens when demand for the product falls off. The "laws of supply and demand" in classical economics hold that when supply exceeds demand, the price will fall. The fall in price will tend to increase the demand again, so that you may have a fairly prompt readjustment. Production is maintained, but at a lower price. This happens in agriculture during a depression. Prices may drop swiftly, but sales are not greatly affected, for a long time at least, and output is scarcely decreased at all. Just the reverse happens, however, in the case of most manufactured articles controlled by big business. When demand falls off, the price is cut little if any. But the output of manufacturers is reduced almost as rapidly as the demand. Thus the law of supply and demand does not work promptly to restore a balance. When prices are held up and production drops, the intensity of the depression is aggravated. For as one concern reduces output, it lays off workers and buys fewer materials, thus injuring the market for other concerns. An endless chain of diminishments of purchasing power is set in motion.

Some economists talk as if this cutting of production rather than of price were just a foolish policy on the part of manufacturers. Educate them in the law of supply and demand and they will act more intelligently. Or, if they can't be educated, make them compete and they will be forced, like the farmers, to sell more cheaply. But, alas, those in control of production don't behave as the economists say they ought, because they are in the grip of circumstances. The system in which they are enmeshed will not permit them to do so.

When machinery plays a large part in production, and a business enterprise is big and complex, an important change takes place in the character of its costs. It may have borrowed a lot of money to invest in its plant and equipment, and interest on this money has to be paid. Or the plant is represented in its capital structure by large issues of stock, and the first responsibility of the management is to keep paying dividends on this stock as long as possible. There are many items of heavy expense which continue about the same in depression as in prosperity—insurance, rent, property taxes, the salaries of the executives and others who are in control and believe themselves necessary to keep the plant running at all and ready for possible future expansion. These overhead or indirect expenses do not decrease easily as business falls off. Indeed, the overhead cost attributable to each article produced increases as the output falls. It is difficult indeed to cut this part of the costs of production, so that prices may be reduced, when the demand for the product is falling.

The other part of the expense of production, composed principally of labor and materials, can be reduced easily by producing less, by laying off men and buying fewer materials. But this does not lead to reduced cost per unit of product, which would be necessary for reduced prices. To cut wages much is not easy, because the cost of living does not fall rapidly in a depression. And wage cuts do not reduce costs of production appreciably, when the labor cost makes up a small proportion of the total cost. If wage payments are 50 per cent of the cost of a product to a given concern, as they are in some less mechanized industries, a cut of 20 per cent in wage rates will yield a reduction of 10 per cent in total costs. But if wages make up only 10 per cent of the costs, cutting them by one-fifth will reduce total costs only 2 per cent. A concern with such a cost structure could cut its expenses only 10 per cent if it got its labor for nothing. It is also difficult to get materials at much lower prices, if they are the product of other manufacturers—steel, for instance. Any savings which are made in the prices of materials and the wage rates of labor are likely to be used to make up for the increased unit overhead costs rather than to decrease prices.

The big corporation, when sales and gross income fall, almost invariably lays off labor, reduces its purchases of materials and cuts its output as demand drops away. This is the natural and easy choice. If, as often happens, the corporation has laid by large reserves and surplus profits, it can use these to pay interest and dividends while it slackens activity, in the hope that the depression will soon blow over. This perfectly natural behavior intensifies the depression and creates greater danger to capital in the end, for, if generally pursued, it reduces the purchasing power of labor and farmers. But it is virtually inevitable in a system where the claims of capital—interest, rent and profits—are the first charges on industry, and are large. What is really happening is that the controllers of industry are trying to protect capital values by shifting the burden of deflation to wage-earners and the more defenseless producers of raw materials, among whom the farmers bulk large. The last thing to which the control of industry is forced is the deflation of capital and the reduction of fixed charges—which can take place, as a rule, only through default and bankruptcy.

Thus a régime of big corporate business, arising from and depending upon rapid technical progress, not only tends to build in prosperity a top-heavy capital structure and a lack of balance between productive capacity and market demand which help bring on depression, but tends to intensify and prolong the depression when it arrives.

4. THE RIGIDITY OF DEBT

We have just seen the part played by corporate long-term debt in making prices more rigid when they ought to fall. In the case of manufactures, the debt itself is a smaller part of the picture than is sometimes believed. The non-legal obligation to enlarge or continue dividends, and the types of fixed and overhead charges other than debt are more influential. In 1932, long-term indebtedness of industrial corporations was only about one-fifth of their tangible asset value as of 1930. Their interest charges are not great enough to be a serious burden except in times of severe depression. Industrial debts were in 1933 but 8.2 per cent of the nation's total long-term indebtedness.

In railroads and public utilities the fixed indebtedness is of course much larger in relation to the assets than in the case of industrial corporations; here the problem is serious indeed. About half the book value of the railroads is represented by bonded indebtedness. Almost the same figure prevails in the electric utilities. All goes well when neither rates nor sales are reduced. But when railroad traffic falls, as in the current depression, serious trouble immediately impends. Early in 1933, 10 per cent of the railroads' mileage was in receivership and about one-quarter of their funded debt was either in default or was saved from default by emergency loans. Railroad rates were scarcely reduced as other prices fell; this was not just because they were under federal regulation, but because, unless reducing rates should lead to a noticeable and immediate increase in the volume of traffic, it would render larger numbers of railroads unable to pay their interest. The bonds are held principally by savings banks, insurance companies, educational and charitable institutions. Here, then, is a terrific instance of rigidity. In a country with such wide distribution of products as the United States, railroad rates are an important element in costs. They simply cannot be reduced in a time of slack business without an immediate and substantial amount of capital deflation, without endangering financial institutions at the very center of our system, in which the savings of millions are invested. The problem is aggravated by the fact that the railroad industry is one of those which have passed the period of rapid growth and have begun to decline in the face of competition from newer industries. (Railroad debts in 1933 made up 11.3 per cent of the total debt of the country.)

The electric utilities have not been suffering so severely from their heavy bonded indebtedness only because they are still on the upgrade; demand for current did not fall off so greatly during the depression. In their case, the chief sufferers were the investors in holding companies, which had vastly overcapitalized abnormally high profits of the subsidiary operating concerns. Nevertheless, the fact that public utility rates do not readily fall, either in prosperity as lower costs arise from technical improvements or in depression as prices of commodities drop, introduces a serious element of rigidity into the price structure. This fact means that costs of power to industry are virtually stationary and an appreciable part of the cost of living to domestic users remains high. The electric utilities might expand their output much more rapidly than they do, if prices were lower. If they did, more unemployed persons thrown out of work in declining industries could find jobs, both with them and with the manufacturers of electric equipment. Public utility debts were, in 1933, 8.9 per cent of the aggregate long-term debt in the nation.

Farm mortgage debt composes only about 6.7 per cent of the total long-term indebtedness of the nation, and only two-fifths of the farms are mortgaged at all. It amounts to but 25 per cent of the value of farm land and buildings, as of 1933. Why, then, the sharp outcry about this form of debt? And why is it a more acute problem than in former generations? The value of farm mortgages doubled between 1910 and 1920—at a time when the demand for wheat, meat and other staples, which was heavy during the war, led to high prices and the expansion of operations by growers specializing in single crops and large-scale production for the market. It is concentrated largely in regions devoted to commercial agriculture; 60 per cent of it in 1933 was in states in the corn belt and the wheat belt—Ohio, Indiana, Illinois, Michigan, Wisconsin, Missouri, North Dakota, South Dakota, Nebraska, Montana. In 1920 the export demand for these products fell sharply and has never recovered; prices declined and have stayed down, falling again precipitately after 1929. But the debt was not deflated; it even increased up to 1928. The rigidity of fixed costs on the farm does not directly affect other costs by holding crop prices up; on the contrary, when markets shrink, crop prices promptly fall and the whole burden drops immediately on the debtor.

Hence the cry for debt relief. The increased commercialization of agriculture, resting on long-term credit, imperils the large number of farmers who have thus been drawn within the orbit of the capitalist-credit structure.

When necessity for debt deflation arrives, the readjustment is more difficult than in earlier times, because the debt is more centrally held. Farm mortgages used to be scattered among neighbors and local banks. The farming class itself was, to a greater extent, both debtor and creditor. But in 1928, nearly a quarter of the farm mortgage debt was held by life insurance companies. Farmers held only 15 per cent and commercial banks 11 per cent. Federal land banks and private mortgage companies held 22 per cent between them. Thus a big financial interest, remote from the farms, has been created which acts to squeeze the last possible cent out of the mortgagor. The lines are drawn for a real conflict between debtor and creditor. And if the creditor loses, as he eventually must unless farm prosperity returns quickly enough, the effects of the deflation are felt throughout the financial system, instead of being confined as in earlier decades largely to agricultural regions where the mortgages were held.

A far more menacing situation—more menacing, that is, not to those who suffer directly by it, but to the economic structure as a whole, lies in the urban real estate mortgages and securities. With the rapid growth of the cities and the prosperity of post-war years, speculative building of both residential and commercial structures boomed. City building is habitually carried on largely by means of borrowed money; at the height of the boom the speculative builder hardly put up any capital or shouldered any risk at all. Credit both for long and short term was showered upon him by financial institutions. A building boom of any magnitude in turn increases industrial activity: the construction industry employs large numbers directly and, through its demand for a wide variety of materials, spreads wages and profits throughout the country. In an unplanned and competitive system, a boom of this sort is certain to overshoot the growth of effective demand for the kind of housing and commercial floor space built. When, for any reason, demand falls off and the flow of credit stops, the necessary readjustment is exceedingly painful and long drawn out.

Urban mortgage debt was nearly trebled between 1921 and 1929. In 1933 it represented nearly one-fifth of the long term debt of the country, and about 60 per cent of the estimated total value of city real estate. It makes up a substantial portion of the assets of big insurance companies, banks and title and mortgage guarantee companies. Half the assets of savings banks were so involved. To reduce this debt would create such financial havoc that there was the stiffest sort of resistance on the part of creditors. Its total amount had not, in 1932, been decreased as much as 1 per cent. Nevertheless, the property on which it was a lien had fallen 40 per cent in value. The rents received by the owners were cut nearly in half, while vacancies increased up to 25 per cent. Meanwhile the other expenses of the owners were not appreciably reduced. Taxes fell but little. Expenses for maintenance, repairs and wages made up such a minor part of expense that the reductions obtainable in them furnished no great relief. As a result, it was estimated that much more than half of these debts were by 1933 in default or arrears.

Nevertheless mortgage foreclosures were not common, because the creditors saw little advantage in taking over the property. The net income which the owner could make was in many cases simply wiped out.

What was the result? There being no profit in owning a building, the demand for new private construction fell toward zero. And there being great risk to the money already lent for building purposes, financial institutions did not dare to lend any more. New building would, they feared, create competition with the old, which would endanger their existing loans. The great construction industry, with all its dependents, direct and indirect, was nearly idle. This hampered the return of activity and employment in all the heavy industries which supply building.

The fact that new construction depends so largely on credit intensifies booms and depressions. On the way up, mortgages and bonds are easily sold; if the actual savings brought together in savings banks, life insurance companies and building and loan societies are not enough to finance them, the more easily expansible loans of commercial banks step in to fill the breach. But each bond and mortgage sold sets up new fixed charges; the interest to be paid (the price of the money borrowed) is fixed by contract for a long period and cannot be reduced subsequently except through absolute inability to pay it. Even then the creditor holds out for his legal rights to the last gasp. Thus the price of money is made rigid; it cannot be reduced quickly, as classical economics holds that prices will be reduced when supply exceeds demand. This has long been the case, but the importance of this rigidity in our system has been greatly enhanced in recent years by the drift of population to the cities, and the larger place of urban construction in our total of production and exchange.

Public debts have also increased tremendously in recent years. The federal debt of course had its big growth during the War, then was gradually reduced until 1929, when it began to mount again during the depression. In 1933 it was 11.2 per cent of the total debt in the United States. Whether it is a serious element of rigidity depends upon the fiscal policy of the government. If the government borrows more during depression in order to maintain or increase its expenditures, it utilizes credit resources which would otherwise be idle—since private enterprise usually can borrow little at such a time—and the spending of the money helps to maintain a higher level of activity than would otherwise be the case. If it then pays off its debt during periods of prosperity, it helps to counteract the expansion of debt incurred at such a time by private enterprise. Thus the government can, theoretically, help to neutralize the injury caused by the rigidity of private debt.

There remains to be considered the method of levying taxes to pay the interest and amortization charges. If graduated income and profits taxes are used, these charges are paid by those best able to pay them, and no appreciable addition is made to fixed costs. But if sales taxes, import duties, excise taxes and the like are resorted to, the tendency is to increase costs of business and stiffen their rigidity.

The trouble is that private interests act in such a way as to prevent the government from pursuing a sound fiscal policy. They interfere with rapid paying off of the debt during prosperity, because this means high income taxes.

For the same reason, they oppose expansion of the debt during depression. They also favor taxes which raise prices instead of those which tap surplus incomes and profits.

State and local government debts are an extremely serious element of rigidity, because the charges upon them are paid so largely out of property taxes. These taxes are not varied with ability to pay, like the income tax, but depend on the assessed value of the property and hence become an element of fixed cost, which tends to hold rents up during a period of depression. When, through dire necessity, property taxes cannot be collected in full, the states and municipalities have to continue to meet capital charges, and hence discharge employees or reduce their salaries, or in extreme cases do not pay them at all. The creditor benefits at the expense of the large and on the whole indispensable class of public employees—teachers, firemen, policemen, engineers and the like. Popular purchasing power is drastically reduced by this item alone. The unemployed, dependent largely on local relief, suffer. The plight of the local government and its employees is made worse when tax collections are so small as to make default necessary. Up to February 1, 1933, 1,120 public units in the United States had defaulted on their bonded obligations. The rapid growth of cities has made this problem far more serious, whenever it arises at all, for it has brought an expansion of fixed debt out of proportion to the growth of the country's population.

Certain theorists, notably the Technocrats, have called attention to the fact that fixed debt has for many years shown a tendency to grow more rapidly than production or than the national income as a whole. They believe this fact is in itself a menace, as if the interest paid on debts were drained out of the national income and did not come back again into the market as a demand for goods and services. Of course those who receive interest may spend it again, just as if the money had been paid out to wage-earners or had been given directly to universities and hospitals or devoted to old-age pensions. The mere payment of large amounts of interest is not in itself a cause of the interruption of economic activity. But in a more subtle and intricate sense, the rapid growth of debt does accentuate the problems inherent in large-scale capitalism. It signalizes the fact that more and more areas of activity are coming within the influence of financial institutions. It creates greater rigidity in costs, so that when a readjustment is required by a falling off of demand, what takes place is a reduction of output rather than of price. It thus prevents the smooth operation of a system which tries to depend on the automatic and unplanned adjustments of laissez-faire. And, since larger and larger sections of heavy industry are dependent on new investment of capital to create a market for their products, any danger to the long-term debt already in existence acts to discourage new investment and thus to injure the important industries making capital goods. The chief difficulty arises when the debt stops growing, as it does whenever the spasms of the system endanger the payment of past debt.

The rigidity of debt charges as compared with other streams of income sticks out like a mountain peak from the recent figures on the national income calculated by Simon Kuznets of the National Bureau of Economic Research. The total national income paid out shrank 40 per

cent from 1929 to 1932. But interest paid shrank only
3.2 per cent, while wage payments in mining, manufacturing, construction, steam railroads and certain other transportation fields had fallen 60 per cent.

So far we have been considering only long-term debt.
Short-term debt, such as is extended by ordinary commercial loans of banks, or by loans on security collateral,
and even debt for slightly longer periods, like that which
finances instalment sales of automobiles, is ordinarily considered of less importance because it is supposed to be
"liquid." It matures so quickly that it is supposed to be
automatically adjusted to the needs of business, and to
furnish no rigid barriers to the necessary changes of conditions. But note how this aspect of the financial system
also creates trouble.

As industrial capitalism grows, more and more people
use banks, more and more payments circulate through
them. Normally about nine-tenths of our payments are
made, not by transfers of dollar bills and other currency,
but by checks—which really are nothing but orders to
the banks either to pay out currency, or more commonly,
to make certain bookkeeping transactions which transfer
figures from one person's account to another's. Most
deposits arise, not because anyone passes currency
through a receiving-teller's window, but because someone
has made out a check to the depositor. And, in the first
instance, most of the accounts on which the checks are
drawn arise from loans made by the bank to the depositor. Thus the major part of our circulating medium is,
at the same time, debt owed to the banks. Expansion of
payments, meaning increased business activity, can arise

only from two sources: (a) because the circulation of payments is more rapid or (b) because the banks are increasing the total of their loans. Contrariwise, when the bank loans are not being constantly paid off and renewed, or when the banks are not expanding them, business must slow down.

Now it is easy enough for payments to flow rapidly and for bank credit to expand when business is booming. There is no lack of flexibility here; on the contrary, the flexibility on the way up is customarily too great; loans will be made for all sorts of purposes which in the end will turn out to have been unsound. But when the turn downward comes, a large part of this so-called "liquid" credit is likely to freeze up. When a large number of businesses and individuals are slow in paying their debts to one another, many are necessarily slow in paying their debts to the banks; some bank loans cannot be paid at all. Under these circumstances the banks are reluctant to make new loans, and the total circulation of purchasing power is reduced.

The banks will be certain to have loaned a lot of short-term money on the collateral of stock-exchange securities and real-estate bonds. In many cases the purchasers of these long-term instruments will have bought them, not out of real savings, but out of the money loaned them by the banks. Thus bank-credit has helped mightily to finance the capital boom. And when the capital boom collapses, the bank credit in turn shrinks and freezes. The borrower is sold out when the value of his securities sinks. This further depresses the market price and cancels a large number of loans. The total of credit is thus reduced. Eventually, as in the recent depression, the banks are

likely to find themselves the possessors of a lot of securities which are so low in value that the loans made against
them cannot be repaid by selling the securities. The same
thing may happen with loans against commodities. Bank
debt, and consequently the circulating purchasing power,
simply will not expand under such conditions.

All this is serious enough, but when, as in the United
States, banks begin to fail and depositors thus lose confidence in the banks themselves, the stage is set for at
least a temporary collapse of capitalism. There is nowhere near enough currency in the whole country to pay
cash in full to every depositor. After enough depositors
have demanded and received cash, the banks must close,
because they cannot pay out any more. When all banks
are closed, our circulating medium has literally been
decimated.

A similar expansibility on the way up, coupled with
rigidity on the way down, is exhibited by instalment
credit. The industrial system is equipped to produce more
of almost everything than people have cash enough to
buy. This is especially true of the more expensive things
like automobiles. We therefore offer them credit for the
purpose. During boom times it is easy to expand this
credit without appearing to take unsound risks. People
have jobs; expectations are high. One family after another mortgages its future income to buy cars, furniture,
refrigerators, etc. Ninety-nine per cent of these loans may
be well within the capacity of the borrower to pay—if
general misfortune does not arrive. But after a while,
almost everybody in a buying mood for the articles for
sale has been loaded up with all the debt he can carry.
The demand for new durable goods therefore stops ex-

panding at the old rate. As we have seen in the early sections of Part II of this book, when demand for automobiles, for instance, *stops expanding*, the production of automobiles *falls*. Thus you have one of the factors starting a depression. Unemployment spreads, incomes shrink. Instalment collections may for a while—and apparently do—hold up pretty well, because the debtors do not like to lose the valuable property now in their possession. But they will stop buying other things to pay the instalments. And instalment credit stops growing; new loans are made in smaller quantities as old ones are paid off. This restricts the demand for new goods and deepens the depression. The original rapid growth of instalment credit has helped bring on a depression and has made it more difficult to recover from one.

The point to note is that the use of credit—bank credit and other short-term loans—assumes a constantly more important place in the operation of our system as industrial capitalism advances. The instability to which it gives rise without social planning is therefore progressively more dangerous.

5. OTHER INTERNAL RIGIDITIES

There are other important and growing elements in our system which increase the difficulty of readjustment to changing conditions of demand and supply. Let us list and describe them briefly.

Inelastic demands. The classical argument is that, in order to increase the demand for a given article, it is necessary only to decrease the price. If supply for any reason exceeds demand, and the price is allowed to fall, the demand will grow, and a new balance will be brought about. We have already seen that, in numerous important cases, the price does not readily fall. But suppose the price does fall, will the demand necessarily increase? There are many cases where this does not easily happen, and these cases are important. Take soft coal, for instance. Coal is used mainly for making steam—a power supply for industry and railroads. It forms a minor part of the costs of those industries which use it. Their demand for coal depends upon the market for their own products. If the supply of coal exceeds the demand for it at any given time, and the price falls, this does not have any effect upon the need of coal users for power. It may induce some of them to use coal instead of oil or gas, but this effect is limited. The demand depends chiefly, not on the price of coal, but on the operation of a whole system of production. Wheat is another kind of instance. The demand for wheat is dependent mainly on the eating capacity of a given population and on dietary habits of long standing. Changes in the price do not have great effect upon the amount consumed.

These two examples are typical of two great classes of products, the number and importance of which increases as industrial civilization advances. One—that class typified by coal—may be called goods, the demand for which is incidental to a larger process; their sales depend on a whole and complicated institution of production. The other—that typified by wheat—may be called goods which are regarded as necessities and have already approached the upper limit of their possible consumption. People do not eat much more bread, no matter how prosperous they may be, and they will continue to eat bread to the bitter end, as long as they have any money at all.

In both cases the demand is inelastic—it does not respond readily to price changes.

Service Products. In an advanced industrial civilization, there are an increased number of wants which are satisfied by workers who do not add to the total quantity of physical goods, but handle them, transport them, sell them; or indeed perform services having little to do with goods at all, such as barbering, running beauty shops, writing books or teaching. In all cases where such human services are important, the labor cost is high, even though the wages of the individual may be low. In retail stores, for instance, wages of clerks add much to the prices of the articles sold. It is the cost of paying milk drivers that makes up a large part of the spread between the farm price of milk and the price at your back door. Even when wholesale prices or farm prices or factory prices decline, the retail price cannot be reduced nearly as much without cutting wages. You cannot reduce the cost of education without cutting teacher's salaries, or of putting out fires without cutting firemen's wages. But it is not easy to reduce wages, even where there are no unions to protest. For one thing, people have to eat, and the retail prices which they must pay for food remain relatively rigid, because of the very retail clerks' wages which have not been cut. This is, in a sense, a vicious circle.

The same lag operates on the way up. The factories are becoming more productive, let us say, and the wages of those performing services ought to be increased so that they can buy more. But no comparable advances in efficiency are being introduced in their occupations. No increase in their wages can be paid without increasing the price of their services. This is not always easy. Wages of public employees, for instance, tend to lag behind rising wages in industry. If you are trying to operate a system which depends on flexibility of prices to keep automatically in balance, here is an important obstruction. The increasing numbers in service occupations prevent sufficiently rapid changes.

Uncontrollable supplies. When supply exceeds demand, says the classical rule, and demand cannot be increased by the fall of prices, the supply itself will fall. Producers, seeing that people really want less of that particular type of goods, no matter how cheap it is, will devote their capital and energies to something else which is wanted more. Thus the productive energies of society will be directed toward making those things a larger amount of which is most needed. The producers forced out of the line in which the glut exists will be those making little or no profit—in other words, those having the highest costs. Thus, efficiency is enhanced in the industry where the excess supply arises. Does this really happen in our world?

In many cases it either does not happen at all, or happens with such slowness and difficulty that immense trouble is caused to everyone. When crop prices fall, farmers often raise more rather than less, in order to try to keep up their incomes. A farm is not only a unit of production but a home; being a farmer is not only a way of production but a way of life. It is a long and painful process to force farmers out of production. Those who are forced out in times of stress are often the more efficient rather than the less. They have borrowed money to invest in buildings, stock and machinery which reduce costs on a large output. But when prices sink below a certain point, the interest charges and taxes cannot be paid and the mortgage is foreclosed. Meanwhile the primitive farmer who does everything by hand and has inferior soil will stay on, simply by exploiting himself and his family, by subsisting at the poverty level.

In the coal-mining industry, a long-continued excess capacity which drives prices down does not limit the potential production of the industry. The extra mines, the reserve supplies of coal still exist. Unduly low prices caused by a persistent oversupply hampers the mines with the largest investment in efficient machinery, and leads to an attempt to reduce costs by an extreme exploitation of labor. Year after year, intermittent operation keeps a labor supply in the neighborhood of the mines which is larger than is needed. Readjustment of supply does not take place, and a premium is put upon economic waste in production of the chief source of power, upon which industrial civilization depends. The whole of industry, needing an expanding market, suffers immediately because of the poverty of miners.

There are numerous other instances in which we can observe the degenerative effects of the chain which leads from oversupply and reduced prices, neither to expanded demand nor to reduction of supply, with an influence for greater efficiency, but to continual excess of capacity, extreme exploitation of labor and gross economic waste. This is likely to happen wherever (a) technological advance tends to increase the supply and (b) the demand is inelastic and (c) natural or other conditions hamper a decrease in productive capacity.

Is it any wonder that, observing the effect of uncontrolled supply in such industries, many business men try to organize in such a way as to limit output and keep prices up? The trouble with this policy is that such organization is often most successful in industries where demand is not inelastic, where lower prices really would increase demand.

Another and more subtle trouble, which cannot be dealt with by any industry acting for itself, is that many a demand which seems inelastic at a given time would not be so if all industries at once lowered their prices and thus increased their employment. The reduction of output by industries which can manage to make the reduction decreases the demand for the products of industries which cannot manage it, and the total reduction of buying power reduces the demand for the products of all industry.

6. THE RIGIDITIES OF FOREIGN TRADE

When growing production could not be sold at home, the old formula required selling it abroad. The nations which first develop machinery and large-scale production sell their surplus manufactured product to more primitive or backward regions, accepting in part raw materials in exchange, and in part allowing payment to be made by a growth of debt in the new and developing country. The exports from the old country, financed in this way, gradually build up factories in the new country. When their product in turn becomes large, international competition arises among manufacturers. As the backward regions with rich resources are progressively developed, the possibility of applying the old formula diminishes. Then the inhabitants of all the industrialized countries must consume more of what they themselves produce if it is to be sold at all. According to the theories of orthodox economists they could do this if freedom of trade, of price changes and of income changes were permitted. But here rigidities and barriers are introduced, at the behest of capitalist interests, by governments themselves. Tariffs and quotas are established to hamper international competition.

The orthodox economists are commonly called "internationalists," the business men and politicians "nationalists." After over a hundred years of internationalist teaching, the world is drifting closer than ever to a congeries of closed economic systems. We have approximations to them now in Germany, Russia, Japan, and Italy; the British Empire is groping toward economic unity; France and the United States are both turning their eyes inward.

The economic doctrine now called internationalism is nothing less than laissez-faire, applied on a world-wide scale. If competition is free, it holds, the producers having the lowest cost will get the bulk of the business. This will benefit people as consumers, for they will pay the lowest possible prices. It will benefit them as producers also, for if the price of everything is as low as the most efficient practices make possible, more goods will be made and sold. The world's division of labor will be allotted naturally, according to the fitness of each region to produce, according to its raw material and its skill, according to its geographical location as a center of trade. If prices are uncontrolled, they will act promptly to adjust unbalanced demand and supply. Falling prices will restrict output and enlarge demand; rising prices will act contrariwise. The wider the markets, the broader will be the choice, the more numerous and the compensating price forces, and the greater the stability. Capital, by seeking investment in the places offering the highest return, will tend to develop and so to enrich the more backward regions, to make more abundant the goods which formerly have been scarce. A linking of interests by trade and investment across national boundaries will prevent war. This happy development depends, of course, upon certain conditions. There must not be monopoly. There must not be interferences with price movements on the part of the state, by such means as tariffs or aid to cartels or price-fixing. Capital and labor must move about freely. Wage rates and interest rates must both be readily flexible, according to demand and supply. There must be stable currencies, and their relative values must be so nearly unvarying as to facilitate trade.

It is unnecessary to elaborate further these conceptions; they are well enough known. What is not so well known, however, is that laissez-faire is not a "natural" economic order, which inevitably prevails except when some "artificial" action is taken to interfere with it. It did not exist when Adam Smith wrote. He was, as Leverett S. Lyon has written, a propagandist for an "economic plan" —a plan which he thought would render the largest possible benefit to everyone. This plan has never truly failed, because it has never fully been tried. England, educated by the Manchester School and governed over long periods by the Liberals, probably has come closer to applying it than any other nation. But all her ingenuity and all her skill in government have failed to enforce many of the prerequisites of true laissez-faire. We may perhaps say that she at one time came almost as close to it as Soviet Russia has come to a successfully planned socialism, but certainly no closer. Conservatives habitually say that socialism, though logical, cannot work because it is contrary to human nature. The same criticism can be applied with greater force to laissez-faire. The experience of over a century has abundantly proved that laissez-faire is contrary to human nature. It is an economic plan which is so far from realizable as to be utopian.

The very title of Adam Smith's famous book shows that it was, in part, propaganda against the preëxisting system of exclusive nationalism. "The Wealth of Nations," he called it. The old conception, commonly known as mercantilism, was that nations profited by selling without buying, by accumulating foreigners' money, just as private merchants try to expand their sales as much as possible while limiting their purchases to the utmost, and so to pile up more money than their neighbors. But of course the only use of money is to buy, and Adam Smith correctly showed that if nations do not spend abroad they cannot really grow wealthy from trade. You cannot eat money, or wear it, or build a house out of it.

The system of mercantilism, against which the Manchester School directed its propaganda, was in full course before the American Revolution and played a large part in causing it.

The phrases about freedom and natural rights embodied in the Revolutionary literature, and eventually enshrined in the Declaration of Independence, thus had, as Charles A. Beard and other historians have proved, a solidly material content. One might have inferred that the revolutionists were fighting Adam Smith's battle; that they were dedicating the new continent to economic "freedom" and laissez-faire. It is true that they wanted freedom of trade for themselves. But not for others. Hardly had the infant nation begun to draw breath when Alexander Hamilton persuaded it to build up manufactures by a protective tariff. Freedom from English restrictions was not enough. We had to restrict England in turn. Never since then has the United States moved very far toward freedom of trade. Its drift has been in the opposite direction. A society in which production is controlled by profit-seeking capital is bound to seek freedom for specific groups of capital or specific national aggregates by hampering the freedom of other groups or other nations to compete. There is no sufficiently powerful agency to enforce the interest of all against the interests of the parts.

The welter of trade restrictions which have grown up since the late War are often attributed to the War itself. That is in part true, but far from the whole truth. The more serious part of them have been imposed during the depression beginning in 1929. They were natural, one might even say inevitable reactions to that depression. When there is not enough trade to go round, the economically powerful producers in each nation believe that by tariffs and import quotas they can assure themselves at least the "home market," and they act on that belief. Prices of wheat have been held far above the world price in France, Germany, and Italy by these means. Under governmental stimulation, wheat growing has expanded so much in each country that the peasants would be ruined if wheat were let in freely from the United States, Canada, and the Argentine. As a result, wheat growers in the exporting countries have been ruined. Is it not utopian to expect that the government of any nation will sacrifice its own farmers for the benefit of those elsewhere so long as it has power to protect them? The same logic applies to manufacturers. Even more nearly inevitable have been the restrictions on movements of gold, of capital, and of foreign exchange. When prices fell, it was harder to pay debts incurred at higher price levels. Nations whose exports were shrinking could not meet their debt charges. The inflow of credits ceased; capital began to rush out as internal finances cracked. That took gold away. Banking and monetary systems simply had to be propped up by forbidding the shipment of gold, by controlling the export of capital and the exchange markets. It is no good to know that these acts in turn helped prevent trade from reviving. The only route to trade revival by means of free movement of money seemed to be through universal bankruptcy, and no nation was willing to permit that amount of deflation if it could be avoided. Laissez-faire asked too much of human nature under the circumstances.

But the depression in turn, it is sometimes said, was caused by the War, which was an interference with the "natural" economic order by the "artificial" measures of wicked diplomatists, military men, ambitious rulers. Both parts of this statement are too simple. The world has suffered many depressions without war. There was no war preceding the gloomy nineties, which in many respects are comparable with the past few years. Connection between the War and the speculative overexpansion of 1928 and 1929 in this country is pretty remote. The War did not cause the immense inequality in the distribution of income, which, in the opinion of many, led to overinvestment and the inability of the masses to buy enough to keep the factories and the farms busy.

The War of course superadded many elements of unbalance to an already topheavy economic structure. But the Kaiser and the Tsar, Poincaré and Sir Edward Grey, the Hapsburgs and the rest did not act in a vacuum. They were not living in the fourteenth century. Competition for markets was back of the rivalry for colonies and the struggle for sea power. We must not forget the push of Germany to the oil of the Near East, the desire of Russia for a warm-water port, the Berlin-Bagdad Railway, the struggle for the coal and iron of the Ruhr and Lorraine. Promoters of peace have been busy arguing that nations which expect to profit by conquest in the modern world are simply deceiving themselves; they cannot win. But the argument is irrelevant to the actual motives and behavior of nations subject to the influence of special interests. Oil companies can win; steel makers can win; armament purveyors can win. The "artificial," political interferences with economic health arose in large part from economic forces themselves. Economic nationalism, in spite of the theories of laissez-faire, flourished mightily before the War. Those who attempt merely to restore pre-war economic conditions are attempting also to restore the War.

Internationalism, then, is not a good word with which to describe the program of the orthodox economists. Their purposes are excellent; if they could be achieved the result might be called internationalism. But these purposes cannot be achieved by the means which they approve. The attempt to bestow freedom upon business by an absence of governmental interference merely results in the growth of powerful business groups which seek to restrict the freedom of other groups, of consumers, of government itself. Government may try to let alone, but profit-seek-

ers will not. They will in the end use government to exe-
cute that multitude of interferences which they favor.
Government may, to be sure, under the pressure of small
and helpless competitors, try to prevent the restraints imposed by big ones. A generation of such attempts in the
United States does not encourage us to hope much from
regulation to enforce competition, so far as internal policies are concerned. And internationally, it has completely
lost the battle against protective tariffs. Adam Smith's
plan, while preaching internationalism, favors the conditions under which the worst features of nationalism arise.
A doctor would be no more foolish if when treating a drug
addict he should content himself with shaking his finger
at the patient for using narcotics, while leaving about
large quantities of morphia and a hypodermic needle.

The financial and trade relations between the older industrial countries of Europe and the United States are a
prime example of the dilemma of capitalism when a newer
country develops a surplus of manufactures. The expansion of industry in the United States was to a great extent
financed with European capital. Until the War of 1914,
we were a debtor nation. Europe consumed large quantities of our wheat, meat, cotton, copper and other raw materials; we imported European manufactures. But we did
not import, for many years, enough to pay for our exports. We had a surplus of exports over imports—what,
in old terminology, was called "a favorable balance of
trade." A "favorable" balance of trade means merely
that a nation is giving away to foreigners a lot of precious
goods for which it is receiving nothing currently in return.
The reason we could contrive to do this is that we were
paying Europe debt charges on what she had previously

lent us. That was why we could sell abroad our surplus wheat and cotton.

In the course of time, we should have built up enough capital here, and lent enough abroad on our own account, so that it would overbalance the debts owed by Americans in Europe. We should have become a creditor nation by a gradual process, and the currents of our trade might gradually have been readjusted to the necessity of importing more than we exported. Even so, the readjustment would have been difficult. Producing and consuming habits are not easily altered. But the War caused us to become a creditor nation within two or three years. The European belligerents, in order to buy all the supplies they needed from the United States, first sold their investments here in large quantities, and then began to borrow from us. Through this new borrowing, our "favorable balance of trade" was for a time greatly increased, thus making the inevitable readjustment all the more difficult.

After the War—in 1920, to be exact—the readjustment began, with disastrous results particularly to American farmers. But then a revival temporarily moderated it. Without collecting the debts incurred during the War, we proceeded to make a lot of new loans in Europe. Especially after the inauguration of the Dawes Plan and the stabilization of currency in Germany, our bankers extended large credits there. For a time this sustained our exports; we still had a "favorable" balance. But here was a new and anomalous situation—a relatively new country was sustaining its exports to an old and developed country by making loans to it. The old countries had for years had a surplus of imports over exports, which they could buy because they were creditor nations and foreigners had to pay them interest. But now Germany had become a debtor nation and was buying abroad only by means of new borrowing. When, for any reason, the new borrowing ceased—as cease it must eventually—Germany could no longer buy abroad the goods she needed, and we could no longer sell in Europe the goods we were accustomed to selling. Our plight was intensified by the fact that other European nations as well had a diminished purchasing power. We are still making vain attempts to collect the European debts which we can never collect— unless, before they are canceled or written off, we can make the necessary readjustments at home to use more imports and either produce less of what we export or consume it within our borders.

What has happened, essentially, is that a great amount of capital and credit, irresponsibly expanded by a gigantic banking and investment system, and flowing in directions contrary to the customary channels of trade, has collided with the more rigid necessities of production and consumption of real goods. If American cotton production is not to be cut nearly in half and wheat farmers are not to lose their export market, we must fail to collect Europe's debt to us and must admit a lot of new European manufactures and consume them in addition to what we are now using. All possible means of readjustment are resisted to the last gasp by interested groups. It is much easier for this sort of dilemma to arise in a highly developed capitalist system than in one in which finance plays a smaller part.

7. THE SIZE OF THE COMMUNITY

One further item must be added to the great changes traceable to technical progress and the growth of industrialism—the country has, socially speaking, been growing much smaller, and the vital community of interest of the majority of its people has expanded to include almost everybody in it. It is a commonplace to say that communication and transportation facilities have reduced distances miraculously, that the interweaving of production, trade and finance over vast territories has made the people of one section closely dependent on what happens in any other. But the implications of these statements are often not fully realized. The facts make possible nation-wide social and political movements more easily than ever before, they smooth the pathways of propaganda and agitation, and they simplify the task of anyone attempting centralized administrative control. They make the objectives sought by these movements and the policies of centralized administration immediately important to every citizen. The United States is to-day scarcely larger than Rhode Island when the union was founded.

8. THE SUM OF THE CHANGES

Looking back over our analysis of the basic changes in capitalism which may point to a growing incompetence of its ruling classes to deal with the situation in which they find themselves, and of the rise of new classes to power, what do we find?

We find that technical advance, proceeding continually, makes necessary more rapid readjustments of the elements of our system. It requires substantial expansion of the purchasing power of the masses of the people, through rising money incomes or falling prices of goods made. It requires mobility of labor and capital from declining industries to growing ones. It requires continual changes within the structure of costs and prices.

At the same time, the technical progress, impinging on a system of private ownership of capital and of productive facilities, makes possible ever larger concentrations of wealth and power on the part of a few. These few act in such a way as to diminish the possibilities of readjustment. They attempt to stabilize prices when prices ought to fall, they increase the area and rigidity of fixed costs. While the necessity of flexibility increases, the obstructions to flexibility thus grow more formidable. The net effect of the centralized capitalistic control is to intensify booms and depressions, to concentrate the gains of the system when we are on the upgrade, and, when we are on the downgrade, to throw the first and major losses upon the less protected and less powerful sections of the population—wage-earners and small salary earners through unemployment and wage-cuts, farmers through drastic price reductions consequent upon their lack of control over output. Eventually, however, this loss returns upon the owners of capital themselves, because profits or even interest payments cannot be maintained in a highly developed technical industry without selling large quantities of goods to the masses of the people. This necessity is enhanced by the drying up of the possibility of export surpluses or "favorable balances of trade."

All this does not mean that capitalism breaks down once and for all, that it cannot be renewed after a crisis and a painfully enforced readjustment. But it does mean that the spasmodic character of capitalist progress is increased, that crises are likely to be more severe in their social effects, and recovery more difficult. Booms may be shorter and sharper. The chills and fever of capitalism, observed since its infancy, shake and burn its whole body more drastically as it approaches old age. Social and political strains are correspondingly increased.

When we examine the changes in population, we see that they tend both to increase the difficulties of private capitalism and to modify the status of the capitalist. As population growth slows down, industry can no longer find an expanding market solely in increased numbers, values cannot float up so rapidly on the filling up of a continent. There are not so many immigrants to exploit. There is less opportunity to become an independent business man or farmer. The class distribution changes. Population is concentrated about industrial and commercial centers; city ways become dominant. The number of employees grows larger in relation to the number of employers; more are employed by the big concerns. There develops a large new class of employees—those engaged in professional and service occupations. They show signs of outnumbering in the not-distant future those engaged in production of actual physical goods. The capitalist as owner and enterpriser becomes decidedly less important; many of his functions are taken over by the highly trained technicians. The intellectuals are restive and their influence expands. The manual workers, though their numbers are now declining in proportion to the total, become more essential to the smooth operation of industry as their numbers decline.

It is quite conceivable to-day, as it was not when capitalism began, that production and distribution could be carried on at least as well if all the legal "owners" should be buried in an earthquake. The importance of the employees, both as consumers and as producers, is immensely enhanced. In actual fact, if not in political form, the rise in the community of the new classes is clearly visible. Their power is as yet largely potential; it is not well mobilized. Most of them have no good idea of what is happening to them, and most, probably, are still loyal to the old régime and the old ideas. But the pressure of events is making them restive. The old is cracking; something new is rising to take its place. The first essentials of the long revolutionary process are present.

PART III

THE CRISIS OF THE THIRTIES

I. THE EBBING TIDE

UNDER the "New Era" of Coolidge and Hoover, twentieth-century capitalism had reached a triumphant climax. Though, under the surface, the changes described in Part II had been progressing rapidly, on the surface there appeared to be a smooth and rising current. There were still, it is true, projecting reefs and marginal whirlpools, but they were ignored by most people. The markets for the surplus which farmers had learned to produce for war needs were steadily being diminished by increase of crops in the food-importing nations; the disparity between crop prices and industrial prices which had appeared in 1921 was never fully corrected; a spirited agrarian movement arose. Bituminous coal mining, cotton textiles and other industries were in continual difficulties. Various pools of unemployed kept alive the issue of "technological unemployment." There was a large amount of political and financial corruption, a growing tendency to racketeering and gangsterism. Nevertheless, because of the general upsurge of production and profits, the building boom and the automobile boom, and the chances for making easy money by speculation, the dangers and injustices were ignored by the main forces of opinion and power. During this period the propaganda of the ruling classes themselves firmly impressed upon the public mind the conceptions that the possibility of increased mechanical production was virtually boundless, and that everybody had a right to hope that he could become, not merely comfortably fed and clothed, but rich.

But then the tide began to ebb. So pervasive was the optimism that, at the beginning, almost nobody took notice of the danger signals. These appeared long before the stock market plunged over a steep place into the sea in the fall of 1929. There had been minor recessions of the business cycle in 1924 and 1927, but the expansive tendencies of production and capital growth took us over them with scarcely a jolt. (The strength of the La Follette movement, which had polled nearly 5,000,000 votes in the Presidential campaign of 1924, was largely a leftover from the events of 1919 to 1921.) The first sign of real danger to the new era was the fact that residential construction turned down in 1928 and began to drop steadily. The housing shortage created by the War had been made up. There were still, of course, millions of people without decent homes, but the supply of housing had reached, indeed had overreached, the limits of effective demand on the part of those who had enough money so that it was profitable to construct new dwellings for them. Early in 1929 the construction of industrial and commercial buildings began to fall also. Business and manufacture were more than adequately equipped to supply all that people could buy. If observers had clearly understood the important part played by the construction industry in keeping business active, if they had realized how serious a symptom a slackened demand for durable and capital goods is, they would have taken alarm at this development. Overbuilding and overinvestment—in relation to the effective demand of ultimate consumers—had done its work.

Production of automobiles began to fall in June, 1929. Thus the greatest industry making durable consumers' goods—aside from the construction of dwellings—indicated that at least a temporary saturation point of demand had been reached. Fewer people, at the existing level of wages and prices, were buying new cars. And, with construction and automobile manufacture shrinking, the general curve of industrial production turned down. There was less demand for such things as steel, lumber, cement, which serve as materials for durable goods. Meanwhile the production of perishable consumers' goods such as food and clothing, which had increased less in the boom, shrank little or not at all. It was not until much later in the depression that they were affected.

The stock market went on booming after the real depression started. People avid for speculative gains paid little attention to the drop of the output from which industrial profits are derived. Stocks rose so high that their yield, at the prices paid for them, was less than the interest on money borrowed to buy and hold them. But what did that matter to people who were buying stocks not in order to receive dividends, but in order to resell them promptly at a higher price? As long as some one else would buy as foolishly, speculative purchasing could continue.

The whole process was, of course, rationalized by the theory that business profits would keep on increasing in the future as they had in the past few years. Failure to see the underlying difficulties made this theory persuasive. People overlooked the fact that this rapid increase of profits was itself at once a symptom and a cause of deep maladjustments. It was a symptom of the fact that the reduced costs of production arising from technical improvement were not being passed on quickly enough to wage-earners and farmers, and hence that popular purchasing power for the products of mass production was not advancing so rapidly as the capacity to produce. It was a cause of overbuilding and overinvestment in relation to popular demand, since it created huge corporate savings to be reinvested in productive equipment, and attracted other savings and credit to the capital markets. If speculators had been conscious of such maladjustments, they would have taken prompt alarm at the fall of the curve, first of building construction and then of industrial production in the industries making durable goods.

One group of economists especially shared much of the blame for misjudgment of the situation. This was the school which laid great emphasis on monetary and credit matters. According to them, there was no danger so long as the average of commodity prices was fairly steady. Booms and depressions, they thought, were caused by rising and falling prices. These in turn were caused by monetary and banking policies. All you had to do to maintain prosperity, once you had it, was to keep prices steady, and all you had to do to keep prices steady was to pump more money and credit into circulation when prices started to fall, or to pump some out when they started to rise. Now, it was an outstanding feature of the prosperous period between 1923 and 1929 that there was relatively little fluctuation in commodity prices. On the average, they neither rose nor fell far. It was commonly supposed that management of credit by the Federal Reserve System had a good deal to do with this. At any rate, the comparative steadiness of the average of prices soothed any fears in the hearts of many economists.

Professor Irving Fisher, an eminent leader of this school, was so misled that he actually saw no danger in the stock-market inflation up to the very moment of collapse. With steady commodity prices and rising industrial profits, why should there not be perpetual prosperity, and why should not the price of shares go on up forever? That was, indeed, the logical conclusion from his monetary theory. The fact that it did not turn out so seems to have taught this school of economists little or nothing. All through the depression they have continued to talk as if all you had to do in order to bring back prosperity and keep it was to manage money in such a way as, first, to cause rising commodity prices, and, second, to keep prices steady when a proper level has been reached.

Many economists and business men who did not swallow whole the monetary theory, or expect the prices of stocks to rise forever, still felt that the inflationary boom on the stock exchange was just an isolated phenomenon. They thought it merely a speculative craze depending on too easy an extension of credit by the banks; and, when the bump came, they expected that a sufficient downward correction of stock prices would take place without much effect on the business of the nation. The common expression of this point of view was that business itself was "fundamentally sound." If our economic structure had indeed been fundamentally sound, this expectation would have come true; the fact that it did not is a sign of how deep-seated the trouble was.

When the stock-market crash began, industrial depression was already well under way, both in this country and abroad. The depression was not caused by the crash; that was just one among many factors, which helped to intensify it after it had begun. We have already traced the start of the decline of industrial production in the United States: residential building began to fall in 1928, building as a whole early in 1929, automobiles and the average of industry's output in June. The cumulative effect of these events began to show in a fall of wholesale prices in July. The decline of wholesale prices had already begun in France by February, in Germany, Great Britain, Italy and the Netherlands by March. Wholesale prices of many commodities are set in a world market; their fall evidenced a shrinking world demand which must be reflected in this country as well. Liquid funds had flowed from Europe in large quantities to augment our speculative boom; it was probably the withdrawal of such funds in October which started the deflation of the Stock Exchange. Some were withdrawn because the danger signals were more clearly recognized abroad than at home, some because the money was needed to pay the costs of the depression which was already progressing in the countries which had sent us speculative funds.

It needed only a slight push to topple the structure. When everybody is buying in the hope, not of holding but of selling again, everybody will begin to sell when it is clear that prices are falling. And then panic is inevitable.

2. THE HOOVER RESISTANCE

President Hoover, who had had a great reputation as an economic engineer and humanitarian while prosperity

was on, gradually disappeared at the small end of the
telescope of public esteem after depression set in and
deepened. It was generally believed, by the time the election of 1932 arrived, that he was in some personal way
responsible for what had happened, that he had done
nothing to stem the tide, that he was a model of stupidity,
weakness and indecision. In view of the fact that the
Republican administration had assumed the credit for
prosperity and had promised a chicken in every pot and
two cars in every garage, that was poetic justice. Politics
works in this way; it is fortunate that it does, otherwise
we should never be rid of defeated generals. Nevertheless
the popular judgment was incorrect. President Hoover
was merely the representative—and a representative
somewhat above the average—of the ruling economic
classes in the United States. The responsibility for what
happened was not his alone, but theirs. Almost everything he had done or failed to do was in consonance with
the best judgment and the prevailing opinion of those who
exercised actual economic power in the nation. They controlled the party that elected him, a large part of the
press, and business and financial organizations throughout the country. The President was governed by the
forces that made him. They were just as stupid, bewil-
dered and helpless as he.

It was a reflection of their short-sighted interest, for
instance, which before the depression had led him, first
as Secretary of Commerce and then as President, to try to
force upward American exports without accepting enough
goods in return to pay for them—not to speak of accepting enough goods to pay Europe's debt charges to us also.
He bowed to these forces, possibly against his better

judgment, in signing the Smoot-Hawley bill, with its heightened barriers against imports, even after the onset of depression. They saw no more danger than he in financing our export surplus by lending to Europe—especially to Germany—large new sums with which to pay for what we sold. Only a few of them recognized any inconsistency between this course and demanding payment in full of the war debts of the Allied governments.

The business and financial community stubbornly resisted, as did Mr. Hoover, the agitation of the farmers caused by the shrinkage of European markets for our war-expanded wheat production. When it finally became politically necessary to do something for the wheat farmers, the governing classes cooked up a scheme which made the trouble worse. The Federal Farm Board, unlike such plans of the farm forces themselves as the McNary-Haugen bill and the debenture plan, did not recognize that any solution of the trouble must in some way deal with the shrinking export market and its effect upon domestic prices. It assumed that there was no persistent problem of overproduction in this country, that surpluses were a matter of economic accident only and would soon be offset by shortages. Only on such a theory was it sound to attempt the "stabilization" plan of buying with government funds the surplus stocks of wheat in order to maintain the price, without making any provision to sell those stocks or to cover the probable loss in doing so. Since the basic theory was untrue, the result of this device was only to maintain too large a wheat production without having much effect in raising prices, and to keep hanging over the market the large government stocks, which eventually helped to break it during depression.

Another example of Hoover ineptness which was in line with the judgment of dominant opinion in the country was his prescription for the soft-coal industry. For years this had been riddled with overcapacity, low wages, unemployment, economic waste, labor troubles. If any industry ever required unitary management in the public interest, this one did. Yet Mr. Hoover advised us that its troubles would be solved merely by engineering improvements in particular mines, and by competition, which, he believed, would cause the less efficient to go out of production and would equate demand and supply for coal. At the same time he approved a wage agreement for one part of the industry (the Jacksonville agreement) which did not cover another large part, where exploitation of labor had free sway because of the absence of unions. He did nothing to bring about control of the non-union fields. The result was, naturally, further expansion of overcapacity, more wage-cuts and bankruptcies, and an even sicker industry. But Mr. Hoover's poison-prescription for the industry was not invented by him. It was favored by a large part of the coal operators themselves, by the conservative president of the union, and by orthodox economic opinion.

These preliminary considerations throw light on Mr. Hoover's policy in the face of depression. The popular legend is that he had no plan, that he did nothing. Quite the contrary; he had a very definite plan and acted promptly upon it. His conception of the affair was based upon the prevailing opinions—that the business of production and trade was itself fundamentally sound, that the only trouble was a speculative collapse in the stock market, that the main job was to insulate business against the possible reactions of this collapse. The only enemy, he thought, was fear. And he also believed that private business, disorganized, predatory and planless though it really was, formed the bulwark of stability rather than being one of the weakest members of the foundation. Therefore he called together the leaders of business and labor and asked them to agree to proceed with their activities as if nothing had happened. Employers were to keep on expanding their plants, ordering their materials, producing and selling. They were not to reduce prices or wages. Labor was not to rock the boat. Government, for its part, was to push public works. If everybody was assured that everybody else would act in this way, fear would be banished, confidence would prevail, and business would not lose its fundamental soundness.

It is important not to scoff too readily at this plan, because if we do, we shall not draw the correct inference from its failure. If the assumptions of Mr. Hoover and the ruling economic classes had been correct, it would have worked. Its ineffectiveness proves, not that Mr. Hoover was a solitary dunce incapable of action, but that the depression was caused by something more than the collapse of stock speculation, and that business could not, under its existing régime, coöperate for any such purpose as he set forth. Business was not fundamentally sound. Production could not be maintained because, under the circumstances, the goods could not be sold. Employment and wages could not be guarded against shrinkage. Markets had definitely been lost—markets abroad, for we had ceased lending there or buying as much as we should —markets at home for automobiles and houses and other durable goods, because a saturation point of sales had been reached in reference to the purchasing power of the ultimate consumers. Public works could not be expanded sufficiently because the government had not planned in advance or accumulated enough funds to do the job quickly or on a large enough scale. And, to cap the climax, few at the conference had any abiding faith that anybody else there would live up to his promises. There was no binding obligation, in a competitive order, to do so.

Mr. Hoover's next important move was to reduce income taxes. In the light of subsequent events, this looked like simple madness. If one assumed that a serious depression was unavoidable, that in a depression the government would have to spend large sums for relief, for stimulation of public works and the like, and that it was desirable to keep the budget as nearly in balance as possible, one would obviously favor the collection of at least moderately high taxes from those best able to pay. But neither Mr. Hoover nor his supporters did assume that a depression was inevitable or that large public spending would be necessary. On the contrary, they were wedded to the prevailing tax theory of Secretary of the Treasury Mellon, of most others with large incomes, and of the economists who gave them theoretical support.

According to this theory, prosperity proceeds from the rich downward. Take care of the big incomes and the small incomes will take care of themselves. More specifically, don't tax the rich too much and they will have more money to invest; their investments will buy new capital goods and stimulate new construction which will furnish employment and profits to the small fry. If this theory was sound during prosperity, it was doubly sound when depression was threatened. The President had asked business men to continue to build and produce. To cut the income taxes of the rich was obviously an encouragement to them to do so. It would release more private funds for this purpose; it would assure a larger gain to any investor who prospered. The folly of the measure was not simply the folly of Mr. Hoover, it was the folly of the ruling classes themselves, and of their theory about national wealth. It was the folly of assuming that, in an advanced technical world, new investment will be made, or anything can be earned on it, unless there is a corresponding increase in the incomes of the masses who must buy the goods and services which the investment will produce. Or, to give the erroneous belief its due credit, it was the folly of assuming that large earnings and investment by the rich automatically assure that the masses will have enough income to buy what is produced. The failure of the Mellon income-tax reductions either to perpetuate prosperity while we had it, or to restore it after it was lost, are pieces of the same fallacy, and should teach us the same lesson.

As the months went on, attention became concentrated on governmental reports of employment and business activity that were far more optimistic than the facts warranted. A whole series of cheerful predictions by public and private authorities, which were always followed by new disasters, became a public laughingstock. A standard joke called attention to the fact that all Mr. Hoover had to do in order to send the stock market down was to predict recovery or talk of the famous corner, around which prosperity was supposed to be. But these were not plain lies, given out for fatuous political purposes. They were fancy lies, honestly told in pursuit of a calculated policy. Mr. Hoover undoubtedly believed that if he told them vigorously and credibly enough, the very telling would make them come true. They were in complete harmony with his plan and his analysis of the situation— which was that business needed only confidence, that the only enemy was fear. If recovery had come promptly, he would have been hailed as a great prophet; under-emphasis on the worst of the true situation at a time when knowledge of it would have served only to undermine the confidence upon which recovery depended would have been regarded subsequently as high statesmanship. The trouble was not that Mr. Hoover did not act, it was that business could not be saved by the injections of optimism in which his action chiefly consisted.

Nothing, perhaps, reveals the intellectual bankruptcy of the ruling classes more clearly than their course in raising the tariff in the spring of 1930. The tariff had long been the Indian snake oil of the dominant industrial interests. It was the patent remedy for everything. It had made manufacturers rich, and manufacturers had made America rich. Every depression had been caused, we were told, by reducing it or efforts to reduce it. Now, in their extremity and their fear, the Republicans returned to it as a dying sinner returns to his childhood faith. What matter that an increase in the duties would make it still harder to import the goods necessary to pay for the wheat and cotton which our farmers were already having difficulty in selling abroad? What matter that it would help to cause default on foreign debts to us, already hard to pay? What matter that the home market, which it was supposed to corral for our industrial producers, was already shrinking because of the inability of consumers to buy enough industrial products at the prices charged? Those who controlled our government, like those who controlled the government of every other important capitalist country, tried to resist depression by making it harder to buy and sell. They used a time-honored method of defending themselves at the expense of others, unconscious that if others were pushed over the abyss, they themselves would be pulled after.

So business and the President together went on whistling in the dark, carrying on, doing everything as usual that their habits and training and beliefs had taught them to do. But in spite of all promises and efforts to maintain production, one menacing fact made it impossible to do so. *Goods could not be sold as fast as they were made.* After a short time of producing ahead of orders, any business man could see the result in his own stockrooms. A prominent statistical concern sent questions to a large number of corporations concerning the growth of their inventories during 1929. Between the beginning and the end of the year, stocks of unsold goods were reported to have increased as follows:

Office equipment	13 per cent
Copper	15 " "
Retail stocks	16 " "
Iron and steel	18 " "
Agricultural machinery	22 " "
Oil	22 " "
Electrical equipment	27 " "
Foods	30 " "
Railroad equipment	35 " "
Household products & supplies	40 " "

Meanwhile individual consumers had, by the million, ceased replacing the stocks of durable or semi-durable goods which they had bought—automobiles, houses, rugs, furniture, and even clothing.

Under these circumstances, manufacturers could not and did not keep their promises to maintain production. The government was able to expand a little its public works program. But the construction of residences in the first six months of 1930 was only half the amount of the first six months of 1929. So great was the decline in private construction that public works could not anywhere near compensate for it, and the total of building fell off. Men and women lost their jobs in factories and in the building trades.

The dispute over the number of unemployed caused a census to be taken in April, 1930. It revealed what was supposed to be a reassuring fact—that there were "only" about 2,500,000 persons who had had jobs, were now without them and were actively looking for them. But in addition there was another large number, not announced, who thought they still had jobs but were not working because they were "laid off" or on compulsory "vacation." That most of these remained unemployed for months and years we subsequently discovered. The census did not count at all the young people and others who had never had jobs but now were forced to seek them, who were as truly unemployed as anyone.

The wage truce soon was broken by employers—reductions in rates began in the spring of 1930, gathered momentum in various concealed ways, and finally poured so rapidly through the cracks in the dam of promises that they swept it away.

The confidence game reached an absurd climax when, in the fall of 1930, the Lions Clubs sent out a broadcast telegram asking everyone to hold a "business confidence week" beginning October 19th.

But the second winter of depression was shortly ahead, the jobless were growing in numbers, unemployment relief was essential, and the great drive began to feed the hungry and house the shelterless by the improvisation of private charity. Heroically the ruling classes had prevented us from following the horrible example of other nations in establishing a "dole." Consequently we had no reserves built up by unemployment insurance with which to cushion the drop into joblessness. We had no reliable way of distributing them, such as is provided by a public system of labor exchanges. The defensive reaction against this criminal error was to pretend that private charity could do the job, that it was not a "dole," that it injured the self-respect of the recipient less than would payments out of a fund accumulated for the purpose during prosperity.

In the Hooverian attitude toward unemployment you can see an almost perfect example of the unfitness of the old conceptions, and of the people who hold them, to cope with the situations which technical advance has brought about in a capitalist order. It consists of a series of delusions, each resting on an outworn truth. These delusions are sincerely held; they seem like noble principles to those who believe them. Their effect, however, is to throw the inevitable losses of the system as much as possible on the most helpless participants in it—the unemployed workers. They are self-protective devices, for the most part unconscious, of the old order. And their ultimate defeat is a surrender by the old order itself.

The first delusion is that we have a system in which personal effort determines the material welfare of each individual in it. If a man is really able, he will be rich. If he is merely competent and industrious, he will surely have a job. Only those who are lazy or unemployable are unemployed. To admit that an unemployed person has a right to live at the expense of others is to undermine the basis of capitalist civilization. A long time ago, this used to be approximately true. During the depression it stood in absurd contrast to a situation in which there were no jobs for at least a third of the industrial workers. If a third of the workers are lazy and unemployable, our civilization is doomed anyway.

The second delusion is that each depression is the last, that it is an unhappy accident in a normal progression of prosperity. By installing a few reforms, we shall prevent the next one. When we are prosperous, we should not do anything to prepare for the next depression, because to admit that depression might come is to destroy the confidence which is essential to a continuance of prosperity. This was moderately true in a primitive and expanding capitalist order. At least its falsity did not have irremediable consequences. But now it is the height of folly.

The third delusion is that, while certain unfortunate people always need help, and at some times more people need help than at others, the obligation to help them is not a social one, but merely the moral imperative of private generosity on the part of those who feel charitable. And there are enough charitable people, of small means and large, to succor the needy. It is all right to "give until it hurts," but decidedly wrong to be taxed until it hurts, if the taxes are used to repair the human damage of a broken-down industrial system. This delusion was shattered against the fact that a considerable proportion of the necessary relief had to be shouldered by local governments and paid out of taxes from the beginning, that as time went on, much more than half the relief came from this source. The delusion threw the burden, first on the relatives and friends of the unemployed, in city and country, who could least afford it and had least responsibility for the occurrence of the crisis, and then on local governments dependent for income on property owners already groaning under the weight of local taxes. Eventually, as we shall see, we had to come to a full-fledged national dole in the CWA and other devices.

Now, there is no shining merit in unemployment insurance or in a national contribution to the relief of unemployment. Both involve grave difficulties and abuses; neither is a good substitute for full employment. But the point is that capitalism in crisis is inevitably forced to practice something of the kind, as the lesser of evils. The point is that this necessity is not avoided by maintaining the old individualist pretenses. And the point is that once the nation has admitted that there is a collective, public responsibility for the compensation of the unemployed, it has also admitted in principle that there is a collective, public responsibility for running industry in such a way that mass unemployment shall not occur.

The exponents of the old order with unerring instinct sensed these implications, and did their inadequate best to avoid the great moral defeat which was involved in the abandonment of their attitude toward the unemployed. But they could not prove to a whole nation in poverty that the poverty of each is his own fault. Especially so, when a year or two before they had been in undisputed command of the situation, and had told everyone that if he would but follow their example he would shortly be rich. Or when the existence of technical capacity to produce almost limitless wealth had been driven home with pile-driver publicity.

3. THE SECOND PHASE OF HOOVER PLANNING

When it became necessary to acknowledge that the first Hoover plan of holding the industrial *status quo* and injecting confidence had failed, there ensued a long, weary period of waiting. The country waited while production declined, prices fell, incomes shrank, the number of unemployed increased, mortgages were foreclosed, banks and insurance company assets wore away, banks failed. The longer it tried to pump up confidence while these things went on, the less possible it was to have confidence. The confidence-pump squeaked and leaked, and finally stopped altogether. The administration waited for the "natural" end of the depression and the "natural" beginning of revival. Meanwhile its principal action was negative. It resisted all suggestions and agitations for more governmental activity. It turned a deaf ear to the growing clamor for enforcement of the anti-wage reduction agreement, for some form of public unemployment relief, for a different kind of help to the farmers, for a large public-works program based on borrowing. Although this latter course had been endorsed by Mr. Hoover many years before when it had been suggested by economists as an anti-depression measure, and although he had actually inaugurated it in a small way in the first winter after the Wall Street disaster, he now turned against it because he was convinced that it was more important to balance the budget. The two things were in obvious contradiction. Anything he could do which involved large borrowing might weaken the securities market and discourage new private investment—and he relied upon private investment to start revival.

This was the period which gave rise most of all to the legend that the depression President was a spineless mass of jelly in the face of the nation's difficulty, that he was incapable of action. Yet he was still pursuing a definite policy, a policy endorsed in theory both by the financially powerful and by the conservative economists. It was a slightly different one from that which he had attempted to practice at the beginning, to be sure, and yet the two were related. The first theory had assumed that there was nothing much the matter, and that if everyone could be induced to believe this, there would be no danger. The second theory had to admit that there was something the matter: in some mysterious manner, the system had got out of kilter. But the way to remedy the disease was to let it run its course without interference. The economic order was a self-compensating one, and if left alone would get into balance. If wages were allowed to sink, that would reduce costs, profits would therefore reappear and furnish a bait for production, output would increase and employment would turn up. Existing goods would wear out, inventories would reach a minimum, and finally simple necessity would require enlarged production. Disparities in prices would be corrected by the force of competition. Prices that were too high would be driven down.

Inflated capital values would perforce be written off. The disappearance of weaker banks would strengthen the others. Eventually the banks would adjust their assets to lower values and begin to lend again. All that was necessary was for the politicians to keep hands off, and resist agitation for action which might either interfere with these "natural" readjustments or frighten those who had money to lend and invest. This was the reason for trying to balance the budget and resisting the appeal for larger Federal expenditure on any form of relief or construction.

There is a logical connection between this and the first policy, divergent though they were in their prescriptions. The first policy had assumed that no real danger was threatened, because it had always assumed that the system was self-compensating. If the economic order were naturally one which worked well, why expect serious difficulty? But when difficulty came, the trust in self-compensation dictated that no further "artificial" action be taken.

There is something to be said for a program like this. It will very likely work, if given enough time and allowed to proceed to a conclusion. That has been demonstrated in the discussion of a collapse of capitalism in Part I, Section 3, of this book. If production, employment, wages, prices, and capital values are allowed to sink low enough, a point will somewhere be reached at which a new balance of economic factors can exist and advance can begin. That point may be zero. It may be so far back that in order to regain it we must retrace the steps of half a century of business and financial development. But somewhere along the downward course it lies, even if it is so low that it demands a complete rebuilding of capitalism from the ground up.

What this theory does not anticipate is the social and political cost of a logical deflationary program. It does not see that on account of the powers of resistance which have been built up by concentrations of industry and capital, certain important prices and values will not be sufficiently deflated until the majority of the citizens have been reduced to a misery which they simply will not endure. It does not acknowledge the power which capitalist interests possess over the government itself, or foresee that they will use the government to prevent, if possible, their own deflation.

That is exactly what eventually happened to Mr. Hoover's program. He was adamant against public relief of the unemployed, of the distressed farmers. He was adamant against unbalancing the budget for an employment-creating building program. But the time came when the financial shoe began to pinch too hard. Railroads, insurance companies and banks were in danger. The better bonds might be defaulted. Deflation began to eat into the basic financial structure of private capitalism. And at this point, Hoover abandoned laissez-faire. He threw government credit into the breach. He did it because those who controlled railroads, insurance companies and banks convinced him that it was necessary. They convinced him that if their wealth went, everything would go. Capitalist society, when the logical implications of a deflationary program began to be imminent, simply could not take it.

The persistence with which debt-capital was protected during the deflation of everything else is shown by esti-

mates of the national income prepared for the National
Bureau of Economic Research by Simon Kuznets. Here
is the drop in the streams of income paid out to various
classes of income-receivers; between 1929 and 1932: *

> Wages dropped 60 per cent.
> Dividends dropped 57 per cent.
> Salaries dropped 40 per cent.
> Interest dropped 3 per cent.

(The figures for wages and salaries include mining, manufacturing, construction, railroads, but not trade and other occupations. The salaries figure include the big salaries which
dropped little or rose, as well as the small ones.)

Interest payments had even increased from 1929 to
1930.

Mr. Hoover at first stimulated the creation of a private
pool to rescue menaced financial institutions, and when
that did not work satisfactorily, he asked Congress to
establish the Reconstruction Finance Corporation. This
governmentally owned company, with an initial appropriation from Congress and the right to borrow more
money, lent funds to banks, insurance companies and
railroads in many cases where shrinking incomes threatened their solvency. In this way the government tried to
protect the great capital hoards against the onslaught of
the deflation which it was allowing to proceed unham-
pered in the earnings of workers, farmers, and business
income in general. This was, in reality, gambling on the
hope that a turning point would be reached before serious
inroads had been made on fixed capital investments. But
this gamble was increasing the rigidity of the most rigid
element of the system while doing nothing to stop the
decline of the most flexible. It was as if, when breaks ap-

peared in a levee, the engineers should strengthen the parts which were already the strongest while doing nothing about the parts which were giving way. Thus capitalism repeated a characteristic performance; it prevented action in behalf of the more unfortunate in the name of laissez-faire, while calling upon government to employ deliberate interference with the free play of economic forces to protect the centers of economic power. The net result was to weaken itself.

Before the policy of artificially sustaining capital values developed, however, attention was distracted from the domestic muddle by dramatic events abroad. By 1931, depression was smashing the intrinsically weak and crazy structure of international trade and finance. Nations, no one of which could produce all that it consumed or consume all that it produced, had been trying to act as if they were independent economic units. They were raising tariffs and other trade barriers against one another and thus deepening the crisis of all. When the flow of international credits dried up, the inconsistency of the existing debt framework was revealed: Germany, for instance, which had built up its entire economic structure on the basis of an excess of imports over exports, and had before the war paid for this excess by the earnings on its foreign investments and shipping services, now had to pay foreigners the interest on the debt it had itself accumulated after the War, not to speak of reparations. The fall of prices made all debt payments more difficult, even aside from the drop in the physical volume of trade.

It was necessary to knock over only one financial domino in order to upset the whole row. Germany, in her extremity, tried to establish a customs union with Austria and thus beat down at least one wall of the barrier about her. France became frightened at the political implications of this approach to "Anschluss," and vetoed it. Directly or indirectly, French financial interests, which had been extending help to Austria, caused the withdrawal of credits from her, and the first domino went over with the collapse of the Creditanstalt. German financial institutions, which were also involved in Austria, were already weak enough so that this endangered them; a bank holiday ensued in Germany. London, which had been sending short-term credit to Germany to earn the high rates of interest there, thus became involved. The British credits were frozen. The French and others who had large liquid funds in England withdrew them rapidly. Thus gold flowed out from London in immense quantities. A Labor government in Britain, being overthrown by a bitter attack, on the basis that its domestic spending endangered the gold standard, was succeeded by a National government, which promptly was forced off the gold standard, by the sudden excess of outgoing payments over incoming ones. Controls were established over German exchange, to hold Germany's gold reserves at the expense of foreign trade and payments. The exchange value of the pound sterling, unlinked from gold, fell. Other countries closely dependent on British trade promptly followed her off gold.

If anything were to be saved out of this confusion, the first step was obviously to get rid of the burden of political debts—reparations and war-debt payments. The main source of political payments was Germany: she owed reparations principally to France and England; France owed war debts mainly to England and in much smaller measure to us; England owed war debts to us. We were, according to contract, the ultimate recipients of the flow. It was therefore up to us to move first. After much pressure, and too late to prevent most of the damage, President Hoover suggested a moratorium on war debts and reparations, and the suggestion was accepted. At Lausanne, the recipients of reparations agreed virtually to their cancellation, expecting that war debts would be canceled in turn. The Lausanne meeting was regarded at the time as setting the course for further action to clear up the tangle of trade barriers, private debts and currency instability. So far, in spite of several attempts, the world has scarcely moved an inch further along the line laid out at Lausanne.

These events abroad prevented any prompt improvement of business through a revival of exports. To say this is not, of course, to say that revival would have come if the row of financial dominoes had not fallen and the gold standard had not been weakened. Entirely aside from the additional restrictions on trade produced by the financial crisis, each capitalist nation had long been striving to increase its exports without increasing its imports, and the inevitable result of this policy on world markets is a surplus of goods for sale, falling prices and depression. There can be no market where everyone wants to sell and no one wants to buy. The United States had been a chief offender in this respect. It therefore came with bad grace from our administration to blame the rest of the world for our failure to recover. This ignored the effect of our policy upon the rest of the world. It also ignored the immense obstacles to recovery in the internal economy of the United States itself, and within each of the other nations concerned. To say that the depression was international, though true enough, was only a convenient alibi for each national government. Depressions do not occur in the middle of the Atlantic and Pacific oceans, or solely along international boundaries.

What really had happened was that the international gold standard and the international debt structure had broken under the strain of continued depression. Their breaking was not an accident; if it had not come about in this precise way, it would have come about in some other. And the nations which left gold, being thereby placed in a somewhat more advantageous competitive position with regard to exports, were subsequently able to moderate a little the full force of the depression within their borders. Their gain was others' loss, in the shrinking world markets, and to that extent the United States was injured. But neither the gain nor the loss was great; the volume of world trade had become so small in any event that shifts in its sharing were of relatively little consequence. British prices ceased falling rapidly, but British trade hardly increased. If Britain had never left the gold standard, we still could not have sold abroad much more wheat or cotton or automobiles or agricultural machinery.

Two more devices of Hoover planning remain to be discussed briefly. One was work-sharing. This was, in reality, unemployment-sharing. It had no influence whatever on the amount of work to be done. It meant merely that the work—and the pay for it—should be distributed more evenly. It meant giving jobs at extremely low wages to some of the unemployed, at the expense of the wages of the employed. It transferred some of the burden from the shoulders of those who were giving charity to the shoulders of workers who were less able to pay for it.

The other was the effort to stimulate business by an easy credit policy. Interest rates had been kept low ever since the beginning of the depression, but credit obstinately refused to expand. The Federal Reserve Banks began to buy government bonds. In this way they accumulated about $500,000,000 of excess reserves. In prosperous times, such action, by increasing the liquid assets of member banks, tends to stimulate more lending. If the member banks sell the bonds to the Federal Reserve, they thereby accumulate funds. Private persons who sell bonds presumably deposit the proceeds. Thus the banks receive large amounts of money, either currency or "bank money"—i.e., deposits on their books—which is not earning any interest. The theory was that they would be forced to lend this money in order that it might earn something. An expansion of reserves in the Federal Reserve Banks can, under ordinary circumstances, lead to an expansion of lending by the member banks about ten times as large as the growth of reserves. This was thought to be an easy and simple way of enlarging the amount of purchasing power in circulation. It was a moderate type of inflation.

But it did not work. The ordinary capitalist machinery failed here as it had elsewhere. The people who needed the money, and who would have to start buying if the rest of the business machine were to operate, could not borrow from the banks. Wage-earners of course could not borrow; farmers could not. Business men who were already weighted down by debts and had shrinking markets were not good risks. Banks are accustomed to lend only to concerns which have business prospects. It is one thing to believe that if the banks would simultaneously expand loans to the whole business community, all would begin to buy more and everybody would have better prospects. It is another to expect individual banks to start the process by lending to individual customers at the bottom of a depression, without being assured that all the other banks were going to do the same thing and thus that all loans would be made more safe. Banks, though part of a system which, on account of its close interrelationship, requires collective action, do not act collectively because they are privately owned, profit-seeking enterprises. The proponents of the credit-expansion cure were thinking of the banks as if they were a single system, a social instrument. They ought to have been, but they were not.

Furthermore, the banks were afraid even to take risks that normally they would regard as good. A large part of their assets had become frozen in real estate loans, in bonds and stocks that had shrunk amazingly in value. To attempt to turn these assets into cash at the prevailing prices would bring certain disaster. The always considerable number of bank failures was growing. Nobody knew when depositors in large numbers might begin withdrawals. The instinct of self-preservation therefore led banks to keep as liquid as possible. They took advantage of the Federal Reserve policy, first to reduce their indebtedness to the Reserve Banks, second, to accumulate cash. The banks were themselves the first and largest hoarders. The self-preservative action of the part of individual banks had the same result as the effort on the part of each business to throw depression losses on others. It deepened the depression, and made the situation more dangerous for all. Rapidly the banks slid toward the crisis of March, 1933. The more they apprehended the calamity, the more they did to make certain its arrival.

Mr. Hoover was reported to be very angry at the banks for their failure to expand loans and so to stimulate recovery. In this he reflected the unpopularity of the banks among mortgagors who had been foreclosed or threatened with foreclosure, among borrowers on collateral who had been sold out, among depositors who had lost their money by failures, among business men and farmers who could not borrow to meet current obligations. The "international" bankers were unpopular because of the collapse of foreign ventures, the investment bankers because of the loss to investors in security issues. All this irritation was given point by the beginning of a long series of revelations concerning prominent bankers who had served their own interests by shady practices at the expense of the public. Thus a split appeared in the citadel of capitalism itself; various sections of the ruling classes began to quarrel, as they always do when an old order gets into serious difficulties. Logically, however, neither the President nor the other objectors had a very good case. The bankers were merely acting on the prescriptions of rugged individualism. Comparatively little of the trouble was caused by outright dishonesty. You cannot expect one section of the community to act collectively for the general good when other sections do not do so, when it is not organized to do so, and when all have been nourished on the principle that if each unit acts in its own interest, the interest of all will be served.

And so the closing months of the Hoover administration saw a complete rout of everything he had tried to do, because he had followed the prescriptions of the ruling groups themselves, and these prescriptions led to illogical and unworkable policies. At the beginning, business men could not effectively coöperate to maintain the *status quo,* since that status was impossible to maintain. Confidence could not be restored by optimistic statements, because more than confidence was lacking. A policy of governmental non-interference permitting deflation to work through to its logical end, could not be carried out because capitalism itself would not permit deflation of the most rigid elements in the structure, which needed deflation the most. Contradictory international policies which had long been followed caused an international crisis which interposed a further obstacle to recovery; belated and partial action was ineffective; the reparations and debt moratorium merely held the crisis in solution. And the effort to stimulate credit expansion by the banks was mired in the dismal swamp of financial individualism. Hoarding increased, gold withdrawals swelled, Michigan and then other whole states declared banking holidays in order to save what reserves they had and throw the burden elsewhere. The burden of withdrawals, not only for hoarding but to carry on current business, rapidly became concentrated on New York, and by March 4, 1933, the whole banking complex was tottering. Panic was on.

4. FERMENTATION

While the governing classes of capitalism under Hoover thus blindly sought a way out, American society was disintegrating, and from this disintegration there arose new ferments, new outcries, new pressures. Before turning to these strange movements, let us pause for a moment to check up on what had become of the more important factors in our economic life.

The total physical output of goods in the United States was reduced 37 per cent between 1929 and 1932. The shrinkage ran all the way from about 6 per cent in agriculture to about 72 per cent in construction.

The income paid out in the nation shrank 40 per cent. In shrinkage of income, construction was the heaviest sufferer, with 72 per cent, and mining and manufacturing followed not far behind. Agricultural income was not quite cut in half (it dropped 46 per cent).

The number of people working in the various occupations of the country, including employers, between 1929 and 1932, was reduced 33 per cent—just about one-third. In construction, 56 per cent stopped working, in manufacturing, 48 per cent. The number of unemployed was reliably estimated as 14,400,000 in 1932.

Those wage-earners who did have work in the major industries suffered a reduction in income per capita, of 32 per cent—almost one-third. The cost of living meanwhile had gone down only 20 per cent.

Total income paid on account of property ownership, including interest and dividends, was cut 30 per cent. Interest, of course, shrank very little.

(The above figures are taken from the Studies of Frederick C. Mills and Simon Kuznets made for the National Bureau of Economic Research.)

Neither this nation nor any other had ever in the last century been submitted to such economic strain in time of peace. The imagination simply cannot encompass the dislocation and suffering, physical and mental, which is symbolized in these abstract figures. Gradually the pressure began to wear through habitual ways of doing things, traditional ideas, and existing loyalties. People in increasing numbers stopped waiting hopefully for something to turn up, and began to stream off in new directions. The vat bubbled and boiled.

One of the first dramatic outbreaks which attracted the attention of the country was the bonus march. Outwardly and formally, this was one thing; inwardly it was another. The conventional attitude toward it was that it represented the climax of the long effort to raid the Treasury by veterans who considered themselves a specially favored class because they had fought for their country. Really, however, it was composed of a rank and file at their wits' end for a means of sustenance, who seized upon the best excuse they could think of to enforce their claims upon organized society. They now wanted the money, not really because they were veterans, but because capitalism in collapse offered them no way of feeding their wives and children or keeping a roof over their heads. They poured into Washington and settled upon vacant spaces as near the heart of the city as they could, in order to impress upon Congress their needs and those of others at home, whom they represented.

After some days of nervousness in which the Washington police under General Glassford managed to prevent embarrassing incidents, the government succumbed to panic and decided to show "a firm hand." President Hoover simply could not endure this continued demonstration of the extremities to which the crisis was forcing the unfortunate. He did not like to meet unemployment and want face to face. He was enraged at the thought that he might after all have to use Federal funds to support idle people. Unable to cure the disease which was eating the vitals of the country, he struck at this outward symptom which had come uncomfortably near. The army was called out to disperse this pitiful remnant of the ex-army. With grenades and firearms and tear-gas, it drove them out and burned their improvised habitations. Washington was treated to the sight of a one-sided battle in its streets, between the well-fed and -equipped forces and those who once had been called to the colors but were no longer needed and therefore were cast aside. Washington did not like the spectacle. Neither did the rest of the country. It did not help matters when the army, having killed an ex-soldier in the mêlée, buried him in the national cemetery with military honors. Such honors, if appropriate at all, would better have been extended to the living. The marchers straggled back on the roads from the capital. They erected monuments to the memorable occasion by adding to the number of "Hoovervilles" all over the country, where homeless men were for a time allowed to live undisturbed in their packing-boxes.

Another phenomenon of which the nation gradually became conscious was the army of drifters, many of them young boys and a few of them girls, who began by going about the country looking for jobs because they could not find work at home and could no longer be supported by their relatives, and ended by sustaining themselves by their wits, as confirmed vagrants. The freight trains were full of them; they thumbed their away along every automobile highway in the country.

From another quarter there arose dramatic signs of resistance. Farmers, long accustomed to pleading for legislative relief, turned to direct action. They organized in defense of their homes when these were threatened by wholesale foreclosure. A group of neighbors would crowd into a foreclosure sale, bid in the house, the implements and the live stock for a pittance, and return them to the owner. Outsiders were given to understand that it would be unhealthy for them to bid. In some cases threats of hanging directed against agents of the creditor, or even against a judge or sheriff, prevented the sale altogether. So dangerous did the resentment against foreclosure sales become that insurance companies granted a voluntary moratorium, and laws making moratoria compulsory were passed by numerous states. The Supreme Court later sustained this legislation.

The unemployed in cities and towns began to organize and act. Sometimes the leadership was local and spontaneous; often it was stimulated by radical groups like those of Communists, Socialists or the Conference for Progressive Labor Action. "Hunger marches" were mobilized. Demonstrations demanded more adequate relief—and often got it. Flop-house committees in Chicago, backed by a demonstration of five thousand, demanded a three-foot aisle space between beds, and clean sheets in municipal lodging houses. When a family was to be evicted, neighbors would gather and protest. Pitched battles with the police often resulted. After the furniture of the unfortunate household was removed to the sidewalk and the authorities had left, the crowd would often put it back. In extreme cases, when the landlord persisted in evicting, the house itself was wrecked. In one city, unemployed plumbers and electricians would go about reconnecting gas and electric wires, and by-passing meters, after the utility company's emissaries had cut them off. In other places, the unemployed groups were more moderate in their actions. They would seek to locate and distribute surplus supplies, organize barter exchanges, try to find odd jobs for their membership.

The growth of barter exchanges was one of the most interesting developments, in regions where the collapse of capitalism was most complete and where a more primitive type of civilization had persisted in any case. There was surplus food on the farms, surplus labor in the towns. Neither could be exchanged for the other because the possessors of neither had the money. What simpler than to exchange on the barter basis? Gradually the movement extended to the barter of old possessions such as furniture, and of new handicraft products and services. As it extended, the use of some sort of money was necessary for the most complicated and roundabout exchanges, and so scrip was printed for the purpose and paid out by the central organizations. The most active and ambitious of such movements were the National Development Association in Utah and the Midwest Exchange in Dayton, Ohio. Others existed in California, Washington, Oregon, and a dozen other states. But this instinctive attempt to rebuild capitalism from the bottom up, though it helped the relief of perhaps a million unemployed persons at the height of its development, was doomed to failure as a widespread and enduring remedy. It could not supply either the goods or the chance to labor that can be furnished in our technical civilization only by complex and expensive mechanical processes. The owners of the essential industrial plants would not barter their products or allow the unemployed to use them. Without possession of the centers of the industrial system, those who returned to barter could pursue their activity only around the handicraft fringes. And that did not offer much scope. If for no other reason, the back-track to a primitive civilization of local exchange is barred by the fact that without the employment of mechanical industry, a population of the present size cannot be kept alive.

With this ferment of activity went an even larger ferment of ideas. Literally thousands of schemes to end the depression were invented and pressed upon the government, the press, and persons who were supposed to have any sort of influence. As an editor of a magazine which dealt with public problems, I can testify that if, during the years 1931 and 1932, I had conscientiously analyzed every scheme which came to me I could have done nothing else; I should have had to employ a large staff of research assistants and secretaries. Even then there would have been on my desk a mountain of unanswered mail and unreviewed books at the end of the period.

Some day a social historian may classify this mine of material. He will find that a large section of it suggests doing something about money or credit. There is an almost endless variety of ways by which the volume of money might be increased, and it is natural for persons who have not enough money to think that more ought to be provided. The suggestions included remonetizing silver, issuing greenbacks, devaluing gold, issuing bonds as legal tender, abandoning a metallic standard altogether and basing currency on ordinary commodities, issuing stamped scrip, taxing unused bank deposits, distributing credit to consumers. The more the inventor knew about the operation of our present system, the more ingenious he was in devising means to make his expansion of purchasing power effective and to guard against the dangers of runaway inflation. In addition to these monetary schemes there were others bearing on other aspects of the system, such as shortening working hours, forbidding new inventions, extending the barter system to machine industry by letting the unemployed work in idle factories, giving subsidies of one sort or another to business so that it could begin reinvestment in capital goods, and insuring the banks against loss if they would lend business enough to start production on the level, say, of 1926.

The inventor of each of these schemes believed, in almost every case, that if only people could be converted to his idea and the government would act accordingly, all would be well. But each scheme embodied a basic fallacy. This was that the economic system was, normally, a successfully operating mechanism, that it was all right except for a flaw in one part. They believed the system was like an automobile motor which had unaccountably stopped; some applicants for the job of repair thought the trouble was in the carburetor, others thought it was in the spark plugs, or the generator, or the distributor, or the coil. But the real significance of these multifarious suggestions lay in the evidence they gave that we had never designed a motor adequate for the load being carried, and in the reflection they provided of the mental restiveness which is a symptom of social change. The fact that most of them were not consciously revolutionary or that they did not contain formulæ for shifts in power is relatively unimportant. Each constituted a challenge to existing authority, for each demanded a change in practice which would be instinctively resisted by those in command. And all together can be compared with the confused ferment of religious ideas which accompanied the Puritan revolution in England, or the outbreak of controversy which preceded the French Revolution.

One school of thought in particular flared, for a short time, into an amazing prairie fire of popularity. Technocracy was a revealing symptom. It was a more direct challenge to the existing order than any of the particular schemes noted above, because it attacked the "price system" as such and called for the abolition of money entirely. It predicted a complete economic collapse, and hinted that when this occurred, engineers would be called upon to run things sensibly. Thus it visualized a thorough change. The chief items in its argument were old conceptions dressed up in new language, but they were fundamental and important conceptions—the revolutionary character of technical progress in making it possible to produce more goods with less labor, the fact that there is a relation between technical change and unemployment, the inadequacy of the traditional monetary and price system, the gravity of the debt problem, the basic position of energy and natural resources in supporting the population.

Part of the easy vogue of Technocracy was due, of course, to its more vulnerable characteristics. It stated most of its theses in a greatly exaggerated form. It was announced (incorrectly) as having the official blessing of the assembled scientists of Columbia University. It dressed up the old conceptions in a new package with an attractive new label; it was described as being something totally new, abolishing politics and economics, having no traffic with outworn ideas such as those, not only of the standard economists, but of economic planning, socialism, communism or fascism. Also, it was supposed to fore-shadow an inevitable change. All this gave it a powerful appeal. Brand-newness was good, since all we had known seemed to do us little service, and anyway we were sick of talking about the familiar. Change was good, since we didn't like what we had. Inevitability of change was particularly good, since it appeared to mean that we did not have to worry about effectuating the change. The exaggerations in stating the case for Technocracy had a dramatic value. Also the obscurity of much of the language it used, and the top-lofty scorn for all other theories, gave it an impressive intellectual swank, especially to those readers who were so innocent as to believe that difficulty necessarily indicated profundity. There was some justice in Professor Charles A. Beard's remark in a preface to one of the books about it, that its popularity was due to the fact that "the source of our distress is exposed in words difficult to understand and the cure handed to us on a shining new platter."

Nevertheless its ready acceptance also owed much to the fact that it came very close to a bull's-eye in hitting the popular instinct concerning what was the matter. There is a shameful folly in the existence of want in the midst of plenty. We could, if things were only managed correctly, have an immensely higher standard of living. What we need is a new management. It must be a technically competent one, not tied to pecuniary motives and pecuniary traditions. The chief trouble is with the way in which we organize the distribution of the goods. That way is variously called "the price system," as by the Technocrats and by Thorstein Veblen before them, or individualism, or laissez-faire, or capitalism. As a result of the

Technocratic discussion, these generalizations sank into many more minds than before, and they remained long after Technocracy as a cult had gone the way of Eugenie hats.

In more conservative circles, the realization of deep flaws in our system was intensified. The two-volume report on "Recent Social Trends," from which much of the statistical information in Part II of this book was drawn, is a veritable landmark in the mental shift of the intellectuals—not of the more irresponsible literati who had little grounding in the academic standards of social science, but of those with high prestige in our universities and scientific societies, the leaders of opinion among teachers and professional classes. Even a slight shift here is of greater significance over a long period than the excursions of the more mercurial. Its influence will be pervasive and enduring.

When President Hoover in 1929 appointed the Committee of experts to report on social trends, he probably had no idea what serious flaws in our culture it would disclose. The depression had not begun; reports of other commissions had been utilized by political supporters of the administration as much to celebrate our civilization as to indicate that great reforms in it were needed. But when the Committee reported at the end of 1932 it had found an immense amount of change: various forces "have hurried us dizzily away from the days of the frontier into a whirl of modernisms which almost passes belief." [1] And the chief element of instability, it discovered, was the lack of balance between those things that have

---

[1] This and the succeeding quotations are from "Recent Social Trends in the United States," Report of the President's Committee on Social Trends; by permission of the publishers, McGraw-Hill Book Company, Inc.

changed and those that have not changed enough. It
spoke of "astonishing contrasts" as between "splendid
technical efficiency in some incredible skyscraper and
monstrous backwardness in some equally incredible
slum." The Committee could not speak more plainly on
this subject. "It is the express purpose of the review of
these findings . . . to direct attention to the importance
of balance among the factors of change. A nation advances not only by dynamic power, but by and through
the maintenance of equilibrium among the many forces.
. . . Unequal rates of change . . . make zones of danger
and points of tension. It is almost as if the various functions of the body or the parts of the automobile were
operating at unsynchronized speeds."

The Committee was not given a code of social standards
by which to evaluate what it found, nor was it entrusted
with the task of recommending a program. Nevertheless
there inevitably appear hints of both in its work. A mass
of statistics would be meaningless unless they were ar-
ranged about problems, and problems do not arise unless
we make some assumption about what ends are desirable.
The central assumption is stated by the Committee as
follows: "We may hold steadily to the importance of
viewing social situations as a whole in terms of the inter-
relation and interdependence of our national life," and of
viewing problems "as those of a single society based upon
the assumption of common welfare as the goal of common effort." The far-reaching implications of this statement may escape the eye. It sounds like a truism, or like
a formula which does not fit us at present, since we are
not really "a single society" seeking "common welfare"
by "common effort." We are a congeries of self-seeking

individuals, groups and classes. But the Committee did not pretend that we are now anything else. Only in the light of a valuation which is so far from fitting the facts, does the enormity of the facts appear.

The Committee wished to achieve balance, not by suppressing the rapid changes in technology. "On the contrary, it holds that social invention has to be stimulated to keep pace with mechanical invention." The implications of this statement are also far-reaching. It gave no support to those who want to "go back," to seek refuge in "fundamentals," to have a lower standard of living, to establish self-sufficient farms, to seek a way out by barter and handicraft. Nor was it sympathetic with attempts to restore laissez-faire, to liquidate this depression merely in order to pursue the old round of expansion and collapse.

The policy which it recommended was derived from these bases. "Social problems are products of change," and "social changes are interrelated." But there are lags among the changes, which bring maladjustment. The delays "may arise from vested interests resisting change in self-defense, from the difficulty with which men readjust familiar ideas and ideals, or from various obstacles which obstruct the transmission of impulses from man to man." The varying changes not only give rise to dangers, but hold out great promise of betterment. "The objective of any conscious control over the process is to secure a better adjustment between inherited nature and culture. The means of social control in social discovery and the wider adoption of new knowledge."

But the effort to do this cannot be merely a happy improvisation by a few. Neat panaceas are a delusion. It is "a job for cumulative thinking by many minds over years to come. Discovery and invention are themselves social processes made up of countless individual achievements. Nothing short of the combined intelligence of the nation can cope with the predicaments here mentioned." There are, however, certain indispensable prerequisites to such an effort, as follows:

"Willingness and determination to undertake important integral changes in the reorganization of social life, including the economic and the political orders, rather than the pursuance of a policy of drift.

"Recognition of the rôle which science must play in such a reorganization of life.

"Continuing recognition of the intimate interrelationship between changing scientific techniques, varying social interests and institutions, modes of social education and action and broad social purposes."

How were these preparations to be achieved? First, by an emphasis of thinkers upon finding the *meaning* of our wide knowledge. Important contributions by individuals emphasizing the focus of social problems, rather than merely assembling data, as in the recent past. We have had many fact-finding agencies; the next development "may find more emphasis upon interpretation and synthesis." Next, a development of more governmental planning, and advance thinking by official bodies. Third, a going organization of social scientists (perhaps through the Social Science Research Council), both "for the consideration of *ad hoc* problems and for more and continuous generalized consideration of broader aspects of social integration and planning." Fourth, there might emerge "a National Advisory Council, including scientific, governmental, economic (industrial, agricultural and labor) points of contact, or other appropriate elements, able to contribute to the consideration of the basic social problems of the nation." Whatever the approach, however, "the type of planning now most urgently required is neither economic planning alone nor governmental planning alone."

Revolutionary critics will be quick to point out that such a program says little of the conflict of class interests which may interfere with its execution, or warp its direction. But the Committee did not overlook this realm of discussion. It "does not wish to exaggerate the rôle of intelligence in social direction. . . . Social action, however, is the resultant of many forces among which, in an age of science and education, conscious intelligence may certainly be reckoned as one."

If we do not make progress by the methods here described, there are alternatives "urged by dictatorial systems in which the factors of force and violence may loom large. In such cases the basic decisions are forcibly imposed by power groups. . . . Unless there can be a more impressive integration of social skills and fusing of social purposes than is revealed by recent trends . . . there can be no assurance that these alternatives with their accompaniments of violent revolution . . . can be averted. . . . The Committee does not wish to assume an attitude of alarmist irresponsibility, but on the other hand it would be highly negligent to gloss over the stark and bitter realities of the social situation, and to ignore the imminent perils in further advance of our heavy technical machinery over crumbling roads and shaking bridges. There are times when silence is not neutrality, but assent."

These are words which are likely to be quoted by future historians. The report is in itself a revolutionary portent and a revolutionary act. It constitutes one of the most important of the processes of a great social change —what is called by the Committee "the formulation of new and emergent values." Without this sort of activity by leaders of intelligence, no social revolution, whether violent or non-violent, ever occurred.

It will be noted how the report of the Social Trends Committee emphasizes "planning." For years a few had been talking of the necessity of economic and social planning, of regional planning. This type of idea came into much greater prominence during the depression. It is a prime example of the broad sort of idea characteristic of pre-revolutionary and early revolutionary periods. It is not like the specific panaceas discussed above; it does not concentrate attention on the faults of a specific part of the social machine. It challenges, rather, the basic conception by which the old order as a whole had always been explained and justified in the minds of the leaders of opinion. The old order was supposed to be automatically self-adjusting rather than planned or consciously controlled. The belief that it was self-adjusting was what provided the moral sanction for individualism in economic affairs, for competition and laissez-faire and private profit-seeking. To say that our economy must be planned was to introduce a conception precisely opposite to the whole complex of ideas by which the old order had been rationalized. It implied as basic a challenge to the old order, in the realm of the mind, as the introduction of the idea of natural rights and liberty had carried to the pre-capitalist order in the seventeenth century.

duce better results. But the moment such acknowledgment is made, the questions are raised, what objectives shall be sought? and, Who shall do the planning and exercise the control? Those who govern through the institution of the private ownership of the means of production thereupon strive to keep in their own hands the power to set the objectives and exercise the control. Thus they must accept public and acknowledged responsibility for what happens. The failures become their failures. Their aims and methods must be defined, and must become subject to social criticism and appraisal. Those who are not served by what they do or try to do tend to mobilize in opposition. Any opposition of class interests which formerly has been implicit tends to become conscious. The struggle over the aims of society and the power to run it is thus organized. You have a polarization of forces in a new universe of discourse and action. And the declining economic rulers are likely to repeat old mistakes which in the past have brought disaster.

Another of the significant ferments of the depression was the series of scandals which went far to destroy faith in the bankers and big business men themselves, and, in particular, created a division between the relatively few leaders of capitalism and their hundreds of thousands of passive allies and dependents—the small stockholders, bondholders, savings bank depositors, all those who in former phases of capitalism might have had active supervision over small units, but now were relegated to the minor status of being "owners" of capital without having any real responsibility and power, not even the power to safeguard their property.

With the collapse of Stock Exchange values, the gods

of the speculative New Era crumbled to sand. Investment trusts faded away; foreign bond issues were defaulted; real estate bonds, advertised as perfectly safe investments, became virtually worthless. The Bank of United States failed amid scandal; Kreuger and Toll blew up; Insull's rickety and involved structure of utility holding companies fell in and he had to flee. Shady banking practices were revealed in high places; it was shown how insiders had feathered their own nests while the small depositor and borrower suffered. Mitchell of the National City was tried for alleged income-tax irregularities; Wiggin departed from the Chase National; other rich men had, with perfect legality under an imperfect law, avoided paying a cent of income taxes during depression years while their current incomes were still reckoned in millions and while relatively poor people had struggled to pay the high rates imposed. High-salaried executives of industry were shown to have drawn enormous bonuses while dividends were reduced or discontinued; they had increased their own salaries while cutting the wages of workers to the bone; it was common for many of them to draw far more than the President of the United States. When companies got into difficulties, long and expensive reorganizations provided fat fees for bankers and lawyers while the helpless investor waited in vain to get something out of the wreck. A long book would be required even to summarize the unsavory revelations of the period concerning the way the relatively small group in command of capitalism had piled self-interest upon folly.

Not all bankers and big business men were rascals, of course, any more than all members of the English or French nobilities before 1688 or 1792 were corrupt and tyrannical. Many of the practices which were denounced in the light of depression had been regarded as customary and not dishonorable, by the class which practiced them, during prosperity. But history shows us that when an old order fails to work, the individuals in command, justly or unjustly, have to bear individual blame. Popular resentment welcomes and magnifies every scandal; the pretensions of the rulers are subjected to ridicule. The most vulnerable members of the ruling class are held up as horrible examples. The reaction from adulation of the financially successful under Coolidge to the long series of uncomplimentary revelations about them under Hoover and Roosevelt is a phenomenon with a distinct revolutionary cast. It is a blow to their prestige from which they can never completely recover. If prosperity returns for a time, the scandals will temporarily be overlooked, but in the next crisis more people will be more ready to blame the ruling class. This was a foretaste of what may happen. It was a beginning of the break in old loyalties. More particularly, it signalized a split in the ruling classes themselves, such a split as always precedes any successful attack from without. The small capitalist had been set against the large, for a time at any rate. There came concrete result in legislation about banking, security issue, stock market regulation. These results in turn must lead to other consequences, unforeseen by either party to the quarrel.

5. THE NEW DEAL IS DEALT

The first problem with which President Roosevelt was confronted after he assumed office, and one of the most critical of his entire administration so far, was one which was scarcely mentioned during the campaign a few months before, and one not anticipated by many of the best-informed persons near the center of financial affairs. This is thoroughly characteristic of social crises in a potentially revolutionary period. They arrive with a speed and decisiveness which few persons expect; they compel action on the part of those who, usually, are mentally unprepared to act.

A group of eminent economists meeting a few weeks before the inauguration, to frame recommendations for emergency measures, held the opinion, with one or two exceptions, that the banking structure as a whole was in no danger, and that we were not likely to be driven off the gold standard. On the very eve of the nation-wide banking moratorium, several of the most prominent New York bankers believed that New York could satisfy all demands from the interior, and that confidence could be restored by keeping the doors of the banks open. The fallacy of this view speedily became apparent, and Roosevelt's entry into office was signalized by the order declaring a general banking holiday. During a few anxious days of incessant work and conference, the question of policy was debated. The President obtained from Congress the new legislation he asked for to deal with the crisis; he could, under the circumstances, have had any laws he wanted. The confidence of depositors was restored by the simple device of substituting the prestige of government for that of the bankers. Over the radio the President, in an admirably clear address, assured the public that banks would be reopened as rapidly as possible, and that none but sound banks would be allowed to open. He called in all gold in private hands, and forbade the banks to pay out more. This stopped the tendency to hoard. It looked to the public as if at last we had someone in charge who was not afraid to act quickly and decisively, and who was competent to act. The practical conclusion was enforced that when private enterprise collapsed, the state could successfully intervene. This combination of a man at the helm who had suddenly made good in an emergency, with a demonstration of what government could do, set the stage for further action of the same sort.

Now, the action which lay behind Mr. Roosevelt's words was not really sufficient to justify the confidence which they aroused. He had no direct control over state banks not members of the Federal Reserve System, and a number of banks were in fact reopened which were not sound. Many others were only technically solvent; their funds were largely tied up in investments which were far from liquid. Unless the value of bonds and stocks is restored, the crisis may reappear. Bank managements remained about the same as before. The Reconstruction Finance Corporation, which previously had been lending money to banks, now could increase their liquid capital by buying preferred stock. Thus the strain was temporarily eased. Although technically this action gives the government power to exercise management through part ownership, there is no sign that the power has been widely used. The question of the proper organization and social function of the banking system has not been squarely faced. Mr. Roosevelt skated on very thin ice in taking over responsibility for the solvency of the banks without establishing power to administer their policies.

Temporarily, he got away with it, however, and the reaction from the previous panic had much to do with the

spurt of business which took place from April to June.
About ninety per cent of the total deposits in banks were,
before long, released. While there remained about
$2,000,000,000 of frozen deposits, and whole sections
were for long without adequate banking facilities, the
turnover of the released funds increased so greatly as to
facilitate more active business. Individuals and business
concerns, no longer fearful, began to spend instead of
hoarding. The banks did not increase the total quantity
of their loans and deposits, but those which existed passed
from hand to hand so much more rapidly that the effect
was the same. Heightened velocity was a substitute for
augmented quantity of bank money.

As soon as this storm blew over, the administration began to turn its attention to the rescue of agriculture and
business itself. How did this part of the New Deal origi-
nate? There are two theories about it, one advanced by
the extreme right and the other by the extreme left, both
of which are crude over-simplifications. The theory of the
right is that a small group of professors who had been to
Russia and wanted to destroy capitalism formed a "brains
trust," conceived a well-knit series of revolutionary measures before the election, and put them over on the country
and a reluctant Congress through dictatorial power of the
President. The theory of the left is that the President
was the instrument of a capitalist plot to establish a
fascist dictatorship, by freeing business from the anti-
trust laws and establishing governmental control over
labor. In doing this, he used as a "front" to deceive the
people a lot of complaisant and muddled liberals and a
number of high-sounding but hollow phrases.

The brain-trust theory is true to the extent that, in an effort to rescue our economic life, the President saw the necessity of enlisting expert advice. Professors of economics and political science and law, people who have studied social problems with some approach to scholarly care, must be called into positions of responsibility when any attempt is made to govern industry and finance instead of letting individual profit-seekers do exactly what they like. In a broad sense, then, the New Deal gives us a foretaste of the rise to power of a new class, and this foretaste does have a distinct revolutionary tinge, just because it indicates a shift in class power. The forefront of the white-collar workers, the productive professions, are just beginning to assume some of the political prerogatives which their actual place in a highly organized industrial society warrants, and to which their superior competence in matters of social theory entitles them. Washington offices are now full of people who talk a language which would have been understood by few members of previous administrations. These persons do sense that great changes in our ways of conducting affairs are overdue, and they are at home in problems of economics, statistics and jurisprudence as former governmental staffs have not been.

The brain-trust theory is completely false, however, in the sense of a plot controlling the administration. In the first place, many of the most important members of the administrative machine are business or other "practical" men who have a disdain for theory and consequently do not see far beyond their own noses. In the second place, there is no unanimity of opinion among the intellectuals and professors throughout the country; the overwhelming majority of them are still, in one way or another, supporters of and apologists for the old régime. In the third place, the very experts who were chosen to advise the administration do not agree among themselves; hence no well-knit plot would have been possible. Liberals in the Department of Agriculture, for instance, like Professor Rexford G. Tugwell or Mordecai Ezekiel, though they became scapegoats for every action which frightened the business or financial community, were by no means satisfied with the monetary theories of Professor Warren; and though the gold policy of the President was attributed popularly to Professors Warren and Rogers, these two were far from complete agreement concerning it. The gold theory of Professor Warren of Cornell (age 59) was attacked in the press as the vagary of a radical young professor, while the opposition to this theory by Professor Sprague of Harvard (age 60) was called the judgment of a great financial expert. And when Professor Sprague, after adopting a position on this subject which was widely heralded in the press because conservative finance approved it, attacked business interests for their tendency to restrict output and keep prices up, little further attention was paid to him. Doubtless he had become suddenly an impractical professor.

The capitalist-plot theory advanced by the left is just as false. It overlooks the tremendous social pressures at work during the depression, the realization by the President, as a skillful politician, that changes were popularly expected and must be made if industrial civilization were to work, the deep sincerity of many of those who were called to help him, and the efforts by the more far-seeing of his advisers to prevent profit-seekers from ruining the show. Whatever the result, the administration was not a purposeful unit which had as a goal the strengthening of capitalism. There were within it right wings and left wings; it was a battleground between opposite interests and opinions. This sort of endeavor may have the weakness of liberalism; its lack of well-defined plan or method and its belief that fundamentally diverse interests may be made to coöperate may lead to a temporary victory of the old order. But this is a different thing from a calculated plot to bring about the triumph of reaction. To condemn it as a conscious cabal is to miss the chance for education which it presents. It is to falsify its place in the development of history. It is to forego the opportunity to mobilize opinion and action about the fundamental questions which the New Deal dramatizes.

It is possible to trace with considerable accuracy the lines of thought and pressure which led to the New Deal legislation. We must go back to the origins of the program in order to be able to judge its results.

1. *Agriculture.*

The long-continued depression of agriculture was one of the fundamental difficulties. Somehow the farmers must be provided with more purchasing power, not only to give them a decent life, but to restore the market which they furnished for city products and to enable them to pay debts which they had contracted and which formed a substantial part of the assets of banks and insurance companies. Now there are only two ways to provide farmers with more income; one is to increase the sales of their products and the other is to raise the prices of what they sell. There was a good deal of evidence to show that in the case of agricultural staples like wheat, pork, and cotton, there was little chance of increasing their sales, and so the correct course was to increase prices. The volume of these staples produced had expanded tremendously during and after the war, and was scarcely cut by the depression. Our foreign markets for them had been gradually diminishing. An effort ought to have been made to expand the foreign markets if possible, but the hope in that direction was slight, and in any event its realization would be long delayed. The domestic market for wheat and cotton, it was agreed, could not absorb all we were producing even if everybody had all the money he wanted with which to buy them. We had always grown large surpluses for export. People tend to eat less bread as they become prosperous, and to buy more expensive fabrics than cotton. In spite of the obvious fact that many were now going hungry and ill-clad, because they had scarcely any money at all, a remedy for that lack would not rescue the wheat and cotton farmers.

Another way of stating the problem was to point out the disparity between agricultural prices and industrial prices. This had been marked even before the depression. And, between July, 1929, and February, 1933, the prices of farm products had fallen 60 per cent, while the prices of manufactured goods had fallen only 31 per cent. Unless industrial prices were to be reduced as much again, and deflation carried through to its painful and logical extreme, farm prices would have to be increased to restore anything like a balance. The farms had taken the depression in the form of a price drop without any appreciable cut in output, while the factories had taken it by a tremendous cut in output, while holding prices up as much as possible.

Now, if the farmers had been able to shut down as the factories did, the restriction of output would have brought their prices up toward the industrial level and helped to restore the balance. But they were not able to do this. Any decree fixing higher prices would have been undermined by the constant flow of products from the farms. The only hope of automatic adjustment was through the slow and cruel impoverishment of hundreds of thousands of farmers and the abandonment of land. Experts therefore attacked the task of bringing about limitation of output through governmental measures.

The domestic allotment plan, invented in its essence by an economist in the Department of Agriculture under Coolidge, and later perfected and discussed by others, came to the attention of Mr. Roosevelt's advisers during the campaign, and seemed to them the best—perhaps, indeed, the only practicable emergency method of bringing about restriction of farm output in the interest of a higher price. Former administrations had advised the farmers to grow less in order to get better prices, but no one farmer had dared to do so because he was sure most of the others would not follow the advice. The new plan was merely a means of organizing the restriction, on the basis of individual contracts with the government. The farmer would agree to cut his acreage. The government would agree to collect from the processor a certain sum of money on each unit of the crop, and turn it over to the farmer who made the agreement. Thus the consumer would pay a higher price, the farmer would receive more per bushel or per pound, and the price increase could be maintained because less would be grown.

This plan, together with the cotton option plan and the land-leasing plan, were ways of effectuating a price increase by offering the price bait in advance exchange for output limitation, instead of waiting for farmers as individuals to limit and subsequently to enjoy the increase. (The processing tax was not to be collected on goods destined for free distribution to the unemployed; and the consumer was safeguarded by the placing of an upper limit on the price rise, at the pre-war parity between agricultural and industrial products.)

The farm bill not only legalized these measures but gave to the Agricultural Adjustment Administration, which it set up, power to do many other things as well— notably to make sure, by agreements with, or licensing systems over the processing and distributing industries, that the consumer would not be overcharged; that the price to him would not be raised more than any increase in the cost of raw materials and the processing tax warranted.

Congress added to this bill an amendment, not an original part of the plan, giving the President various powers to proceed with a limited inflation of the currency. The agitation in the agrarian regions for higher farm prices had largely taken the traditional form of a demand for inflation. The farmers did not understand complicated schemes like the domestic allotment plan, but plumped for the easy panacea. Hence, from popular pressure (not from the experts) arose the gold devaluation and other powers which later assumed such a prominent place in the President's action.

2. *Industry.*

It would be futile economically and impossible politically to embark on this program for the farmers without doing something for city workers, at least one-third of whom were jobless, while those who were working had suffered disastrous wage-cuts. Higher prices for foods and fabrics would undoubtedly mean smaller sales unless the purchasing power of the wage-earners were increased. They must also be enabled to buy one another's products and so provide the market for an industrial revival.

To stimulate industry, an expansion of public works was the stock remedy. A public works bill was thus in order. But at once theoretical and practical difficulties arose. Mr. Roosevelt had promised to balance the budget as a means of restoring financial confidence and aiding the market for private bond issues, which would have to revive if the private demand for construction and capital goods were to increase. But how could he finance a public works program sufficiently large to insure industrial revival, if at the same time he were to balance the budget? The two aims were contradictory. In order to have the required effect, so much money would have to be spent on public works that it would certainly make difficulty for public finance. And then you would be employing a lot of men in construction who really ought to be employed making other things that people used—employed in regular industries. A compromise was therefore indicated, in the form of only a moderately large construction program.

This turned attention to what could be done directly in industry. There had arisen a powerful movement for shorter working hours in order to increase employment. Some employers had spread work by shortening hours; others had increased hours, and consequently were benefiting by lower costs of production. Congress seemed about to pass the Black bill limiting hours to thirty a week. But this proposal raised the question of wages. Many wage-rates were already so low that they were unendurable; what would happen if hours of work were cut while hourly rates of pay remained the same? Through the Secretary of Labor came the demand for an amendment to the bill setting up wage boards in any industry where they were thought necessary, to fix minimum wages. Cutthroat competitors were everywhere trying to escape the losses of the depression by depressing labor standards. It was necessary to set a bottom somewhere and turn the current in the other direction, if the purchasing power of labor were to be increased and either agriculture or industry were to have a market.

At this point various groups of industrialists interposed strong objections. They were willing to have hours cut— but not, by a blanket law, to thirty a week. This would simply put more factories out of production altogether. Still worse would be the effect if wages were raised at the same time. Labor costs being increased, the result would be more unemployment. What was basically essential was a means of controlling the cutthroat competition which had brought about the depressed labor standards. If industry could be assured that no competitor would charge prices which were too low, or would engage in other practices which it considered unethical, it would be enabled to pay the cost of shorter hours and higher wages. Some sort of industrial administration which would have oversight over prices and trade practices was therefore suggested as the best way of achieving the aims of the Black bill.

Thus there came into the picture proposals which had formerly been made for industrial planning—in particular those proposals which visualized "self-government of industry" through associations of employers. The original suggestion for the N. R. A. was derived, not from the "brains trust" but from the United States Chamber of Commerce, from Gerard Swope of the General Electric, and from other powerful industrialists. It was their pressure that substituted this sort of measure for the social legislation embodied in the Black bill, which sought merely to regulate maximum hours and minimum wages.

But both labor representatives and the expert advisers of the administration had a hand in framing the Industrial Recovery bill. They foresaw the danger—many times pointed out in previous discussions of the subject—that if business were to be allowed to govern itself in order to suppress "cutthroat competition," if it were, for this purpose, freed from the operation of the anti-trust laws, and if the police power of the government were put behind its decisions as to prices and trade practices, it would also have the power to suppress legitimate competition, to fix prices which were too high, and to profiteer at the expense of employees and other consumers. Safeguards had to be put into the bill in order to counterbalance the power of private business and to police it in the public interest. Therefore there was introduced the famous Section 7a, which sought to guarantee the right of collective bargaining for labor, and the provisions giving the President broad power to require any information of an accounting and statistical nature and to protect the consumer. There was also written in the provision giving the President power to establish a planning agency.

Section 7a was intended by its drafters not just as a political gesture to placate organized labor, but as a genuine safeguard for the existence of a strong, independent labor movement, which could act as a counterpoise to the power of organized employers and could help to improve and police the labor standards which the act sought to bring into existence. The sections granting the power to require statistical and accounting information were framed with the full knowledge on the part of the experts that unless there were complete publicity of accounts, showing the effect of the decisions of industry upon production and prices, costs and profits, we should have not merely self-government by industry, but irresponsible capitalist dictatorship over the consumer. The section giving the President power to establish a planning agency was inserted with consciousness of the fact that if industries were allowed to pursue their several ends without the framework of a series of policies adopted in the interest of the whole people, the result would be merely confusion and frustration.

Thus arose the backbone of the New Deal legislation— the Agricultural Act and the National Industrial Recovery Act, with its public works section and its industrial section. There were, of course, other important departments of proposed action, such as the establishment of a federal Coördinator for the Railroads, the President's developing policy concerning the price level and currency, the creation of various instruments for debt relief, including not only the Reconstruction Finance Corporation inherited from Hoover, but the Home Owners' Loan Corporation to help mortgagors in the cities, and the reorganized Farm Credit Administration to take over distressed farm mortgages. There was the long overdue Federal Employment Service, the Securities Act to enforce financial responsibility on those who issued new securities, and the experiment in regional planning under the Tennessee Valley Authority. Every important agitation, every pressure, every reasonable idea, had its hearing and usually stimulated some action in response. The President and his staff were like a great sounding board which reëchoed many cries. They provided an immense psychological relief for a nation which, under the stresses of disintegration, had been confined within the narrow bounds of outworn theory. But it would be mistaken to believe that their action was in any broad sense a well-calculated plan. It was an unresolved resultant of confused and often conflicting social forces. It was neither a radical nor a conservative plot, but a facile reflection of the disorderly social scene itself.

The one great change which these first months of the New Deal marked was the general acknowledgment that laissez-faire was dead and should be decently buried; that government must be called in, on a dozen fronts, to do what private enterprise obviously could not do. In Washington you could see now the beginning of constitution-making for industry. The idea of political government is old, but, ever since the rise of capitalism, the sanctioned constitution of industry had been anarchy. The irrepressible disposition of man to arrange affairs had, of course, thrust through to temper this anarchy in dozens of ways. Individuals and groups had carved out great business principalities within which they could govern more or less absolutely. The police power of the state had been invoked to regulate, to check, to oppose. Labor organizations had, in numerous directions, compelled economic government. Competitors had attempted to organize coöperation, just as feudal lords centuries ago combined for mutual protection, in spite of their rivalry. But never until now—except under the extraordinary conditions of warfare—had these forces been brought into focus in this country, with the emergent purpose of acting as an industrial state. I venture to say that, in the eye of the future, the particular policies adopted during the crisis will shrink into oblivion compared with the fact that here economic society struggled, for the first time in the United States, into a primitive attempt to attain order. It is only against this generally acknowledged conception of the need for order that the disorderly elements in the New Deal appear so confusing. Much greater inconsistencies in economic policy had previously been enacted in our anarchic economic society without being generally observed.

No sooner did you begin industrial government than you were faced with weighty and complex problems. Price policy is an illustration. We began with an attempt to raise crop prices to a former parity with prices of manufactures. But this would be inconsistent with a program of much increase in prices of manufactures; the farmers would continually be tagging on behind, just as would the incomes of workers. You might get an inflationary, speculative boom if you let prices skyrocket indiscriminately, but it could not last long, and at the end we should be worse off than ever. These considerations in turn bore upon monetary and credit policy. The issue of money and credit must be accessory to the demands of an industrial plan.

Price policy needed to be elaborated also within the industrial field. What prices ought to be permitted to increase, and what prices ought to be held down? It had already been decided that prices kept low at the expense of starvation wages must be allowed to rise. There was another guide to policy in this respect, already implicit in the different treatment of agriculture and manufacturing as a whole. Agriculture had suffered, not because of reduced output, but because of reduced price. Therefore, restriction of output was the logical course. But many industries, such as automobiles, could, with sufficient markets—which are conceivable—prosper at lower prices. Some industries, however, may resemble agriculture more than automobiles in this respect. Bituminous coal is an example, and probably oil extraction as well. Here restriction and price valorization might be allowed.

Not every case, however, was so clear. Take the manufacturers of railroad equipment, or of machinery, or of building supplies. The extent of their markets seems at any given time to be largely independent of the prices of their products. When railroads, or manufacturing, or construction, are booming, they sell a lot of their products, though they increase prices at the same time. When their customers do not thrive, their sales would not, apparently, be enlarged by any conceivable price reduction. Here the problem appeared to be to arrange the largest steady volume possible for their output, and allow prices such as to be reasonable at that volume.

When it comes to deciding what is a desirable price at any given volume of business, accounting must be called in. What are costs, and what are profits? In the case of an industry which contains units with varying costs, should not the price be judged with reference to the more efficient? The government had blanket authority to require accounting information, but, in addition, the administration of accounting, the decisions made in regard to its intricate problems, and the publicity accorded the results, were of prime importance.

At the accountant's right hand ought to have been the management engineer, developing standards of efficiency, judging codes of practice from the technical point of view, striving to reduce costs without reducing wages, by eliminating waste. His advice was also essential on one of the most basic problems of any effort at national industrial government—how to combine the necessary centralization with the decentralization which is essential to good performance. Complete decentralization means the impossible waste of anarchy; complete centralization the fat hand of bureaucracy.

A desperate puzzle was concerned with the restoration of full employment. Industrialists were almost unanimous in saying that they could return to 1929 output without anything like 1929 employment. Some of them therefore envisaged a large permanent residue of unemployed, to be cast off into the middle ages by being settled on "subsistence farms." Such a program would be disastrous socially, and would also make impossible 1929 production itself, since millions of former buyers would be removed from the markets for industrial goods. The only genuine solution would be much larger output than in 1929, made possible by a larger purchasing power of workers and farmers. But this was difficult to achieve. How, for instance, enlarge promptly the employment of industries engaged in making capital goods, when almost every industry believed it was "overequipped" in relation to easily predictable demand for its products?

This is just a beginning at an enumeration of the tasks which were faced. It ignores detailed social problems, such as decisions as to whether the legally required collective bargaining should be delegated to A. F. of L. unions, company unions or progressive and "outlaw" unions. And it ignores the great social problem whether industrial government under capitalism could reconcile group and class interests; whether the "thin red line" of experts who had at heart the welfare of labor and consumer, who wanted to build a collective economy, could survive the attacks of the reactionary profiteers who were already out for their scalps. If recovery came and the Devil began to convalesce, would he still wish to be good? Or would more drastic changes be enforced by a suffering and impatient populace? What we really created was not a reformed industrial system, but a mixture in which problems would be precipitated with greater clarity, an arena in which sides could be chosen and significant conflicts waged.

6. THE NEW DEAL IS PLAYED

Between the time Mr. Roosevelt took office and June, 1933, there was a spirited revival, which brought some of the curves depicting the average volume of business back nearly to the level of 1923-25. It is fairly clear that this spurt was due to the following influences:

The return of confidence in the banks, combined with the popular enthusiasm over the new administration, made numerous individuals and business concerns ready to spend money instead of hoarding it.

The President announced that we had left the gold standard, and that his purpose was to bring about a rise of prices. This caused both speculators and manufacturers who were short of materials to stock up with commodities, in the expectation that if they did not buy now, they would have to buy later at a higher price. To some extent, the same influence affected the action of wholesalers and retailers, and, to a considerably less extent, of individual purchasers at retail.

The agricultural bill, with its price-raising program, strengthened the impression that rising prices were coming, stimulated the purchase of agricultural commodities both for speculative and manufacturing purposes, and lent some confidence to the industries making or selling goods used principally by farmers.

The National Industrial Recovery Act, with its promise of shorter hours and higher wages, made manufacturers eager to produce goods for stock before labor costs rose, on the assumption that these goods could later be sold at prices justified by the higher labor costs.

There was some increase in the demand for new automobiles, caused by the fact that more old ones, left unreplaced for several years, were wearing out, and that some possessors of these old cars had money enough and confidence enough to contract for new ones. The movement was helped by the great improvement which had taken place in the quality of cheap cars, which made it possible to buy more desirable automobiles at a lower price.

There were, however, two characteristics of this revival which indicated that it could not last long. One was that it was confined very largely to the industries making consumers' goods; like cotton textiles and shoes; most of the heavy industries scarcely felt it, and it was in the heavy industries that the greatest volume of unemployment existed. The other was that it was not accompanied by sufficient mass purchasing power. The increased production was accomplished without equal increase in factory payrolls, since neither hours nor wages were yet changed, and the ability to produce more per man-hour had increased markedly during the depression. In effect speculators and industry were stocking up in advance expectation of substantial growth of retail demand, without doing much to supply the purchasers at retail with the money to create that demand. Subsequently, having "beat the gun," as General Johnson said, they would have to slow down in order that the consumers might catch up. In so far as their activity raised prices, they made it that much more difficult for the consumers to catch up. The movement was a speculative flash in the pan.

In June the National Industrial Recovery Act was signed, and soon thereafter the cotton textile code was approved, establishing minimum wages—very low minima, but still higher than many mills had been paying—reducing hours of work, abolishing child labor, restricting the hours which a mill might operate, and installing control over the installation of new machinery, on the theory that the industry was overequipped. The reforms in labor conditions which it embodied were such a dramatic reversal that they overshadowed everything else in the public mind, as well as in the mind of the administration. It was believed of supreme importance to extend these reforms as soon as possible throughout industry. The theory was that by the simultaneous reduction of hours and increase of wage-rates the codes would help to restore the purchasing power of the wage-earners and thus provide a market for the goods which were being piled up in storerooms and on retail shelves. If this were not done quickly, a discouraging slump would follow. Furthermore, if codes were adopted in only a few industries but not in others, the industries which had complied would suffer. Their costs would be raised, but the markets for their goods would not be enlarged sufficiently to compensate for the cost increase. They could not sell their goods solely to their own employees, and the employees of industries not under codes would not have enough money to buy.

The administration therefore was alarmed by the slowness and reluctance with which other important industries set about the code-making process. Many of them disliked the labor sections—not merely the necessity for improvement of hours and wages, but the provision for collective bargaining which the law made it compulsory to insert in every code. The alarm at delay gave rise to the President's Reëmployment Agreement—the Blue Eagle campaign. Every employer in the country was asked by the President to reduce hours of work to a maximum of 40 per week, to raise wage-rates so that those who already had jobs would earn at the shorter hours as much as before, to take on whatever additional employees this made necessary, and not to raise prices more than was honestly required by the increase in costs. The display of the Blue Eagle rewarded the signers of the agreement, and its absence conveyed a threat of public reprisal to recalcitrants—provided the public were enthusiastic enough about the scheme to exercise discrimination in their purchasing. This blanket agreement was admittedly difficult to enforce, and involved a lot of ballyhoo and propaganda. Few people were in a position to find out whether it was really being carried out by the signers. Even in the labor provisions there were countless evasions, and nobody but the employer himself could possibly know whether he raised his prices more than the increase in costs warranted; even he could not do so in many cases because of the general lack of good cost accounting.

The Blue Eagle was obviously a stop-gap, and attention was again directed toward getting through the permanent industrial codes which were destined to take its place. The speed with which it was believed necessary to improve labor conditions led the administration to emphasize this phase of the matter at the expense of the others. Instructions were sent out to rush through codes which would take care of wages and hours, leaving other provisions in a primitive stage if necessary. These could be reviewed later and revised. There were a score of major industries, and hundreds of minor ones; in the haste and turmoil it was impossible to thrash out all their problems in detail. Business men themselves knew little enough about these matters, and the government was certainly not prepared with competent experts on the manifold problems of industry, as they might affect the public welfare.

In this mighty effort to get industry codified quickly, the approved method was persuasion of business. The law had provided that the President could modify the provision of any code before approving it, and if any industry failed to agree upon a code or to present one which the President approved, he could impose one upon it such as he saw fit. Any code, when approved, governed all the members of the industry, whether or not they had agreed to its provisions, and violators could be punished. The law gave the President power, if necessary to enforce a code, to impose a licensing system upon an industry and to decline to license any member who failed to observe it—that is, to deprive him of the right to do business. But it was a governmental policy not to exercise these powers. Some entertained a doubt as to whether the courts would hold the legislation constitutional. Others believed that the whole system could work only through the voluntary coöperation of business. Though General Johnson threatened to "crack down" on numerous occasions, he did not do so during the first critical months except by pounding his fist on his desk and using picturesque language. Certain close observers in Washington described him as a sheep in wolf's clothing. The underlying conciliatory attitude of the N. R. A. toward business soon became generally known, and was used by business in gaining what it wanted and preventing what it did not want. The fear that business might fail to coöperate and might create a situation necessitating that an issue be taken to the courts kept the administration from pressing any policy which it thought would arouse the hostility of any important business man.

In the idealist phrases of the President, the N. R. A. was described as a great coöperative effort. Labor, consumers and industry were to be partners—"industry" meaning, in New Deal language, the owners and executives of industry. But the practical result, in view of the underlying social and economic situation, the urge to make haste, and the policy of conciliating business, was that business ran the show, labor got consideration only when it could create enough disturbance, and consumers had no vote and very little voice. The executive members of the N. R. A. staff were, almost without exception, men with a business background and were often former business officials. The drafting of the codes was done by employers; in only a few cases where unions happened to be well organized and powerful did their representatives participate in the original code deliberations. The completed draft went to the executive staff to be briefly reviewed in order to see whether technically it complied with the law. It then went back to the employing body or the trade association concerned, for minor revision. After this revision a hearing was held on it, at which anyone having an interest had an opportunity to speak his mind.

During these hearings, labor and consumers were supposed to have their chance. In particular the Labor Advisory Board and the Consumers Advisory Board were expected to safeguard the interests entrusted to their care. The members of these boards were, on the whole, honest, conscientious and competent. But their status was ambiguous. They were not direct representatives of labor and consumer interest, but were appointees. (The Secretary of Labor appointed the labor board, General Johnson the consumer board.) Their function was advisory only; they had no real power except that which might be embodied in the pressure groups behind them. Organized labor having a certain amount of such power, the Labor Advisory Board sometimes was effectual in changing a code by its representations. But there were no powerful organized pressure groups of consumers, and the Consumers' Advisory Board was, as a rule, ignored. When it warned of the future dangers of a certain policy, its warnings were brushed aside because they were said to be based on conjecture and not on "facts." When it asked for pertinent facts it could not bring about the installation of any system of collecting them from organized industries. When it issued reports, these reports were sometimes denied circulation by the publicity men of the N. R. A., through whom all press releases had to pass. In any event little attention was paid to what it said. Professor William F. Ogburn, of Chicago University, one of the first members of the Board, early resigned in protest against its impotence either in obtaining requisite information or in gaining consideration for its advice. Every item of his protest was subsequently justified by events.

After the hearing, and any revisions consequent upon it, the code was accepted by the N. R. A. and sent to the President for signature. Occasionally strong representations to him resulted in further changes, which he could impose as a condition of approval. But in the nature of things, not many such changes could be made by the busy executive of the national government. When approved, the code had the force of law. It was then administered by a "code authority" which was often identical with the executive body of the employers' or trade association of the industry. In some cases "representatives of the public" were added to these code authorities—that is, appointees of General Johnson. They were always in a minority, they usually had a voice but no vote. Ordinarily they were themselves business men. In spite of strong protests, no direct representative of consumer or labor sat on the code authorities. These authorities were under the supervision only of General Johnson's business-minded administrators and deputy administrators. Self-government of industry turned out to be self-government by the business executives of industry, self-government by trade associations and employers' associations. The "coöperation" with labor and consumers was non-existent, as was their representation in the actual government of business.

But was not this all subject to governmental control in behalf of the whole community, based on thorough information and economic planning? That was the common assumption. Theoretically, by law and by organization chart, it might have been so, but actually it was not so. General Johnson said, when pressed on this point, that the President, acting through him as head of the N. R. A., represented the consumers and the general public. There was a small board of Cabinet members, all of them busy with their own tasks, which had technical supervision over the N. R. A. There was also a larger Executive Council, popularly called the "Super Cabinet," which was supposed to consider questions of general policy in the whole administration effort, and which was composed of the Cabinet and the heads of the various important economic agencies of the government outside the regular departments, like the R. F. C. and the Railroad Administration. These, too, were executives busy with their own jobs. Practically speaking, General Johnson ran the N. R. A.

You could look in vain in Washington for a board of experts, of men trained in economics, statistics, or engineering, whose sole business was to assess what was going on, to recommend concrete objectives and judge the concrete progress made toward them. There were men in the government capable of doing such work, but they were scattered and had minor duties. You could look in vain also for any single headquarters of information, of statistics and charts, which would be necessary as a basis of national planning. There were masses of statistics scattered about the various government bureaus. There was a Central Statistical Board, which did excellent work in reviewing and coördinating these statistics and attempting to fill in the gaps. But there was no agency to put the statistics together, to interpret them in relation to the program itself. There was nobody responsible for trying to answer such questions as, What progress are we making in enlarging the purchasing power of farmers and wage-earners? What progress are we making in restoring a workable balance of crop prices and prices for industrial goods, or of factory costs and factory prices? The participants in the effort—not only the governmental executives, but the business men and farmers and workers—had only the vaguest idea as to what was happening.

General Johnson had in the N. R. A. a division of Research and Planning, but it was just as much his stepchild as the Consumers' Advisory Board. For months it did precious little research and almost no planning. There was a rapid turnover in its chiefs. It apparently was not given authority to obtain from the industries under the N. R. A. the information which would be necessary in order to know even the most important things about what was going on. The trade associations specified their own kinds of accounting and their own statistical methods. They gave only such information to the government as they wished to give. This information was almost useless for purposes of control. In February, 1934, months after most of the important codes had been adopted, the American Statistical Association, in the open hearings on the N. R. A., was impelled modestly to suggest that this government agency ought to require financial reports from members of industries which had received permission to limit output or control prices! It ought to have some elementary means of knowing whether they were profiteering at the expense of the public. The Association made a long series of statistical recommendations, all of which were nearly as elementary as this. One would have thought that a government which had talked so much about planning would have attended to such A. B. C.'s at the very beginning. Its failure to do so can hardly be attributed either to ignorance or to stupidity. The situation was that private industry wanted to keep control in its own hands. It did not want the government to exercise any authority over output or prices, or to know anything about the costs and profits of individual enterprises. And the administration let it have its way.

The only supervisory body to which industrial planning functions were explicitly assigned was a large, volunteer committee consisting exclusively of business executives and appointed by the Secretary of Commerce. From this committee industrialists were chosen to serve on the Industrial Advisory Board of the N. R. A. It seldom met, and if it did any planning at all, it planned in the interest of private business.

Even the labor provisions of the codes, on which the administration laid exclusive stress at the beginning, failed to work with anything like reasonable satisfaction.

The standards of minimum wages themselves were often extremely meagre. They covered only the lowest paid groups in the industries; most codes contained no provision about raising the wages of those in more highly skilled occupations. The maximum hours permitted were in many cases longer than the hours actually worked during the depression. Even low standards need to be enforced. There is no other instance on record of a government adopting such important labor legislation without at the same time trying to build up a competent administrative machine for inspection and enforcement. But in this case no effort of the kind was made. Employers were supposed to act in good faith. When complaints of violations and evasions began to roll in, a "compliance" division, with voluntary boards all over the country, was set up to try to *persuade* employers to obey the law. Naturally its success was not brilliant.

The only possible chance of enforcing good labor standards under these conditions was through powerful, independent organization of labor which could police industry in all its nooks and crannies and bring recalcitrant employers into line. Encouraged by the verbal sanction which the law gave to collective bargaining, workers began to organize all over the country. A wave of strikes appeared in protest against the multitude of evasions and abuses, and for the purpose of enforcing collective bargaining. In spite of the lack of preparation of the A. F. of L. or many of its affiliated unions to handle mass organization, new members poured in. But at the same time, the employers in major industries who had always been bitterly opposed to unionism prepared to evade the collective bargaining provisions of Section 7a of the Recovery Act. They set up company unions or "employee representation plans" as a means of fighting independent labor organization. Such unions have no real power to bargain, because they are confined to one plant or one employer, their constitutions or by-laws are drafted by the employer, their elections are held under his supervision, they have no dues or such small ones that they cannot build up strike reserves, and their officers are employees, whose expenses or salaries as officers are often paid by the employer himself. Employees are induced to participate in them and to avoid genuine unions by a combination of rewards and intimidation. Five times as many workers were regimented in new company unions as joined independent unions in the first few months after the passage of the Recovery Act.

A National Labor Board, set up to adjust disputes, could not operate efficiently because it had no full-time, salaried members and possessed an inadequate staff. It was overwhelmed with work. The volunteer members often did not attend its sessions. In numerous cases where employers declined to recognize genuine unions, clearly desired by a majority of the employees, or to consent to hold or abide by the result of an impartial election to find out what kind of representation the employees wanted, the Board was unable to enforce decisions supporting true collective bargaining. Occasionally when it persuaded workers to call off strikes by a promise of upholding the law, it left them in the lurch by failing to make good its promises. Regional labor boards were equally impotent. The N. R. A. declined for many months to use compulsion on employers to obey the labor sections of the law as interpreted by the Labor Board. By a policy of evasion and resistance many non-union employers prevented successful labor organization in their plants. In spite of his unwillingness or inability to enforce the law, General Johnson discouraged strikes, even in cases where they were for the purpose of establishing the legal right to bargain, with the hollow assertion that the law and the government were giving labor ample protection. The first settlement under the N. R. A. which prevented a great strike—that achieved in the automobile industry—was won only at the price of recognizing the employer-dominated company unions on an equality with the independent ones.

While the first concern of the administration in starting the N. R. A. was to enlarge employment and increase the purchasing power of labor, the first concern of most of the employers and trade associations was to increase the prices of the goods they sold. They used the freedom given them and the haste of action on the part of the supervisory authorities to write into the codes every device formerly developed by them to evade the anti-trust laws and control prices. Only in the raw materials industries was outright price-fixing sanctioned, and in one of these—petroleum—the code, having by accident been more carefully developed in the interest of the public and handed over to Secretary of the Interior Ickes for administration, specified public power over the prices set. But a majority of the other codes contained indirect price-fixing devices, under no public supervision whatever. The most common of these was the open-price system, according to which every member of the industry was compelled to file with the code authority a schedule of the prices he intended to charge. As a result, pressure could be and was put upon those listing the lower prices, in order to make prices uniform at the highest level set by any competitor. Other provisions prevented "selling below cost" and the cost was so defined as to be actually above the cost of the more efficient competitors. Uniform accounting systems were installed as a basis for setting prices, and in many cases these accounting systems specified the use, not of the actual costs of individual manufacturers, but of arbitrary percentages or figures far above the lowest costs in the industry. They also included heavy allowances for capital charges and depreciation, often without recognition of the fact that with a large output such overhead costs would be much lower per unit than with a small output. Costs figured on the basis of small output thus led to prices that would make large sales and output impossible. There were prohibitions against the increase of productive capacity, and allocations of production which kept in operation the less efficient concerns, so that prices had to be fixed high enough to cover their costs and profits. Codes with a price-raising tendency naturally restricted output indirectly. And many codes restricted output directly, with an indirect effect on price.

From the beginning, experts on the Consumers' Advisory Board protested vainly against the employment of these devices without adequate public control, and it was not long before their warnings were justified by developments. At hearings early in 1934 to give voice to the rising tide of consumers' protest, few individual consumers naturally were present—they could not afford to come to Washington and they did not have the statistical basis of "facts" which General Johnson always demanded from objectors. But large buyers like cities, universities, states, and mail-order houses appeared with a wealth of evidence. Prices had risen rapidly; price collusion was proved by hundreds of cases in which an offer to buy had produced uniform bids; even requirements that the product comply with the buyers' specifications was sometimes denied by the manufacturers. The Mail Order Association of America produced statistics to show the effect of the price-fixing by business. The prices of those articles which were under no codes or under codes free from price-fixing provisions were, on December 15, 1933, 18 per cent below 1926 and 7 per cent below 1929. The prices of articles under codes which contained outright price-fixing provisions were, on December 15, 1933, not much more than 1 per cent below 1926 and were 3 per cent higher than in 1929. The prices of articles under codes containing open-price provisions were, on December 15, 1933, 11.2 per cent higher than in 1926, and actually 23.3 per cent above the boom level of 1929! Meanwhile prices of farm products were not much more than half of the 1929 levels. Open price provisions were present in most of the important industries, especially those in which, like steel, prices had fallen relatively little anyway.

The stock reply of industry to such damaging complaints was that since the agricultural program and the inflation program were raising raw material prices, and since the labor policy of the N. R. A. was raising labor costs, manufacturers had to increase their prices in proportion. Had not "cutthroat competition" been responsible for the decline in labor standards? Must not the "chisellers" be controlled if labor itself were to gain purchasing power? Had not a general program of rising prices been announced by the President? Indeed, conservative critics had complained from the beginning that the N. R. A. would retard recovery by placing a heavier burden of costs on industry without increasing its earnings, and would thus damage the profit incentive to production. Under the circumstances, the attitude of industry toward prices was inevitable. And under almost any circumstances organized industry, if given power over prices, will increase them.

But the reply overlooked the really important essentials of the matter. All the evidence went to show that prices had been increased, not merely enough to cover increased costs, but much more besides. The government had had no accurate means of telling currently what the increases in costs were and whether the price increases were merely sufficient to cover them or were greater than that. Even if it had known, it had, under the N. R. A. machinery, no means of reducing unduly high prices. Furthermore, the action of the trade associations and code authorities was contradictory of the whole purpose of the recovery program. You cannot increase the farmers' purchasing power unless the prices of the crops that they sell rise more rapidly than the prices of the industrial products that they buy. The program, in this respect, would have required holding industrial prices down while farm prices were rising. And you cannot enlarge the employment and purchasing power of industrial workers unless their earnings increase more rapidly than the prices of the products which they buy.

If, every time industry pays farmers more and wage-earners more, it jacks up its prices correspondingly, it blocks the correction of any existing lack of balance be-

tween popular purchasing power and equipment to produce. If it jacks up its prices more than its rise in costs,
it aggravates that lack of balance. The only sound policy
for most important industries was a policy of low prices
to stimulate large production. The real trouble with these
industries, from the point of view of the total economy,
was not low prices but small sales. Their fixed charges
on unused investment and other items were eating up their
profits. Labor cost was unimportant beside the high overhead due to limited output. That a low-price policy was
not carried out is prima-facie evidence of the fact that
there was no national planning and no control of industry in behalf of the whole people. The trade associations
did exactly what many persons, including the author of
this book, were on record as predicting they would do if
given the function of planning and control—they raised
prices and restricted output, thus diminishing the flow
of goods on which any rise in the general standard of
living must depend. Later we shall give some figures to
indicate the results of the confused policy.

Meanwhile the Agricultural Adjustment Administration was pegging along at its task under great difficulties.
It began its crop restriction programs in cotton, wheat,
and tobacco. Growers agreed to reduce acreage in return for one form of bounty or another. As in industry,
there was a considerable amount of "chiselling" by individual producers. The poorer acres were usually held
out of production, and in many cases more fertilizer and
more intensive work was applied on the acreage culti-
vated. The weather favored a bountiful cotton crop—it
turned out to be in fact little smaller in 1933 than in 1932.

The agricultural authorities declared that without the control it would have been much larger. At any rate a combination of factors helped the restriction program to increase crop prices. The rapid piling up of inventories by the textile industry in the early part of the year enlarged the demand for cotton. The depreciation of the exchange value of the dollar gave a temporary stimulus to bull speculators and to foreign purchases. Japan and other foreign governments began accumulating supplies in anticipation of possible war. Emergency expenditures by the Surplus Relief Corporation and other governmental agencies helped to enlarge domestic demand. Total farm income in 1933, including rental and benefit payments, was estimated to be $3,271,000,000 as compared with $2,113,000,000 in 1932, an increase of nearly 55 per cent. This was far from a recovery to normal, and agricultural prices still lagged behind industrial. The benefits failed to reach down to the tenant farmers of the South, many of whom were thrown on relief because of acreage restriction. Nevertheless, the fact that some farmers had increased purchasing power was registered in larger sales by the mail-order houses, and to some extent by sales of new automobiles and agricultural machinery.

On the other half of its job, however—regulating the processing and distributing industries so that higher prices received by farmers would not be pyramided on the way to the consumer—the Agricultural Administration was not successful. There was a division in its ranks between those who wanted strict control and those who wanted industry to have its head as it did under the N. R. A. One faction was powerful enough so that codes

or agreements proposed by industries, which did not
contain sufficient safeguards of the consumer in the matter of prices and standards, were not accepted. The
other faction was powerful enough so that, when industries failed to produce satisfactory codes and agreements,
no regulation was imposed upon them by the government.
The result was that few codes or agreements over industries came into being under the A. A. A. After long delay
the President broke the jam by a characteristic compromise which failed to face the issue; the pro-industry
faction was removed from power in the Agricultural Administration, while most of the industries in question
were transferred to the jurisdiction of the N. R. A., under
whose complaisant auspices they could gain everything
the A. A. A. had, in the public interest, denied to them.
The report of the Department of Agriculture itself at the
end of the year showed that retail prices of textile and
many food products had risen more than the increase in
costs of crops, of labor, and of the processing taxes justified.

Another dangerous tendency began to appear in the
agricultural program. A good case may be made out for
the restriction of wheat and cotton production, so long as
our whole surplus cannot be sold abroad at prices which
would provide a living to the growers. It is probably true
that we have been raising more of these crops than we
could possibly consume at home, even if there were no
unemployment and the standards of living of city workers
were trebled. The same is not true, however, of most
other crops. The population of the United States, by and
large, has never consumed nearly so much milk, lean
meats, butter, fresh fruits and vegetables as it ought to

do in order to have a wholesome diet. If it did do so, there would be no domestic surplus of any of these crops, and the agricultural problem might be solved, in time, by a shifting of farmers from wheat and cotton growing to the cultivation of the higher types of food. The only sound way to work toward this end is to increase the purchasing power of city consumers. But there was constant pressure to limit output of food instead, to extend the restriction programs to all the food crops. This was actually done with some types of fruit and was seriously proposed with milk. Raising the retail price of milk and oranges at a time of unemployment and semi-starvation is almost criminal.

Here, too, the industrial administration rather than the agricultural administration was primarily to blame. The dairy farmers unquestionably needed higher prices because of the prices they had to pay for the industrial products they bought and because of their undeflated debts. Inefficiency and profiteering in the distributing industries made it impossible for them to gain higher prices without higher prices being charged to the consumer. The behavior of capitalism in industry pushed the farmers along a road which further injured all concerned.

The phase of the President's program which caused perhaps the most acrimonious dispute, and which occupied the most prominent place in public discussion for weeks at a time—his money policy—was in fact one of the least important. It was discussed mainly from two opposed points of view, one of which favored inflation and the other of which opposed it. Both were beside the point, because it was, in the nature of the case, impossible to achieve much inflation by any kind of monetary policy alone, and it will be impossible to avoid it if and when it comes, by any purely monetary policy. In order not to complicate this brief summary with the many intricacies of the problem, it may be well to sustain this contention merely with the listing of a few propositions which appear to be self-evident.

Since nine-tenths of our payments are normally made with bank checks rather than by transfer of currency, any expansion of currency would have to be tremendous in order to have any appreciable inflationary effect.

It is not the quantity of money printed, or the kind of metallic or other base behind it, which determines its "value," its effect upon commodity prices and business activity, but the volume in which it is actually spent by somebody, and the rapidity with which it circulates.

Money spent by private business enterprise is almost entirely money arising out of credit, especially bank credit. In order that inflation may take place through private spending, it is necessary for bank credit to increase. This cannot occur unless business is becoming active for other reasons, since business will not borrow, and banks will not lend, unless there are profits in sight. Credit expansion therefore is an *accompaniment* of business revival and cannot be a prime cause of it.

Hence, anything you may do to increase bank reserves, whether by acquiring more gold, or devaluing it, or going off gold altogether, or adding some new element to reserves, will have no effect in expanding business unless business is, on other grounds, ready to expand. Insufficient reserves may limit credit expansion, but as a matter of fact bank reserves in the United States were ample during prosperity and had been more than ample during the greater part of depression, even before we left the old gold standard.

If private spending does not expand, the only other possible spending agency is the government. Unless a revival occurs in business, the only possible source of inflation is governmental spending. This is a problem of the budget, of appropriations, taxation and borrowing, and not of the kind of money used.

The only difference in governmental spending between printing money and borrowing it is that if the government spends fiat money it is not burdened by interest charges and hence the spending is limited only by the wish of governmental authorities, while if it borrows the money, there is a limit somewhere imposed by the state of the government's credit. Nevertheless, governmental spending can bring about a substantial inflation through borrowing, without printing greenbacks, or going off the gold standard, or debasing the currency in any way, as was proved during the War.

The gold standard has only a slight relevance to the problem of inflation. A nation need not have inflation if it is off gold, while it can have inflation without going off it.

The principal effect of the gold standard is in international payments and international trade. It links together the values of the various currencies which are based on gold. This means that if prices are falling in one gold-standard country, there is a depressant effect on prices in other gold-standard countries, and vice versa.

President Roosevelt therefore acted quite logically in

going off gold in the spring of 1933, and on refusing to go back to it at the insistence of other nations at the London Economic Conference. He had embarked on a price-raising program in the United States. This would have been inconsistent with remaining on the gold standard as long as other important countries had not also embarked on price-raising programs. But they had not done so and declined to do so—notably France, which feared inflation above all things.

In so far, however, as President Roosevelt counted on going off the gold standard as a *means* of raising prices in the United States, and not as a mere safeguard of a price-raising program to be achieved by other means, he was leaning on a weak reed. Such an effect could be achieved only in two ways: first by a psychological stimulation of speculators, which was bound to be temporary, and second, through foreign trade. As the exchange value of the dollar sank foreigners could buy here more cheaply and presumably would buy more—until our prices rose enough to compensate for the fall of the dollar. This influence would act slowly in a time of depression; it would affect only a minor proportion of American business; it might merely push down prices in foreign countries instead of raising our prices; its competitive nature would stimulate retaliation abroad by more tariffs and quotas, which would tend to decrease international trade as a whole and would in turn react against us. On the other hand, we should have to pay more for what we bought abroad, and this would raise our prices insofar as the increased costs did not diminish our foreign purchases and thus lower prices of our imports in foreign currencies.

Even successful achievement of a price increase by such means would thus be fruitless in the end. The volume of our trade, the consumption of goods by our people, would be no greater and probably would be less because of the disturbance to world trade. The only kind of price rise to be desired is one which is accompanied by expanding consumption and activity.

When the President finally went back to gold at a lower value of the dollar, neither the anticipated calamities nor the anticipated benefits of inflation had occurred. We were still wallowing in depression. All the attention distracted to the monetary maze had prevented adequate consideration of far more important problems, such as expansion of public works and relief, enlargement of consumption and employment, correction of price disparities. We were left merely with gold reserves increased by 80 per cent in their possible coverage, while we had been unable to employ the excess reserve we already had. The most that could be said for devaluation was that if and when credit inflation should come—which would probably be after we had ceased needing it to escape from depression—it would be even less limited than before by the size of reserves. The stage was set, not for controlled inflation when we needed it, but for uncontrolled inflation after we should cease to want it, inflation through the ordinary banking mechanism rather than through the monetary heresies by which conservatives had been so foolishly frightened. After devaluation, the country was again face to face with the fact that the only two ways in which a rise in prices could occur was either through a business revival or through increased governmental spending.

Both the industrial and the agricultural programs were thus going awry, while the monetary policy had inconclusive results. What about the program for direct governmental stimulation of activity through public works? The Recovery Act had carried an appropriation of $3,300,000,-000 for this purpose. This was too small, in proportion to the national income, to have a major effect even if spent promptly; Mr. Roosevelt's concern for balancing the budget had kept the total down, just as Mr. Hoover's concern for the same end had prevented any substantial program of the same sort. And it was not spent promptly. All sorts of difficulties were encountered. There was no large spending program ready, because of a lack of advance planning. Months must elapse after a project is conceived before any men are actually employed on it, on account of the need for surveys, plans, authorizations, legal work, bids and red tape of all sorts. The administration was concerned to prevent politics and graft in such a huge amount of spending; this entirely proper caution caused delays.

The ordinary works of the Federal government are a minor part of the total of public building; even these were held up by cautious budgetary authorities. States and local governments, even with the aid of the free grant of 30 per cent of material and labor cost which the law allowed, were often restrained from embarking on building by the fact that they were already embarrassed in meeting their fixed charges and either could not or did not desire to borrow more. There were few new types of construction which did not run into the obstructions raised by private enterprise. Housing, for those whose incomes were so low that they never had been able to afford decent dwelling places, offered theoretically an almost unlimited opportunity to spend; practically it was limited by such things as high land values in congested centers, the opposition of the real estate interests to public competition, the fear of banks and other financial institutions that their real estate assets would be injured, the failure to get together on any adequate plan. The law allowed grants and loans for public power plants, but the privately owned utilities did everything in their power to obstruct such projects, and that was a good deal. By February, 1934, more than six months after the appropriation had been made, only about $50,000,000 of the $3,300,000,000 appropriated had actually been spent on public works. This does not include the sum earmarked in the bill for roads, or the sums taken out of it for naval building, or the other sums taken for emergency relief. The money will eventually be spent, but its spending will extend over two years or more. It will be stimulating, but only mildly so.

The main channels through which the government actually got more money into circulation, outside of the agricultural benefit payments, were by emergency measures such as the Civilian Conservation Corps—which was a mere drop in the bucket—the Surplus Relief Corporation and the Civil Works Authority. The Surplus Relief Corporation bought pigs, coal, textiles and other things direct from producers for distribution to the unemployed. It furnished some help, but its activities were not prominent in the whole picture. The C. W. A. was a godsend to many of the unemployed and to local governments embarrassed by the drain of relief. It really did spend money in moderately large amounts, and quickly. About

$1,000,000,000 was distributed through it in the winter of 1933-34. This spending helped trade and the industries making consumers' goods. And just because it did succeed in its purpose, it had to be abolished. The President became frightened by its drain on the budget. Local employers protested at the competition it offered in the labor market. Because it was free from ordinary red tape, political corruption appeared in it. Most of all, the administration feared the effect of having millions of persons dependent directly on the Federal government for sustenance and employment, persons who would use pressure and political influence to enlarge their compensation and enhance their security. The government was holding the bag for the failure of private industry to provide jobs. As long as it did this, and private industry failed to absorb the unemployed, the government would be between the devil of being obliged to deny the demands of those accustomed to depend on it, because funds from taxation were insufficient, and the deep sea of unlimited inflation through spending currently large amounts out of borrowed or fiat money. That the failure of industry to pursue a policy of ample production could lead to a dangerous pressure for unplanned government spending was soon proved by the passage of the soldiers' bonus over the President's veto.

Until the spring of 1934, however, the danger of too much spending was potential rather than actual. The present fact was too little spending. The great deficit expected from the huge budget which the President submitted to Congress early in 1934 was not, as was popularly supposed, the result of expenditures which would actually put money into circulation, but mainly of debt salvage. It was really a continuation of the Hoover R. F. C. plan of substituting government debts for private debts in order to prevent deflation of the assets of financial institutions. This involved, for the present, a mere exchange of debt instruments, not an increase of money in circulation. No new appropriation was made for public works. The President continued his policy of trying to balance the ordinary budget by cutting the salaries of government employees and reducing their numbers—at the very time when he was urging upon private industry the opposite course. His financial plan was an almost exact replica of that of the former President, but was carried to a greater extreme. It was to hold down current expenditures to the utmost, while enlarging the government's liabilities by an immense program of debt salvage. This amounted to a big bet on recovery, without planning for sufficiently large governmental expenditures which, if private industry did not revive, constituted the only way to stimulate recovery. If he should lose the bet, the government would face a choice between repudiating its debts, thus causing a catastrophic deflation of capital, and carrying out an immense budgetary inflation in order to pay the debts.

What were the net results of these policies? Between March and June, production had increased rapidly because of the rebound from the bank holiday and the general anticipation of inflation. During this period wages and payrolls were increased only a little. In June the National Industrial Recovery Act was signed; in August the Blue Eagle campaign went into effect; by September a number of the more important industries had been codified. During the N. R. A. period from June to December, industrial production steadily declined, until it reached down almost to the low of the depression. Between June and September, while the Blue Eagle campaign was under way and the labor provisions of the codes were going into effect, there was an increase in payrolls and employment, in spite of the decline in production. This was undoubtedly due to the provisions of the codes concerning maximum hours and minimum wages. But, beginning with September, factory employment and payrolls fell again. The average earnings of those employed also declined slightly. Meanwhile, on account of the rise in prices, the cost of living had gone up. Here are the figures of the Federal Reserve Board. They are index numbers based on the average of 1923-1925 (not adjusted for seasonal variation).

	Factory Payrolls	Factory Employment	Average * Per Capita Weekly Earnings
June	46.2	72.1	64.1
September	57.6	75.2	76.6
December	53.1	74.8	71.0

* Computed by dividing Column 1 by Column 2.

Meanwhile, according to the U. S. Bureau of Labor Statistics, the cost of living had risen 5.3 per cent between June and December.

At the end of six months of the New Deal in industry:

There were still between 10,000,000 and 12,000,000 unemployed.

Although factory payrolls had risen nearly 15 per cent, the cost of living had gone up 5.3 per cent. The purchasing power of the workers was thus not greatly increased, in view of the need for enlarging consumption and output of goods, and of the capacity of industry to produce them. Since the more important codes had become effective, the purchasing power of labor had actually declined.

The purchasing power of the average individual worker who was employed was actually reduced from the beginning of the industry control. His money earnings rose 3.7 per cent between June and December against an increase of 5.3 per cent in the cost of living. (This is not necessarily an accurate index of what happened to the earnings of those employed before the N. R. A. went into effect, since the addition of new employees at the minimum wage levels would tend to drag down the average. Such figures are not too accurate in any case. But the errors are probably not great enough to invalidate the conclusion that most of the employed wage-earners gained little or nothing in purchasing power.)

As for the farmers, their gains occurred before the N. R. A. went into effect, and were whittled down afterwards. Wholesale prices of farm products, according to the U. S. Department of Labor, rose from an index number of 40.9 in February, 1933—their depression low—to 60.1 in July. In the same period, the wholesale prices of all commodities other than farm products and foods rose from 66.0 to 72.2. (Both figures are based on 100 in 1926.) Though neither got back to the 1926 level, and though prices of farm products had, even in July, not risen so close to it as prices of other products, still the price disparity between the two kinds of goods had been narrowed. After July, however, the spread widened again. The index of farm-product prices fell from 60.1 in July to 55.5 in December. The index of prices of other commodities rose, as the N. R. A. codes began to go into effect, from 72.2 in July to 77.5 in December. The benefit payments made to farmers for restricting production somewhat moderated this widening of the price disparity, but by no means reversed the trend. The N. R. A. invalidated the advance toward price parity which the A. A. A. was seeking.

Professor Frederick C. Mills, in his chapter on Economic Recovery in "Social Change and the New Deal" [1] shows that the price disparities which he had previously indicated were serious in the development of the depression were somewhat moderated between February and July, 1933, but thereafter were aggravated. His figures have a direct bearing on the operation of the codes. Between July and December, the prices of producer's goods for ultimate human consumption—that is, the materials to be made into food, clothing, automobiles and the like —did not rise so rapidly as the prices of these goods after processing and manufacturing. The manufacturers' margins were widened. Other evidence goes to show that they were widened much more than would have been justified by any increase in labor costs.

The natural result was a growth in profits. No detailed or comprehensive profit figures are available, but a summary of the financial results of 810 large industrial corporations in 37 industries, published by the National City Bank, is enlightening. Whereas these corporations showed an aggregate net deficit of $45,802,000 in 1932, they had an aggregate net profit of $440,643,000 in 1933. Of the 37 industries, 21 lost money in 1932, but only 9 did so in the succeeding year. It is impossible to say how much of the change was due to the larger volume of business in

[1] University of Chicago Press.

1933—the Federal Reserve Board's index of industrial production stood at 76 in 1933 as against 64 in 1932. But wider margins between costs and selling prices undoubtedly played a large part. The most striking gain—indeed, the only gain of really magnificent proportions—in the first months of the New Deal was the gain of the recipients of profits.

These figures threw a curious light upon the argument by those conservatives who had criticized the N. R. A. because they thought that by raising raw material prices and wages it would increase industry's costs at the expense of profits and would thus destroy the profit incentive and curb production. After July, raw material costs and wages were raised less rapidly than industry's prices, and profits were enlarged. But the moment profits began to grow, production declined. Here is the monthly industrial production index of the Federal Reserve Board for 1933, adjusted for seasonal variation:

January	65
February	63
March	59
April	66
May	78
June	92
July (N.R.A. began to operate)	100
August	91
September	84
October	77
November	72
December	75

What limited the growth of production was not the lack of profit margins, but the lack of sufficient growth in demand from farmers and wage-earners. The N. R. A.

had failed to follow the policy which the conservatives feared, but the result was nevertheless that which they predicted.

In the early months of 1934 an upturn of business appeared again, and was hailed on many sides as a beginning of a general revival. But cautious critics pointed out the following indisputable facts:

Much of the business activity represented a normal seasonal bulge. In addition, much was due to the money the government had been pouring out through the C. W. A. and the farmers' benefit payments.

Some of the indices—like those for department store sales—were higher only because prices were higher; volume of goods sold in department stores was actually less than a year before, at the bottom of the depression.

The gradual growth of government expenditures on public works, and railroad buying financed in large part by government money, were important factors in the rising production of steel and other heavy industries.

Government expenditures on relief, farm benefits and construction were thus at last beginning to "prime the pump." But the fact remained that as rapidly as the government brought water to the pump, industry carried it away in its own pail. The priming water was instantly diverted to wider profit margins, which, through higher prices, tended to restrict output again. The question was, how far production and employment would increase under these circumstances, and whether the pump would keep on flowing after the government stopped priming it.

All this governmental activity, hastily improvised as it had been, was of an emergency nature and designed to promote recovery. The N. R. A., to be sure, was conceived as a permanent government of industry, but the action taken under it was directed to the immediate future rather than to long-term reform. What about the more permanent program of the New Deal?

In finance, nothing fundamental was done. The banks were simply set on their feet again, flooded with reserves, mobilized somewhat more completely under the Federal Reserve System, and plastered with deposit insurance. A technical separation was decreed between commercial banking and investment banking. None of these reforms went to the root of the matter. The Securities Act attempted to compel underwriters, directors and accountants to assume personal liability for their statements in the issuance of new securities, and thus to enforce the ethics appropriate to a system of small, personally managed enterprises in which individuals could know all the relevant facts about their businesses—a system which had long since vanished. The financial community resisted this conservative measure as if it were the extreme of Bolshevism, but there was little to be gained even by a victory of the supporters of the law, since it did not touch the larger problem of directing the investment of new capital according to the needs of an industrial system planned to serve the community. A bill was introduced to police the Stock Exchange and limit speculation; its more important provisions were whittled away by those who had an interest in speculative profits; this too, was unimportant. A speculative capital market is an inseparable accompaniment of corporate, profit-seeking capitalism; something may be done to prevent the big speculative fish from eating so many of the little ones; but the major evils of the market, so far as the functioning of the industrial system are concerned, are inherent in the direction of the uses of capital according to private hope of gain rather than according to social plans for production. In all these financial measures the administration was tossed on the old reformist dilemma, encountered in most attempts to make private enterprise be good: either the police regulations are trivial and successfully evaded, or else they destroy the habitual working of capitalism without setting up anything in its place.

In some respects the most hopeful of the administration's plans was the creation of the Tennessee Valley Authority. There the government actually succeeded—as the result of a fight which had been carried on for years by Senator Norris and the progressive minority under previous administrations—in beginning to develop a publicly owned hydroelectric system which might lower rates and furnish a yardstick by which the practices of the private companies could be measured. Even so, the influence of the private utilities and bankers prevented many parts of the region from setting up local public distributing units. The rest of the T. V. A. program was dubious, to say the least. It looked forward to developing a decentralized industrial region, with people living in model communities in rural districts, raising their own food, and earning what cash they needed in local factories. But the chances are ten to one that the government will neither own and operate the factories nor be able to regulate successfully whatever private plants may be induced to establish themselves in the region. What is to prevent the employers from exploiting the population and furnishing "cutthroat competition" for other manufacturing centers, in which workers cannot raise their own food or enjoy such cheap rent and power? As long as the total of the nation's production and consumption does not expand to the capacity of the existing plant, the Tennessee Valley plan can succeed only at the expense of some other part of the country. Its very chance of contribution to the national life is limited by the same central problem that limits the government's whole endeavor. Neither recovery nor reform can be built on the maintenance of general scarcity.

The attempt to do something with the railroads under a provisional régime of Federal "coördination" was hindered by precisely the same difficulties. The railroad companies would not deflate their capital charges by reorganizations and receiverships as long as there was the slightest chance of borrowing money from the government to sustain them, or there was any hope of revived business. Rates had to be maintained at a high level because of the fear of the capital deflation which would be a certain result of reducing them, unless the reduction stimulated promptly a much larger volume of traffic. Many operating economies were theoretically possible, but few of them could be made except by increasing productivity of labor per man-hour. Displaced men could not be absorbed in the railroads or anywhere else, so long as industrial production did not greatly increase. Under depression conditions, therefore, such economies would mean merely enlarging the number of the unemployed.

Quite properly, the law forbade this and railroad labor organizations opposed it. Any real progress in the railroad situation, so long as the railroads remained private enterprises, had to await general recovery, and that must come from somewhere else.

In spite of the ferment of the depression, the shift in opinions and loyalties, the emergence of representatives of hitherto suppressed classes and schools of thought in the new administration, and the great hopes aroused by Mr. Roosevelt's first acts and words, the New Deal thus began to reveal the old contradictions and conflicts. The President never lived up to the implications of the major aims he announced. The program was not assessed for inconsistencies; no informational machinery was set up for checking in detail whether progress was being made toward the announced aims. Continual improvisation threw off some hopeful experiments, but most of them were not followed through.

Since even the sensory part of the planning brain was lacking, the thinking part naturally could not exist. The "brain trust" was always a picturesque fiction. What there ever was of trustification in brains succumbed to the free competition of ideas. Washington swarmed with people, official and otherwise, who had their own views about how things are going. It was full of separate projects for action. Able persons discussed these matters around luncheon and dinner tables, at chance meetings. Ideas and projects of all kinds—good, bad and indifferent—went up to the President; he asked advice and took what action seemed right to him at the moment. As a consumer of facts and brains, however, he was like a housewife in a great department store, without an expert testing bureau. He was not afraid to try new ideas— which is good so far as it goes—and he was a remarkably shrewd and resourceful buyer. The fact remained that individuals were thinking as individuals, and most of them were thinking so hard about the small problems for which they are directly responsible that they had little time to think about the big ones.

Mr. Roosevelt did a lot of reforestation in our governmental landscape; many were tending the new saplings; but it was nobody's business to look at the woods.

What is the reason for this strange omission? Many of Mr. Roosevelt's trusted advisers favored national planning in the interest, not of separate groups and private profits, but of the social good. He had spoken of it himself, and had embarked on the sort of program in which the logic of the effort led straight toward it. Perhaps the lack was due to the circumstance that most of the men who might do the job were overworked with detail. Perhaps it was due to Mr. Roosevelt's own volatile temperament. But there was a more basic obstacle. Business distrusted any mobilization of knowledge and of analysis. It distrusted the power which might grow from it. Active, executive arms of the New Deal feared those to whom thinking might be delegated. The closer the executives were to business interests, the more they distrusted anything which did not smack of the "practical" —that is, of action without reflection, of day-to-day adjustments among interests, not related to general principles. Business itself, one infers, would have made any non-business planning board a center of attack; indeed, it acted instinctively to prevent any from being created.

There lurked behind the scene a fundamental conflict of purposes.

In this happy-go-lucky manner, the President tried to keep all factions and schools of opinion contented. But in the nature of the case he could not kept the executives of private capitalism contented if he really took from them any of their power. Since he was not prepared, either in his own mind or by the organization of social and political forces behind him, to press the issue against them, he had to surrender to them. This was called by polite names like "coöperation." He asked private industry to coöperate with the recovery effort; in this exchange it gave the very least it was compelled to give and took all it could. No doubt the President did not understand how much it was really taking. No doubt he deceived himself by thinking that the enunciation of high aims and the drafting of laws really did check it—though no sufficiently competent administrative agencies were created to do the checking.

When Mr. Roosevelt first spoke of himself as a quarterback calling the signals in a football game, and changing his strategy according to circumstances, he thought of his opponents as abstractions—unemployment, depression and the like. He did not recognize that these cloudy figures had features—the features of steel magnates and the rest of the rulers of capitalism.

The first nebulous effort to undertake social planning thus ran afoul of the realities of capitalism. With every passing month, the habitual rulers of the economic régime, broken and hopeless though they had been when President Roosevelt took office, gained courage. They quickly circumvented the miscellaneous efforts of the more socially minded members of the administration to control them. As they gained power to raise prices and increase profits, their confidence returned. All the planning that was effectuated was in their hands; it was good old capitalist planning, which subordinated, not merely most of the socialistic implications in the original Roosevelt program, but the remnants of self-adjusting laissez-faire. Planning had won a sort of victory in public esteem, but the emergent issue now was, what kind of planning ought it to be, who should control it, and to what ends? The stage was set to see what planning in the interest of private profit could do for the nation.

PART IV

THE COMING REVOLUTION

I. WHAT KIND OF PREDICTION?

THE skill for predicting the future of human history still lies, at its worst, in the arts of magic, and, at its best, in the vision of the prophet. Science has made possible accurate prediction in the realms where it has given us the most exact knowledge: astronomers can foretell the movements of stars and comets; meteorologists can, within wide margins of error, forecast the weather. But the science of human behavior is not yet complete enough in its analysis or exact enough in its quantitative assessment of forces so that anyone can speak with intelligent assurance concerning the future of mankind. Those with prophetic insight feel in their bones what is going to happen, but the reliability of their predictions rests upon the representative character of their intuitions. Even the wisest have seldom been able truly to foretell more than the general drift of affairs. They do not know how rapidly the stream of history will run, or what turns and twists it may take on the way to its next destination. Visions of what lies ahead are more frequently mirages than tele-photographs.

But since the future is a continuation of the past and present, we can survey it with something better than a wild surmise. If our view of the components of the present is at all like the reality, it ought to give us hints at least concerning what will follow. Since these hints are

265

the best guides there are, it is well not to be too modest about learning from them what we can. A willingness to predict, and to act on the basis of prediction, is the condition of bringing anything to pass in human history which would not occur in the history of oysters.

Prediction in this sense is not a passive look into a magic mirror which reveals an inexorable fate. It is, in so far as it is like the other predictions of science, a conditional statement. It involves alternatives. The laws of physics tells us that if an automobile is driven off a cliff, it will fall. The result is inevitable, given the conditions; it is a consequence of natural law. But human beings, knowing this law, can choose not to drive automobiles over cliffs. It may be further contended that the sort of things human beings will choose rests in large part with the make-up of that vague abstraction commonly called "human nature." But human nature acts in many different ways, according to the circumstances in which it is placed, and according to the skill and foresight that it is able to exercise. It is a universal attribute of human nature to want food. A savage gives scope to this urge by killing wild animals or eating nuts and fruit. A Wall Street broker does it by dealing in bits of printed paper. Each has been conditioned to foresee that activity of his particular kind will bring him something to eat. Now, put a savage in Wall Street, or a broker in the primeval wilderness, and you could make a prediction concerning his future. You might predict that he would starve. That would indeed be likely—but not quite inevitable. The really scientific prediction would be that *unless* the savage acted like a broker, or the broker like a savage, he would starve. Prediction in these terms would be of some use. It would at least indicate to the persons concerned what sort of thing they would have to do in order to avoid an unpleasant fate. It would be neither magic nor prophecy, but an attempt to apply verified knowledge to the relation between man and his environment, in order that he might foresee the consequences of different types of behavior and might choose accordingly.

This book, up to the present point, has been an attempt roughly and briefly to describe the new environment in which the American people now find themselves, and the inappropriateness to this new environment of old ways of behavior. We are still acting much like savages in Wall Street. Experience ought to teach us that such behavior is calamitous. Will it do so? Only a prophet could be sure about that, and even his assurance might be wrong. But even here, the more humble approach of common sense based on such knowledge as we have has something to contribute. It tells us that in the past, when human beings have been confronted with the breakdown and failure of old régimes, they have found their way through, sooner or later, to new ones better adapted to the times. There is no valid reason why people should not continue to do so in the future. The rest of this volume will be devoted to guesses—frankly speculative guesses, but still guesses founded in part on verified experience—concerning the course by which the present adjustment may be completed.

2. PLANNING FOR PROFITS

During the nineteenth century, when the prevailing doctrine was that freedom of action on the part of individuals, with an absolute minimum of governmental restriction, would produce the best possible results for everyone, this freedom became in fact more and more limited. Powerful interests began to plan and control, and to use governmental authority, in order to enhance their own wealth. But for many years this activity was masked under the assumption that we still had a self-adjusting mechanism of individual enterprise and competition. Meanwhile the individualism came to mean chiefly the freedom of the great rulers of business to do what they liked, thus restricting the individualism of every one else, while the competition was more and more banished from their activities and enforced upon those whom they were exploiting—the industrial workers, farmers and small business men. The crisis of the thirties was marked by a breakdown of the ways of thinking which had masked the reality. All groups and classes in distress turned toward planning and control, under the ægis of governmental police power. Efforts more determined than ever before were made to limit competition even among the exploited, while big business frankly dropped the pretense that it was competitive or was trying to be.

Business interests naturally wanted to confirm those powers of control which they had been exercising in the past, and to extend these powers. This was, as far as separate industries were concerned, a collective movement. In order to gain greater security and to enhance profits, the majority of industrial leaders consented to submit to collective discipline with their fellows, under governmental authority. Only a few prominent industrialists, of whom the greatest was Henry Ford, openly defied this part of the change. Planning for greater security of profits became a reality in most separate industries. Thus, capitalism moved into a stage of higher organization; it accepted consciously the implications which were already developed in its financial centralization and the coöperative discipline of the large corporations.

It could gain the legal right to do this, however, only by conceding, at least in the words of the law, a certain amount of compensating power for organized action to other classes such as farmers, employees and consumers. The potential political power of agriculture, of labor, and of the white-collar classes, the strength of the new ideas which were fermenting in the nation, was already great enough so that the charter given for the purpose of limiting competition in business had to be accompanied by charters for limiting competition in the growing and marketing of crops, in the labor market (through collective bargaining) and in the markets for retail goods (through the powers delegated to the President to require information from business and to protect the consumer.) And there was provided legal authority to create an agency to coördinate these endeavors for the general good. Thus the idea of social planning, as contrasted with the idea of business planning for profits, took its first baby step.

The step, as we have seen, soon was followed by a tumble. It was difficult for farmers to coöperate in restricting output, even with the government as an ally; employers had no sooner accepted collective bargaining in the words of the law and the codes than many of the more powerful of them tried to escape it in fact; the government's legal power to protect the consumer was scarcely exercised at all—its only expression was in the creation of advisory bodies which could do little except utter weak protests against what the government was allowing to be done in other directions, and in the opportunity offered to hear the complaints of buyers who happened to have some organized economic power, such as the mail-order concerns, and a few cities, states and universities. As a result, prices of industrial products were raised faster than prices of crops or wage-rates; industrial profits began to grow more rapidly than farm incomes and payrolls.

This is our starting point for speculation about the future. Now let us suppose that the present tendency is confirmed and extended. Let us suppose that big business, regaining its confidence as it gets further into the black, strengthens its old resistance to control by any other political or social force. Its effective use of the usual propaganda machinery returns as it accumulates the funds to pay those who operate that machinery. Signs that this sort of thing is occurring are plain as day in every direction. Organized business (not forgetting the profit-seeking press) had already emasculated the new Food and Drugs Act, which sought to help consumers not only in avoiding the use of poisons, but in knowing exactly what they are buying and what it is good for. It had mobilized the opinion of a majority of the propertied classes against the Securities Act and the bill to regulate the Stock Exchange—laws which sought to protect the more helpless of the propertied classes against a repetition of the losses which they had so recently suffered. Having prevented the progressives within the administration from doing much, it is now seeking to discredit them altogether as revolutionaries. It has temporarily imposed a brake on further advance of power by organized labor; its employer-controlled company unions have been granted a quasi-legal recognition. It is using with effect the argument that anything it does not want done should not be done because action opposed by business would interrupt recovery.

All these activities of course have but one ultimate end —to nourish the growth of profits. Can we have a business revival on this basis? Can aggregate profits grow any larger, if the more rigid debts, costs and prices are not further deflated, if the purchasing power of wages and farm incomes does not increase greatly? Many critics of the present order have rashly predicted that we cannot, that this collapse of capitalism is final and irrevocable. I am afraid they are mistaken. Business enterprise was so organized that its leading units could make enormous profits even though, as in 1929, equipment to produce was not utilized at anywhere near its full capacity, even though there were a couple of million or more unemployed wage-earners and the average of wages paid was low, even though farm incomes were inadequate. Since then business has, in many instances, written down its capital somewhat. It has probably also widened its profit margins in many cases. Even a slight upturn in production can cause a rapid increase in the rate of earnings, enough to put the bulk of industry beyond any danger of bankruptcy, enough to permit it to resume dividends and begin to pile up surpluses again. Profits can revive for a time even if prosperity is not general.

Government spending for public construction, moderate though it is, plus government loans to railroads, can bring about some increase in production and employment in the heavy industries. Such reductions in hours, increases in payrolls, and growth in farm earnings as the New

Deal has been able to effectuate, plus direct expenditure for relief, can reduce unemployment and expand sales somewhat in the industries selling and making consumers' goods. A growth of dividends, plus the other expansive elements, can stimulate the sales of new automobiles. The rise of profits may eventually cause an upward movement in the securities markets. This would improve the position of banks and other financial institutions; they could lend more freely. Those dependent on dividends and high executive salaries would be satisfied that everything was going well, and their satisfaction would set the tone of conventional opinion.

But such a revival of profits must be distinguished sharply from a complete or durable revival of the nation's economic welfare as a whole. It will probably take years for the urban real estate business to write off its losses, for effective urban demand to press upon the available space in city buildings and apartments, and for the private construction industry to expand to anything like its pre-depression volume. There is no other visible source of demand for durable or capital goods which can push the heavy industries anywhere near to full capacity for long at a time. Consumers' goods industries will not be selling a large enough volume so that a net expansion of their equipment is likely. Restrictions upon new installations, and allocations of production which give the less efficient plants a share of the total output, will slow down the growth of demand for new plant and machinery. Advances in productive efficiency already achieved will make it certain that, at the restricted volume of production, many millions of industrial workers must remain unemployed. There is little likelihood of much expansion in

the sales of farm products either abroad or at home,
under such conditions. Thus there will continue to be a
surplus of farmers. Want in the midst of plenty will be
more real even than in the depression: there may be
slightly less want among the unfortunate, but it will be
accompanied by more plenty among the ruling economic
classes. What we shall have can be described as a business revival in the presence of an industrial and social
depression. Capitalistic planning will have produced a
certain degree of temporary security for profits, on the
basis of a poverty level for large masses of the population. Capitalist industrialism will have executed a strategic retreat, having excluded from its productive processes millions who must find their living, if they can, in
more primitive types of activity.

But such a situation will prove to be unstable even for
capitalism itself. Even if nothing more dangerous occurs,
a revival of this nature must before long wear itself out.
Government appropriations and loans, having "primed
the pump" may be discontinued. The demand for new
consumers' goods, both durable and non-durable, must
stop growing. This cessation of growth will, as always
before, cause an actual drop in production of the heavy
industries, and a consequent recession in other industries
as well. Profits can fall as rapidly as they can rise. It
is likely, under these conditions, that many of the formerly competitive industries, which were in a weak position in respect to the more highly organized ones, will
revert to cutthroat competition in the effort to capture
the limited amount of business, and nothing will be done
to stop them. Their codes will become dead letters. The
whole N. R. A. may even be allowed to lapse, the big

corporations being satisfied to let it do so since they will have got out of it the one thing they wanted—the ability to control their own output and prices even more firmly than before. This practice will of course be retained. If all this happens, we can, within two or three years at the outside, be back where we were early in 1933. The net outcome of capitalist planning will be a return to depression. Its net result in the change of economic institutions will be a strengthening of the very rigidities and a widening of the very price disparities which had previously been the main source of difficulty.

There is another possibility which would engender more prosperity in the meantime, and a more serious collapse in the end. Inflation, which stubbornly refused to operate when it was most needed to start us out of the depression, may suddenly take hold, once business revival is well under way. As a matter of fact, this is what inflation has always done in the past. Everything is set for such an uncontrolled inflation in this country as the world has rarely seen, once it gets a start. The banks, already gorged with excess reserves, saw the effectiveness of these reserves increased by 80 per cent when the gold dollar was devalued. (Though the actual gold in the reserves was sent to the Treasury, the banks received in return, dollar for dollar, gold certificates which are the legal equivalent of the gold.) In addition, the devaluation brought to our shores an enormous amount of new gold, which it will be difficult for us to get rid of as long as we remain a creditor nation and have an export surplus.

The banking system still consists of privately owned units operated for private profit. It will be just as difficult to force them to act as a unified social instrument in limiting the expansion of credit when it ought to be limited as it was to force them to act as a unit in expanding credit when it ought to have been expanded. The Federal Reserve Banks may, it is true, apply corrective measures by raising rediscount rates and selling government securities. But there is likely to be such a cushion in the reserves of the member banks that neither of these measures will be effective unless carried to such an extreme that they will operate too late and will of themselves cause a continued reaction. The banks can, once an inflationary credit movement begins, lend enormous amounts without utilizing the rediscount facilities of the Reserve Banks. Furthermore it is uncertain whether the Federal Reserve authorities themselves will not be influenced by the inflationary psychology of business on the make, or by the political interests which are thinking of Treasury requirements or of the next election. The bottled-up sentiment in behalf of inflation is tremendous; the country is full of people, from big business interests down to humble farmers, who think that all we need for everlasting prosperity is plenty of money and credit.

Another possible source of inflation is governmental spending. The approved theory is that government ought to borrow more and spend more during depression, and that, once revival starts, it should cease borrowing, repay its debts, and taper off its extraordinary expenditures. We have seen how difficult it is for the government to act according to the depression half of the prescription. Capitalism will make it just as difficult for the government to act according to the prosperity half. The kind of revival we shall have, if we have it, will be directly dependent upon governmental expenditures. Any reduction of appropriations, whether for building or battleships, will be almost immediately reflected in a slump of construction and of the capital-goods industries. There seems to be little likelihood that private demand for construction and capital goods will rise enough to fill the gap. Furthermore, since industry is seeking profits by limiting output, there will continue to be a great number of unemployed workers and farmers, and the demand for large-scale governmental relief will continue. It will be extremely difficult for government to resist these demands; if it does, it will assume immediate responsibility for a renewal of depression and misery.

Now, governmental spending can to some extent make up for the deficiencies of capitalism. There is a whole school of opinion that looks forward to governmental spending on a continually larger scale, creating all kinds of public wealth—beautiful buildings, art museums, parks, and what not. This is all very well, though it is far from intelligent social planning if people are given art galleries by public effort when they have never been able to afford enough nourishing food, when the private industries controlling most of the basic necessities of life are still parsimonious in their provision of the essentials of living to the masses. But, in addition to this, there is a fatal flaw in the politico-economics of this line of action.

Expansion of governmental spending must eventually, if it is not to lead to uncontrolled inflation, be met out of tax receipts, not out of borrowing. And these taxes must be levied in such a way that they do not raise the cost of living for the masses, but come rather out of profits and incomes above the average. Is there any doubt whatever that capitalism will resist to the last the imposition of sufficiently heavy income and profits taxes? Government will not be permitted to pay off its depression debt quickly enough, not to speak of incurring immense new expenditures without new borrowing. Heavy taxation of wealth to provide things for the masses which the masses cannot buy is exactly what reactionaries think socialism is; they will resist it almost as solidly as they would resist complete confiscation of their property. It combines all the disadvantages of true socialism with few of its advantages. It approximates confiscation and redistribution of wealth without the social and economic planning necessary to enlarge the total of wealth. Continuation of heavy governmental expenditures after revival, if it occurs, is therefore likely to be financed by further borrowing rather than by taxation, and can thus lead to uncontrolled budgetary inflation.

Inflation, whether proceeding from unplanned credit expansion or unplanned public borrowing, would make the rise of revival sharper and the ensuing drop harder. It would, on the way up, make things more rosy for speculators and profit-makers; it would probably lead to somewhat more production and employment. Conceivably a credit inflation could flow over into the investment markets, attract the issuance of new securities in large volume, and start new urban construction and new expansion of productive facilities in industry. At the beginning, because of increased volume of employment and higher prices for crops, it would enlarge the purchasing power of consumers as a whole. But after the limits of the expansion in employment and the rise in crop prices had been reached, it would sharply decrease the purchasing power of farm and city consumers, because all prices would have risen faster than wage-rates, and the prices of manufactured articles would probably have outdistanced the prices of crops. No inflation can continue forever; it is killed by the disparities of income and prices which it causes.

Capitalistic planning, if it retains its present victory over labor, farmers and consumers in general, can therefore lead only to one of two results: (a) without inflation, to a revival of profits without much revival of anything else, followed by a return to depression; (b) with inflation, to an inflationary boom followed by a crisis. In either case it solves nothing; we shall be back where we were, with whatever political and social changes may in the meantime have come about.

3. PLANNING FOR THE MASSES

The second possibility is that the general aims originally enunciated by President Roosevelt, desired by the more progressive intellectuals, and instinctively supported by labor and most consumers, will be more strongly and effectively sought in practice. These aims are, more equal distribution of income, progressively increased production and standards of living, greater stability of the economic system and more security for everyone. In the minds of most of those who are seeking them, they require, not a complete social revolution, not a confiscation of the property of the owners and rulers of productive capital, but a real regulation of their activities for social ends.

How could progress toward this goal conceivably be made? Some of the most important essentials of advance in this direction may be listed as follows:

Wage rates and hours must be subject to regulation, throughout industry, by forces acting, not in the interest of employers but of labor.

At the same time, prices must be set in the interest of consumers—wage-earners, small salary earners and farmers.

By pushing low wages up and prices down in industries where production has been restricted, larger volume of output may be attained, and employment may be increased. This can be done, however, only by a continual elimination of the marginal concerns, by concentrating production among the more efficient, by a strong emphasis upon utilization of the best technique.

Production must be planned. It must be planned, however, not merely by restriction in industries which are declining or have little possibilities of growth, but by expansion in other industries. Without greatly expanded production in the aggregate, the goods necessary to support a higher standard of living will not be made, and millions will be without the employment and wages to buy them.

Credit must be planned on the basis of the production planning. Short-term credit must be related to the necessity of immediate production in specific industries and plants; it must be extended on the basis of good budgeting. Long-term credit (investment) must be related to the planned expansion of industry.

The essential basis of all this is more complete statistical information than we have, plus publicly supervised accounting which will reveal the true financial status of every individual concern and every industry.

To enumerate even these few general requirements of successful social planning is to show that their attainment must be, even under the best possible circumstances, a slow and arduous process. It is conceivable that President Roosevelt, if he had acted promptly and decisively enough, might have approached them much more closely than he has done. He might, in the banking crisis, have socialized the credit system. He might have taken his stand firmly with labor and enforced true collective bargaining upon recalcitrant employers. It was only necessary to liberate the desire of workers all over the country for genuine unions in order that a great labor movement should arise, which could enforce standards of wages and hours. He might have stood squarely behind the consumers' experts in the industry and farm administrations, and fought the rulers of industry to obtain from them the right kind of statistical and accounting information, to prevent them from employing price-raising devices where these were not warranted. He might have created an expert planning board. He might have called upon engineers to take a larger part in the government of industry, to see that it was efficient. Even so, the struggle would only have been begun.

If the public experts counted upon competition to control prices, as many of them tend to do, they would have to demand a renewal of the political warfare to disrupt monopoly and regulate business practices which, after having been waged for over fifty years, has left big business bigger than ever. A return to competition as an automatic stabilizer is not a return to laissez-faire in the sense of no governmental control; it would involve a stronger central government, exercising a stronger police power, than we have ever had, in order to prevent private price controls from being used. Even then it would not remove many elements of rigidity. If, on the other hand, the experts turned to public regulation of prices, exempting only those in which competition existed to a sufficient extent to keep the economic balance flexible, they would have to wrest from industry the attributes of its private

property which it considers most sacred. When accounting is supervised and its results are publicly known, when
wages and prices are fixed, production is controlled, and
profits managed both as to their amount and as to their
uses, all the important powers of the rulers of business
have been collectivized. The business executive becomes,
if these powers are honestly and effectively used in the
general interest, virtually a salaried manager. Business
and finance are no more ready to lose their property by
this roundabout route than they are to lose it by outright
confiscation. They will struggle, both to prevent and to
circumvent after it is established, either an attempt to
enforce complete competition or an attempt to regulate
monopoly in the interest of the masses.

It is unlikely that any serious effort of the sort will be
made under the present administration, since it allowed
the critical moment to slip. The virtue of the New Deal
will probably be seen, in the light of history, not as successful social planning, but as a step in the educational
process which is necessary if the workers, the farmers
and the professional and white-collar classes are ever to
become sufficiently mobilized and conscious enough of a
program so that they can engage in successful social planning. It has already helped to pose issues, to organize the
struggle about essential problems, to sift people into
groups according to their real interests. This process will
become intensified if revival proceeds, whether by the
temporary victory of profit-making through the creation
of scarcity and the prolongation of unemployment, or
through an inflationary boom. Its lessons will return,
doubly reënforced, in the next depression. Sooner or later,
if not under the present administration, then in a suc-

ceeding one, if not in the next depression, then after several more depressions, a serious and informed attempt at social planning is certain to be made. The classes which live chiefly by the earnings of their daily work will become better organized and more conscious of what it is necessary to do in order to realize the possible benefits of industrial civilization.

This prediction is justified by the basic dilemma of capitalism. Either it must surrender to social planning or else repeat the mistakes and perpetuate the rigidities which lead a badly planned industrial society into crisis. The recurrence of crisis undermines the prestige of its leaders, repeatedly injures its morale. Even at the beginning of the Roosevelt administration, capitalism was forced, by the effort at self-preservation, to grant to farmers, labor and consumers, at least some verbal rights in the law. It was forced to do so, not because any of these classes held a pistol at its head, but because it was frightened by its own internal collapse. Its leaders saw momentarily that unless more purchasing power was distributed, there would be no more profits. After it recovered from its scare, capitalism tried to take back what it had given, but a breach had been cut in the walls. It had made a beginning of the necessary concessions to the forces which had arisen from its failure. Next time those forces may be better prepared, and more substantial concessions may be made. In so far as they are not made, business travels the way to more crises and more loss of morale.

Capitalism will, consciously, fight hard against the drift to socialism. It is, for the moment, the most highly organized force, with the most resources at its command. Its opponents, though potentially more powerful and far more numerous, do not yet understand fully what the battle is about, and are engaged only in a formless guerrilla warfare. Yet modern capitalism is fighting a rearguard action; the more it succeeds in saving itself, the further it must retreat. Every time it advances, it invites a rout. The territory in which it now finds itself is fundamentally hostile. By one route or another it must eventually retire and leave the field to collectivism. Just as feudalism was compelled in the end to give way to the rise of the middle classes and capitalism, so capitalism must in the end give way to the rise of the working classes and socialism.

4. SOCIALISM, COMMUNISM OR FASCISM?

In every advanced capitalistic nation, a movement to control capitalism in the popular interest has arisen. It has social and political expressions—unions, political parties, often consumer-protective movements as well, usually in the form of consumers' coöperatives. In most older countries this movement has been called socialistic; but whatever it is called, the movement as a whole seldom sets before itself the task of the complete and sudden abolition of capitalism. Only a small minority in the vanguard has a thorough social philosophy; most of the constituent bodies and the rank and file, whatever the principles to which they formally subscribe, aim chiefly to make tangible gains in the present, to restrict and regulate the practices of capitalism. No Socialist or labor party in any country has ever yet established complete socialism; these parties merely mobilize the protest against the more uncomfortable results of the capitalist régime, sponsor reformist legislation, seek their aims within the boundaries of constitutionality, and reject violent revolution. They are inveterate compromisers, and fight a running skirmish with capitalism without ever seeking a decisive battle.

In the United States the Socialist party as such has never been powerful; it declined in influence after the United States entered the War; it does not seem likely ever to win broad popular support. Nevertheless the sort of agitation undertaken by socialist parties abroad has been carried on here by other groups; social and reformist legislation has had a wide adherence, there have been minor parties devoted to labor legislation, the trade-union movement has long existed and now at last bids fair to be more powerful than before. President Roosevelt himself mobilized a good deal of this vaguely radical opinion before he took office and just afterward, and his legislative achievements can be compared favorably with those of socialist prime ministers in other countries—socialist statesmen, that is, who have tried to moderate capitalism without abolishing it.

It is entirely possible that political realignments will take place in this country leading to the formation of a party having some real power, and avowedly hostile to the worst practices of capitalism. Such a party would safeguard the rights of organized labor, seek regulatory legislation of various kinds, and try to extend public ownership. On account of the growth of the ideas of social planning, it might even attack capitalism at more significant points than older socialist parties have done. The rise of a social reformist movement of this kind, using constitutional and elective means to accomplish its

results, seems almost a pre-determined accompaniment of
the twilight of capitalism. It is most unlikely that a
nation unready for this sort of development would be
ready for more drastic action, or that it would leap over
the more moderate proposals to embrace the more extreme
ones.

The function of such a movement is conceived by its
intellectual leaders as a gradual substitution of socialism
for capitalism by peaceful and constitutional methods.
Just conceivably it may do this in a nation sufficiently
homogeneous, orderly and law-abiding in its habits, and
without powerful capitalist classes. Nobody can deny
that socialist movements have made appreciable progress,
for instance, in the Scandinavian nations, and that they
may make more without precipitating actual civil war.
In the leading industrial nations, however, where the
forces of finance capitalism are highly concentrated and
wield immense power, Socialist parties habitually encoun-
ter more difficulty. It takes years to mobilize a secure
electoral majority for socialism; large sections of the
population, particularly among the small business men,
white-collar employees and farmers, are restrained from
adherence by their own hopes of individual advancement,
by the persistence of the old climate of opinion in the
press, the educational system and other elements of culture, and by skillful propaganda. Without a secure, instructed and resolute majority in the legislative bodies,
Socialist parties cannot change the essentials of a profit
system. They can tax, they can regulate, they can adopt
all sorts of measures which burden the profit-makers for
the relief of the exploited in one way or another; but they
cannot administer the machinery of production and dis-

tribution upon the efficient use of which any growth of the total material welfare depends. They continually arouse hopes which they are unable to satisfy; they keep the natural struggle against capitalism in solution without being able to bring it to a successful issue.

Such a movement is not without a function. It serves gradually to educate opinion, to provide a rallying point for those who want change. It carries a constant challenge to the defects of capitalism and thus puts pressure upon it to make whatever internal reforms it can. It thus contributes to the historical development of the passing order. Gradually it builds up new loyalties, and provides a medium for leaders outside the service of profit-making enterprises. A further mobilization of this type of movement in the United States would serve to link the historical tradition of democracy and the early promise of American life to the changes which must be made in the future if democracy and opportunity are to have any scope in an industrial civilization, and if large sections of the people are to be secure even in the exercise of the right to life.

There is, however, a danger for a movement of this kind if it lives too long before facing the crucial issue and accomplishing its main purpose. This it is bound to do as long as capitalism remains strong enough to reign. After it grows into an established institution it develops vested interests. Since it is unable to bring about socialism, it instinctively protects its interests by making terms with capitalism. It gradually merges itself into capitalist culture. The long list of Socialist and labor leaders who have become turncoats is a commentary, not so much on the frailty of human character as on the tendency of a specifically revolutionary organization to disintegrate if revolution is too long postponed. An old Socialist movement which is still a minority in a dominant and even moderately successful capitalist nation is like an army encamped for years in a hostile country; it gradually ceases to fight, it intermarries with the neighbors and disappears among the alien population. If it does not rule it must give way. It is absorbed by the native culture.

The failure of Socialist movements up to the present in establishing socialism by constitutional means has naturally given rise to more radical groups and parties who openly proclaim a belief in sudden and violent revolution. Chief among these is the Communist, which rests on the historical prestige of the success of the Communists in the Russian revolution. As capitalism declines, will the masses therefore turn to the leadership of the Communists, and, instructed by them, rise in successful revolt against the old system? They have not done so, in any advanced capitalist nation; there is little sign at present that they will do so in the United States, and the logic of history is against the probability that a revolution will occur in this way.

A revolutionary movement which avoids the dangers of becoming an established institution with vested interests under capitalism, which never compromises, which openly declares the inevitability of violence and civil war, must of necessity remain a minority until after a revolutionary crisis has already begun. In so far as it grows in numbers, it must lost its fighting edge. It attacks and alienates most of the leaders and organizations to which the oppressed naturally gravitate for immediate and possible action as long as the old régime lasts. It outrages the traditional loyalties and beliefs of the masses. It invites suppression, the moment it becomes large enough to be dangerous. Its appeal, if not to zealots, is at least to intellectual giants and moral heroes. Such an appeal succeeds best where a crisis of conflict is in existence; Communists sometimes gain the leadership of strikes. But it wanes when the crisis simmers down; Communists rarely dominate unions which engage in collective bargaining and maintain successful relations with employers.

In order to preserve its discipline and its purity a Communist party must act like a strict religious body, it must enforce the adherence of members to the doctrines which it considers orthodox, it must be rigorous, it must discourage new ideas not already contained in its literature, it must eschew experiment and opportunism. It suffers continually from factions and divisions, from theoretical debate, from the mistakes of inadequate personnel, from jealousy and careerism and empty formulas disguised as defense of the faith. As long as the river of history is not foaming through revolutionary crisis, it swims against the current. The fact that after the immense dislocations and discontent of four years of depression, the Communist Party of the U. S. A. proudly boasted, in the spring of 1934, of a membership of 25,000 is significant of these difficulties.

The critical periods of social revolutions, in which shifts of power are actually registered, are, as we have seen, seldom begun by the accession to power of conscious revolutionaries. They are not accomplished by violent revolts or *coups d'état*. They begin by reforms undertaken by the ruling powers themselves, and by the coming to power of moderates who often give lip-service to the old régime. The rôle of the extremists is played later in the process, after the old régime has virtually given up because of incompetence, and after the moderates in turn have proved their incapacity to secure the welfare of the people. When a revolutionary crisis is at white heat, a small minority of determined revolutionaries can sometimes achieve the leadership of the mobile masses, as they did in Russia in the fall of 1917. But, even there, they did not and could not come to power until after Tsarism had vanished and the moderates had failed. The rôle of Communist or similar parties in future revolutions will be played at a late stage in the proceedings, if at all. In the meantime they are likely to remain agitational minorities, useful in stirring up action and opinion, but impotent to achieve their announced aim. Their vigor in denouncing the impotence and the "treachery" to the revolutionary cause of all other groups on the left does not signify that they themselves have any greater chance of immediate success.

Another type of movement, unforeseen by Marx or other prophets of Socialist revolution, has recently appeared and grown to power in at least two countries. Fascism in Italy and Nazism in Germany have upset the old forms of government, but have not produced socialism. What is the possibility of Fascism in the United States? What are its characteristics, on what does it thrive, and what is likely to be its future?

Fascist groups begin like true revolutionary movements. They mobilize existing discontent among the masses; they try to win the workers, the unemployed, and the small business men who are gradually losing status in competition with big business and suffer especially in industrial crises and financial disorders, whether of inflation or deflation. They appeal particularly to ex-soldiers and the youth. They promise social justice in vague terms. In so far as they have a declared program, it consists in the overthrow of parliamentary democracy because of its incompetence and corruption, the establishment of personal leadership or dictatorship of a single man, and the government of industry by corporations, in which labor and capital theoretically coöperate for the general good. Their chief mark of distinction from the socialistic parties is that they aim to suppress the class struggle and all the workers' agencies formed to carry it on. They oppose even strikes for immediate improvement of the workers' condition.

The aims of Fascist movements, however, are seldom clearly stated and often involve logical contradictions. They claim to be anti-capitalistic; they are likely at the beginning to denounce bankers and talk much of the iniquity of interest. At the same time they take care not to antagonize the leading capitalists and do not propose to confiscate private property in the means of production. They are much more intent upon gaining adherents than upon achieving a thorough reorganization of the industrial system. In doing so they use every demagogic method which occurs to them. They deliberately play down the reason and seek to inflame prejudices and passions. This may be the result of unscrupulousness, or it may be a sincere emotional muddle-headedness. At any rate, they refurbish any traditional slogan or hatred which may serve their temporary purposes. One of the chief of these, in both Italy and Germany, is exclusive nationalism, dressed up in all the panoply of loyalty to ancient tradition, race and aggressive warfare. Brute strength, glory, unwavering loyalty, and the demand for a forced national unity by the suppression of all dissidents, are their trump cards. Dissatisfaction with the operation of capitalism is transmuted into hatred of some group of scapegoats such as Jews or foreigners or traditional labor leaders.

When such a movement becomes large enough to be threatening, it is likely to be subsidized by industrial and financial interests, who fear what it may do if they do not exercise some restraint over it, and also see in it a weapon against the established labor movement. Unless it were so subsidized, it probably would fade out in time before the strength of more stable organizations. And the question whether it will be subsidized or not is undoubtedly dependent upon the power of the traditional labor organizations. If reactionary capitalist groups fear labor enough, they will seize upon an incipient Fascist movement as a means of defense. This happened both in Italy and Germany.

When a Fascist movement gets funds in this way, it can use all the modern technique of propaganda and organization. It can dramatize itself, militarize the unemployed and the ex-soldiers, feeding them, uniforming and drilling them, and using them to harass and terrorize its enemies. It can spread its units far and wide, support a press, and build a real mass organization. Eventually it can control elections, and by a combination of thuggery and intrigue establish itself in power. Then comes the dictatorship of its leader, the outlawing of political democracy and of all opposed or rival groups, the murder or exile of all potential leaders whom it cannot torture or terrorize into submission. Its principal tangible achievement is the destruction of all labor unions and socialistic political movements, and the suppression of strikes and collective bargaining. The owners and managers of industry it leaves virtually undisturbed, except by the taxes which it has to levy in order to make political places for its spoilsmen, and to relieve or make work for the unemployed.

Unlike the Communist parties, the Fascist parties are not swimming against the current in their climb to power. Their unscrupulous attitude enables them to make use of every easy appeal, regardless of whether that appeal would compromise their declared aims or not. But the result is that, once they get power, their pretended ardor for a change in the economic system disappears. In spite of all talk about "national socialism" or the "corporative state" or "planning," these activities come to very little. The reason is that the profit system is left intact, while all the social forces which might have been called in to check or modify it, such as mass political parties, unions or even free liberal criticism, are abolished. Fascism in power still tolerates the fundamental contradictions of capitalism. The natural forces of protest have either been misled into reaction or have been temporarily crushed. But it cannot permanently keep them so, because it cannot solve the economic problem. Indeed, its aggressive nationalism aggravates that problem at one of the crucial points. If the old radical organizations do not survive underground and eventually come back, a split is bound to take place some time within the ruling organization itself, about the self-same issues which previously divided society. Scapegoats, emotional furore, trappings, bold words, brutality toward the defenseless and all the rest will not suffice to perpetuate an artificial and non-functional unity. Essentially, both the Italian and the German brands of Fascism represent a reaction, a swing to the right during a revolutionary period. To many reasonable and humane persons, they seem one of the most repulsive spasms of a dying capitalism.

Anyone can see with half an eye that many of the raw materials of Fascism are lying about within the United States. We have the suffering ranks of unemployed and veterans and farmers, the dwindling numbers of small business men fighting a losing battle against monopoly, the tradition of bumptious nationalism, the racial and religious prejudices, the tendency to violence and brutality, the proneness to organize about vague and mystical slogans. Nothing has been done to the victims of Mussolini or Hitler which is more revolting than the cruelty practiced by lynching mobs in the United States; the lawless suppression of strikes and radicals by violence is an old habit in this country, whether through the organization of Vigilantes, citizens' committees and veterans, or through the hiring of gunmen. We have a much larger class of professional gangsters accustomed to living by murder than had either Italy or Germany, and these would undoubtedly be employed by such a movement. We have seen the Ku Klux Klan—an incipient Fascist movement if there ever was one; we now have our many-colored shirt organizations in imitation of the black and brown shirts; we have Huey Long, who is an almost perfect American counterpart of Hitler in his early stages.

We have the most highly developed machinery for delusive propaganda in the world.

There are, of course, certain offsets. Our tradition of democracy and equality is still much stronger than it ever was in Germany or Italy. We are not suffering from the feeling of national inferiority resulting from defeat in battle, which has been a powerful factor in both of those nations. The attempt to blame our troubles on foreign nations or on the lack of sufficient territory does not carry much conviction. There is another offset which may carry weight with the more intelligent. President Roosevelt in his administration of the New Deal has really established something much like the "corporative state," which is the acknowledged Fascist aim in the control of industry. It is based on the theory of coöperation between controlled capital and labor organized by industries, and, here as in the foreign models, capital keeps the actual power. The independent labor movement, it is true, has not been destroyed here or forbidden to strike, but then we have not actually had an effective labor movement in most of the great industries, and the industrialists have done their best to keep one from growing. What such an organization of our economic life can do is now in the process of being tested. We are by way of trying out the economics of Fascism without having suffered all its social or political ravages. If it succeeds, as is most improbable, we shall not have to undergo the unpleasantness of the political dictatorship. If it does not succeed, and the reasons for its non-success are sufficiently well understood, any American Fascist movement would have to think up a new economic philosophy. It is possible that the New Deal is a relatively painless inoculation against Fascism.

If, however, there develops a strong labor and socialist movement, if there are great strikes, if capitalists see a really serious menace to their power, an attempt to foster a national Fascism in some American form will almost surely be made. No one can predict that it will not for a time hold power. What can be predicted with certainty is that it will not solve the problem of producing and distributing plenty.

No one of the three most prominent organized movements for social change therefore holds a promise of success in the near future. Socialist or reformist activity is not likely soon to achieve major alterations in capitalism. Communism is not likely to abolish capitalism until after a revolutionary crisis has begun in some other way. A Fascist movement may grow and may gain political supremacy, but it will be a temporary and repulsive reaction, not a solution of anything.

A further possibility which might affect the fortunes of all three movements is another major war. The fear of war is greater to-day than for many years. Its political results are almost incalculable, except that it speeds political changes. The last one went far to kill the only orthodox socialist movement in the United States; it eventually brought a social revolution in Russia; it was succeeded by swings of the pendulum both to the right and to the left in most other great nations. The economic results of war we know only too well. It brings, at first, the artificial stimulus needed to give a good counterfeit of prosperity. That is usually followed by inflation, and after the war, an intense deflationary crisis in due time ensues. It is not at all unlikely that, after another major war, revolt against capitalism would become so general that a genuinely revolutionary crisis would begin, even in the United States. It may be that this is the way capitalism will enter upon its final phase. Certainly the forces of big industry and finance can fail to avoid war only at their peril. But the economic nationalism which they foster makes it always possible.

5. DOES THE PATTERN FIT?

At the beginning of this book, it was set forth that the course of recent events in the United States would be examined to see if they fitted into the broad historical pattern of social revolution. This would be a way to try the meaning of current history. As a preliminary to this test, the nature of social revolution itself was first examined. It was conceived as a long historical process, occupying decades or even a century, in which evolutionary change plays an important part. It was not thought of merely as a violent overturn of political power, or as the victory of a mob engaging in riots. Rather it develops by the route, first of basic changes in the way of conducting affairs, arising largely from technical innovations and new ways of organizing production and exchange. These changes are accompanied by new class alignments and shifts of potential power. The old forms of rulership become ill adapted to the new situation; the traditional rulers, acting according to old principles, fail to manage the new institutions expertly. Thus class oppression comes into being, almost unconsciously. The classes which suffer protest against specific evils and injustices. The classes holding power sternly and confidently repress discontent. At this stage the crisis of the revolution is not near. But eventually the suppressed classes begin to rise; the changing institutions convey more power into their hands, reforms are achieved which register that power.

The intellectuals play a large part in revealing the incompetence of the old régime, in ridiculing its corruption, in shifting loyalties to new ideas and leaders. There is a ferment of opinion which prepares the way for a change. People in general lose confidence in the old régime. The old rulers begin to split and lose faith in themselves. Foretastes of a decisive issue come in the form of periods in which the old order temporarily gives way because of its own incompetence, and these periods are accompanied perhaps by unsuccessful rebellion. Eventually there arrives the revolutionary crisis, marked by a simultaneous breakdown of the old order and the arrival of the new classes at the point where they are prepared to take over the control. This is what is usually called "the revolution." After the shift in power occurs, there may be significant violence as the revolution is defended; there are likely to be swings of the pendulum to left and perhaps back again, but in the end a new type of control is established which gives scope to the new institutions and establishes the rule of the new classes.

Let us now look back over our account of what has happened and is likely soon to happen in order to see if the pattern fits, and, if so, at what stage of the revolutionary process we now find ourselves.

1. *Basic Changes*. Profound changes in the way of

conducting our affairs have indeed occurred. There has been an amazing technical development which makes it theoretically possible, for the first time in history, to increase the production of goods with extreme rapidity, and to produce enough to give everyone comparative abundance. At the same time, the technical changes have brought about a dominance of our whole life by machine industry, an interweaving of the interest of all with the industrial complex. And they have facilitated, under a capitalist order, the growth of large enterprises and the concentration of power over them among comparatively few. Such a civilization requires, for its successful operation, a high degree of flexibility and an intricate adjustment of economic factors like prices, wages, investment and credit. But the capitalist organization of industry and finance increases the rigidity of some of these factors at the very time when greater flexibility is needed. It fails to make the necessary adjustments. The management of economic processes according to the hope of private profits throws the whole machine out of gear and tends to produce severe crises. As a result, the possibilities of abundance are not realized; many are reduced to poverty. The first part of the revolutionary pattern thus fits like a glove.

2. *Class Alignments.* These technical and institutional changes have also brought important shifts and alignments of classes. Our civilization has become predominantly industrial and urban. The farmer is largely at the mercy of the behavior of machine industry. The small, independent proprietors in the towns, once the backbone of our culture, are rapidly losing status. Wealth and real economic power is concentrated in a few hands. The

chance to rise by independent ownership and management
is disappearing. Industrial wage-earners have become a
large and important class. Almost equally important are
the white-collar employees. The place of the old business
enterpriser is mainly taken by technical and professional
men. Inefficiency in the operation of the system under
the old rules and rulers, and the crises to which it leads,
cause misery to farmers, wage-earners, white-collar employees, technical and professional men. Even the capitalist classes themselves are divided by a severe crisis. The
majority of legal owners who have no part in management—the recipients of dividends and the small investors
in securities—suffer much more than those at the center
of the system, the insiders in banks and industries who
keep on paying themselves high salaries and bonuses. All
the oppressed classes show signs of becoming restive.
For years there have been agrarian and labor movements
making specific protests and seeking specific concessions.
Both of these have recently become much more active,
and there are also increasing signs of discontent among
the classes socially closer to the rulers of industry—the
white-collar employees and professional men. The pattern begins to fit as to class alignment and opposition of
interests.

3. *Activity of Intellectuals and Ferment of Ideas.* Already the more sensitive of the writers and teachers have,
with surprising unanimity, ceased celebrating the virtues
of the old order and embroidering its traditions, but
rather have been busy exposing its failures and corrup-
tions and ridiculing many of its leading figures. Of
course they are by no means unanimous on programs for
the future. Intellectuals never are, in any revolutionary

period. And so far it is only a few of the leaders among the creative artists and the learned professions who have definitely and consciously shifted their loyalties to a new type of social order or a new class. Most of the ferment in political and economic ideas is concerned with partial reforms, with fancy panaceas and economic gadgets. The great instruments of propaganda—the press, the radio, the devices of advertising, the legislative assemblies—are still pretty firmly under the control of the old ruling class and its ideas. Employees who are concerned in operating these publicity machines, it is true, do not all feel great faith in their activities or loyalty to the principles they are forced to express.

The intellectual ferment is apparently still in its early stages. Its general direction is significant; new leading ideas which challenge the old, like social planning as opposed to automatic regulation through self-interest, are beginning to take form. They have changed the opinions and attitudes of small numbers of persons in key positions. But they are far from being understood by the general public. With any revival of business activity, and a speeding up of capitalist propaganda, popular opinion is likely to lapse into habitual attitudes, old hopes of advance under capitalism will come to life, and the customary process of shutting the mind to any drastic proposal if it is called by a bad name will return. Especially the white-collar and small-salaried classes are likely to be very slow in turning to any alliance with wage-earners or in holding any opinions which are displeasing to the financial and industrial powers.

By this test, it would appear that a revolutionary period has begun, but it is still far from its climax.

4. *Reforms Which Strengthen New Classes.* The oppressed classes have taken a step up in status, through the legal recognition given them in the recovery program. This, it is true, has not yet led to much tangible result, except in so far as it has stimulated the organization of unions and has strengthened collective bargaining—an advance made long ago in most other industrial nations. Nevertheless, even an empty legal grant of power is an important symbol, a toe-hold which can lead to another step up. There are now in the government machinery members of the professional and intellectual classes who are concerned with collecting and putting together the information necessary for social planning, and with making that information of use in the regulation of industry. An obligation to make national appropriations to feed the unemployed has been recognized. The classes who would naturally assume power during a crisis are better mobilized than before, and their leaders are being educated in the problems they would have to face. The upward climb of the workers has begun, though it is far from completion.

5. *The Revolutionary Crisis.* It is clear that we are not now in the critical period of revolution. What the depression of the thirties gave us was an excellent foretaste, however, of the aspect that crisis will assume if it does come. The capitalist system ran into grave difficulties, not because of any opposition on the part of radical enemies, not because of the threat of a revolutionary movement, but on account of the natural behavior of the ruling classes themselves. In no capitalist country were the workers exercising real power over the operation of the system, least of all in the United States, where the

crash was the heaviest. Capitalism came closer to a complete collapse than it ever has done before, and did so because of the incompetence of its rulers to govern a complex industrial civilization. At the bottom of the curve it was on the point of rout. The ruling classes were thoroughly frightened; their morale was at a low ebb. They simply did not know what to do next, and many of them acknowledged it.

This breakdown was accompanied by a ferment of protests and of new ideas. If, at this moment, there had been a large and disciplined movement with a coördinated program for social planning, if the opinion of intellectual leaders and of the general public had been sufficiently prepared in previous years, it is quite conceivable that a real shift in power would have begun. As it was, the candidate who promised a New Deal obtained powerful support, and most of the people would have sanctioned almost anything he wished to propose. The result was for a time mistaken by many observers for an incipient revolution. One of the principal reasons why it was not a revolution was that neither the President nor his advisers nor the people in general were mentally prepared to exercise real power over industry. They handed the system back to the old rulers, with enough help so that they were able to carry on. One of the two necessary factors of a revolutionary crisis was in large measure present—the cracking of the old régime from within—but the other was not. The rising classes were not prepared to take its place. Even so there had to be a gesture toward calling them in to share power.

Capitalism comes out of this crisis the victor, but in the long run weaker both physically and morally. Some time in the future—perhaps not for another generation or two—there is likely to occur another equally serious breakdown of capitalism. If by that time the ferment of ideas has done its work and the rising classes have attained sufficient status and confidence, the two essential ingredients of the revolutionary mixture will be present. If the incompetence of the rulers and their lack of faith in themselves has proceeded far enough, they will either call in representatives of social planning to run industry, or they will retire before a popular demand that new ideas be applied. In such a crisis the resistance that they are ordinarily able to oppose to socialist movements will be immensely weakened. They will themselves be helpless before the vanishing of their wealth. They will have lost popular loyalty. The command of the propaganda machinery by which they are ordinarily able to divide, divert and mislead their natural opponents will disappear, because they will not have the money to pay for it, or to use for compensating their retainers and bribing their weaker enemies. At such a time, probably by peaceful and possibly even by constitutional means, the control of production and exchange may easily pass to one of the more moderate movements opposed to the profit system.

After that, who knows what will happen? It would be pleasant to be able to predict that those who accede to power will be at once wise, efficient and resolute, that the old ruling classes will gracefully bow to the inevitable, that neither violence nor civil war will follow, that a system of socialized planning will smoothly come into being, which almost at once will realize all the beneficent possibilities of a technical civilization. If all this does occur so painlessly, it will be the first time in history that a social revolution has been completed with neatness and dispatch. What is much more likely is that there will be a prolonged period of turmoil and uncertainty, that the moderates will ingloriously fail, that there will be fighting, swings to the left and reaction. It will be a period of terrible discomfort, of mingled heroism and meanness, of the clumsy effort of human beings slowly to adjust themselves to the new conditions of life. Eventually the outcome will be the final disappearance of government by private profit-makers over the means of production, a chance for social management to learn its task by experience. This will not be Utopia. The perfect society has never yet resulted from a revolution. The process will simply be the adjustment of mankind to a new phase, made necessary by its own evolution. The new society will consist of men and women in a new bond of comradeship setting forth on still another voyage to the unknown.

SELECTED BIBLIOGRAPHY

PART I

ADAMS, BROOKS. Theory of Social Revolutions. The Macmillan Company. 1913.

BEARD, CHARLES and MARY. The Rise of American Civilization. The Macmillan Company. 1927.

EDWARDS, LYFORD P. The Natural History of Revolution. University of Chicago Press. 1927.

LENIN, V. I. The State and Revolution. International Publishers. 1932.

LENIN, V. I. The Threatening Catastrophe and How to Fight It. International Publishers. 1932.

MARX, KARL, and ENGELS, FRIEDRICH. The Communist Manifesto.

OGBURN, WILLIAM F. Social Change. B. W. Huebsch. 1922.

TAWNEY, RICHARD H. Religion and the Rise of Capitalism. Harcourt, Brace & Co. 1926.

TROTSKY, LEON. History of the Russian Revolution. Simon and Schuster. 1933.

WHITE, ANDREW DICKSON. Fiat Money Inflation in France. D. Appleton-Century. 1933.

PART II

ANGELL, JAMES W. Financial Foreign Policy of the United States. Council on Foreign Relations. 1933.

BAKER, ELIZABETH FAULKNER. Displacement of Men by Machines. Columbia University Press. 1933.

BERLE, ADOLPH A., and MEANS, GARDINER C. The Modern

305

Corporation and Private Property. The Macmillan Company. 1933.

BRADY, ROBERT A. The Rationalization Movement in German Industry. University of California Press. 1933.

BONN, M. J. The Crisis of Capitalism in America. The John Day Company. 1932.

BURNS, ARTHUR F. Production Trends in the United States Since 1870. National Bureau of Economic Research. 1934.

CHAMBERLIN, EDWARD. The Theory of Monopolistic Competition. Harvard University Press. 1933.

CLARK, EVANS, and Others. The Internal Debts of the United States. The Macmillan Company. 1933.

CHASE, STUART. The Economy of Abundance. The Macmillan Company. 1934.

CLARK, JOHN MAURICE. Strategic Factors in Business Cycles. National Bureau of Economic Research. 1934.

COLE, G. D. H. A Guide Through World Chaos. Alfred A. Knopf. 1932.

DOUGLAS, PAUL H., and DIRECTOR, AARON. The Problem of Unemployment. The Macmillan Company. 1931.

HOBSON, J. A. Poverty in Plenty. The Macmillan Company. 1931.

LAIDLER, HARRY W. Concentration in American Industry. Thomas Y. Crowell. 1931.

LOWENTHAL, MAX. The Investor Pays. Alfred A. Knopf. 1933.

MILLS, FREDERICK C. Economic Tendencies in the United States. National Bureau of Economic Research. 1932.

The President's Committee. Recent Social Trends. McGraw-Hill. 1933.

TUGWELL, REXFORD GUY. The Industrial Discipline. Columbia University Press. 1933.

VEBLEN, THORSTEIN. The Theory of Business Enterprise. Charles Scribner's Sons. 1920.

PART III

BEARD, CHARLES A., Editor. America Faces the Future. The Macmillan Company. 1931.

BEARD, CHARLES A., and SMITH, GEORGE H. E. The Future Comes. The Macmillan Company. 1933.

DAHLBERG, ARTHUR. Jobs, Machines and Capitalism. The Macmillan Company. 1932.

DEARING, CHARLES L., and Others. The A. B. C. of the N. R. A. The Brookings Institution. 1934.

Establishment of a National Economic Council. (Hearings before a subcommittee of the Committee on Manufacture, U. S. Senate, 72nd Congress, on S 6215, 71st Congress.)

FLANDERS, RALPH L. Taming Our Machines. Richard R. Smith. 1931.

JONES, BASSETT. Debt and Production. The John Day Company. 1933.

KUZNETS, SIMON. National Income, 1929-1932. National Bureau of Economic Research. (Bulletin) January 26, 1934.

LAING, GRAHAM A. Towards Technocracy. Angelus Press, 1933.

MILLS, FREDERICK C. Changes in Physical Production, Industrial Productivity and Manufacturing Costs, 1927-1932. National Bureau of Economic Research. (Bulletin) February 20, 1933.

National City Bank. Bulletin. March, 1934.

OGBURN, W. F., Editor. Social Change and the New Deal. University of Chicago Press. 1934.

ROOSEVELT, FRANKLIN D. On Our Way. The John Day Company. 1934.

SCOTT, HOWARD and Others. Introduction to Technocracy. The John Day Company. 1933.

STRACHEY, JOHN. The Coming Struggle for Power. Covici-Friede. 1933.

TERBORGH, GEORGE. Price Control Devices in N. R. A. Codes. The Brookings Institution. 1934.

U. S. Department of Agriculture. Agricultural Adjustment. 1934.

INDEX

Adams, John, 44.
Agricultural Adjustment Administration, 212, 238, 240.
Agriculture, 209.
Agriculture, Department of, 208.
A. F. of L., 221, 232.
American Revolution, 5, 16, 30, 139.
American Statistical Association, 231.
Anschluss, 177.
Antoinette, Marie, 46.
Automobiles, 84, 155.

Balance of trade, favorable, 143.
Bank holiday (U. S.), 183.
Bank loans, 128.
Bank of United States, 202.
Bank money, 206.
Banks, 180, 255.
Bankers Trust Company, 112.
Barter, 188.
Bastille, 46.
Beard, Charles A., 139, 192.
Berlin-Bagdad Railway, 142.
Bible, the, 24, 28.
Big business, 108.
Black bill, 214.
Blue Eagle, 224.
Board of Trade and Economy, 34.
Bolsheviks, 16, 58.
Bonbright, James C., 109.
Bonus March, 185.
Boston Massacre, 40.
Boston Tea Party, 40.
Boycott, 36, 40.
Brain trust, 206, 258.
Brest-Litvosk, 63.

Brinton, Clarence Crane, 50.
Burgesses, House of, 32.
Burns, Arthur F., 77.
Butler, President, 80.

Capital equipment, 83.
Capital, deflation of, 118.
Capital, export of, 141.
Capital goods, 83.
Capitalism, collapse of, 11.
Capitalism, 24, 36, 59, 147.
Carlyle, 20.
Carolina, 32, 43.
Central Statistical Board, 229.
Centralization, 220.
Charles I, 23, 28, 46, 68.
Chartist movement, 53.
Chase National Bank, 112, 202.
Chicago University, 228.
Civilian Conservation Corps, 247.
Civil War, 18, 21, 70.
Civil War (Russian), 63.
Civil War (U. S.), 53.
Civil Works Authority, 170, 247.
Clark, J. M., 84.
Classes, shift of, 67, 298.
Clerical and professional workers, 99.
Coal, 132, 135, 161.
Collective bargaining, 216.
Columbia University, 80, 191.
Columbus, 4.
Committees of Correspondence, 41.
"Common Sense," 42.
Commonwealth, 23.
Communism, 287.
Communists, 187.
Community, size of, 146.

Company unions, 221, 233.
Competition, 115, 236.
Concord, 41.
Conference for Progressive Labor Action, 187.
Constitutional Convention, 44.
Constitutional Democrats, 57.
Constituent Assembly, 57.
Continental Congresses, 41.
Construction industry, 123, 154, 167.
Consumer, 216.
Consumers' goods, 83.
Consumers' Advisory Board, 227, 235.
Corporation, the, 110.
Corporations, control of, 112.
Cotton, 240.
Cotton option plan, 212.
Cotton textile code, 223.
Credit, 82.
Credit policy, 180.
Credit theory, 189.
Creditanstalt, 177.
Cromwell, 23, 28.
Cromwells, 26, 42.
Cuba, 15.
Customs union, German-Austrian, 176.

Daily Worker, The, 7.
Dawes Plan, 144.
Day-Persons index, 76.
Debt, 119, 128, 249.
Debtors, 32, 35, 36, 39.
Decentralization, 97, 104, 220.
Declaration of Independence, 39, 139.
Declining industries, 82.
Deflation, 39.
Demand and supply, 116.
Demand, inelastic, 131.
Deposit insurance, 255.
Determinism, 19.
Devaluation, 245.

Dickens, 20.
Domestic allotment plan, 211.
Domestic and personal service workers, 99.
Dostoevsky, 55.
Drifters, 186.
Duma, 55.
Durable goods, 82, 84.
Dutch West India Company, 31.

East India Company, 40.
Eatons, 42.
Economic government, 218.
Edwards, Lyford P., 17, 20.
Eighteenth Amendment, 37.
Elizabeth, 28.
Employee representation plans, 233.
Employees, 100, 149.
Employers, 100.
Employers associations, 215.
Employment, shifting, 91.
Employment, factory, 250.
Encyclopædists, 46, 51.
Endicotts, 42.
Enterpriser, 106.
Equilibrium, social, 194.
Establishments, size of, 107.
Estates General, 47.
Evolution vs. Revolution, 18.
Executive Council, 229.
Extremists, 69.
Ezekiel, Mordecai, 208.

Factory workers, 99.
Farm Credit Administration, 217.
Farm mortgage debt, 121.
Farmers, 98, 134.
Fascism, 199, 206, 289.
Federal Employment Service, 217.
Federal Farm Board, 160.
Federal Reserve Bank, 180, 275.
Federal Reserve System, 157, 205, 255.
Fisher, Irving, 157.

Flexibility, requirement for, 93.
Food and Drugs Act, 270.
Ford, Henry, 268.
Ford Motor Company, 112.
Foreclosure, 186.
Foreign trade, 136.
Franklin, Benjamin, 38.
Free trade, 137.
Free will, 19.
French and Indian War, 38.
French Revolution, 16, 45.
Frontier, 95.

General Electric Company, 215.
George III, 36, 39.
Georgia, 31.
Germany as debtor nation, 145.
Givens, Meredith B., 100.
Glassford, General, 185.
Gold, 141.
Gold standard, 177, 222, 243.
Governmental spending, 276.
Gradualness, 19.
Grenville, 39.
Grey, Sir Edward, 142.

Hamilton, Alexander, 140.
Hampdens, 26, 42.
Hancock, John, 37.
Hapsburgs, 142.
Henry VIII, 28.
"History of the Russian Revolution," 20, 59.
Home Owners' Loan Corporation, 217.
Hoover, 5, 153, 159, 171, 203.
Hours of work, 86, 214.
House of Lords, 29.
Housing, 246.
Huguenots, 45.
"Hundred Days," 5.
Hunger marches, 187.
Hurlin, Ralph G., 100.

Ideas, ferment of, 189.

Immigration, 95.
Income, national, 184.
Income of property, 184.
Income taxes, 163.
Industrial Revolution, 13, 76.
Industrial Advisory Board, 231.
Industry, 213.
Inelastic demand, 131.
Inflation, 32, 35, 39, 48, 212, 274, 277.
Instalment credit, 130.
Insull, 202.
Insurrection of 1905 (Russian), 55.
Intellectuals, 8, 9, 21, 41, 51, 64, 68, 107, 299.
Interest, 128.
International finance, 176.
International trade, 176.
Internationalists, 137.
Inventories, 166.
Investment, 88.

Jacksonville agreement, 161.
Jacobins, 50.
James I, 28.
James II, 23, 29.
Jefferson, 44.
Johnson, General, 228, 235.

Kaiser, the, 142.
Kautsky, 54.
Kerensky, 16, 58.
King in Council, 34.
Kreuger and Toll, 202.
Kulaks, 63.
Kuznets, Simon, 127, 175, 184.

La Follette, 154.
Labor Advisory Board, 227.
Labor government, British, 177.
Laborers, 43.
Laissez-faire, 137.
Land-leasing plan, 212.
Lausanne, 178.
Law, John, 48.

Lenin, 60, 64, 66.
Leningrad, 56.
Leningrad Soviet, 57.
Levellers, 29.
Lexington, 41.
Lions' Clubs, 168.
Locke, John, 30, 43.
London Company, 25, 31.
London Economic Conference, 244.
Lorraine, 142.
Louis IX, 45.
Louis XVI, 45, 68.
Lyon, Leverett S., 138.

Machado, President, 15.
Machines, 78.
Mail Order Association of America, 236.
Manchester School, 138.
Manufacture, laws forbidding, 34.
Manufactures, debt of, 119.
McNary-Haugen bill, 160.
Means, Gardiner C., 109.
Mellon, Secretary, 163.
Mercantilism, 139.
Marx, Karl, 14, 16, 54, 66.
Massachusetts Bay Company, 31, 33.
Michigan, 96.
Midwest Exchange, 188.
Migration, 96.
Milinkoff, 57.
Mill, John Stuart, 110.
Mills, Frederick C., 79, 83, 184, 252.
Mitchell, 202.
Mobs, 10, 19, 40.
Mobility of labor, 91.
Moderates, 69.
Monetary school, 156.
Monetary theory, 189.
Money policy, Roosevelt, 241.
Monopoly, 115.
Moratorium, banking (U. S.), 204.

Moratorium, international, 178.
Morgan, J. P. and Company, 112.
Moscow, 56.

Napoleon, 71.
National Bureau of Economic Research, 127, 175, 184.
National City Bank, 202.
National Development Association, 188.
National government, British, 177.
National income, 27.
National Industrial Recovery bill, 215, 216, 222.
National Labor Board, 233.
National Recovery Administration, 215, 226, 240, 273.
Nationalists, 137.
"Natural History of Revolution," 17, 20.
Nazism, 289.
Necessities, 82.
Necker, 47.
New Deal, the, 203, 281.
New Deal, results of, 249.
New Era, the, 153, 202.
New industries, 82.
New York, 31, 96.
New Jersey, 32, 96.
Nicholas, 68.
Non-durable goods, 84.
Norris, Senator, 256.
North Carolina, 96.

Occupations, 98.
Ogburn, William F., 228.
Output, physical, 184.
Output, limitation of, 136.
Output per man-hour, 79.
Output per wage-earner, 79.
Overbuilding, 156.
Overhead, 117.
Over-investment, 156.
Over-saving, 88.
Owners of capital, 149.

Paine, Thomas, 42, 44.
Paris Commune, 53.
Parliament, 28, 29, 39.
Paper Money, 35.
Pattern, revolutionary, 296.
Pay rolls, factory, 250.
Penn, William, 32.
Pennsylvana, 32.
Petty bourgeoisie, 99.
Pilgrims, 31, 33.
Planning, 197, 198, 259, 267, 278.
Poincaré, 142.
Population, 94.
Prediction, 265.
President's Reëmployment Agreement, 224.
Price disparities, 252, 274.
Price policy, 218.
Price provisions of codes, 235.
Price system, 192.
Production, 76, 83, 253.
Production, allocation of, 235.
Production, shifts of, 81.
"Production Trends in the United States since 1870," 77.
Productive professions, 106.
Productivity, 79.
Profits, 88, 155, 252, 267, 271.
Proletarian Revolution, 54.
Proletariat, 61.
Property qualifications, 43.
Provisional government (Russian), 57.
Public debt, 125.
Public utilities, debt of, 120.
Public works, 162, 246.
Puritan Revolution, 16, 22.
Pyms, 26, 42.

Quotas, 137, 140.

Railroads, debt of, 119.
Railroad Coördinator, 216.
Railroads, coördination of, 257.
Reaction, 70.

"Recent Social Trends," 100, 193.
Reconstruction Finance Corporation, 175, 205, 217.
Reforms, 68, 301.
Reparations, 177.
Research and Planning, Division of, 230.
Restrictions on international payments, 141.
Revival, 271.
Revolt, 20.
Revolution, sudden, 16.
Revolution, what it is, 66.
Revolution vs. Evolution, 18.
Revolutionary crisis, 69, 301.
Rigidities, 274
Rigidity, economic, 93.
Rigidity of Foreign Trade, 136.
"Rights of Man," 44.
Riots, 19.
Rogers, James Harvey, 208.
Roosevelt, Franklin D., 5, 203.
Rousseau, 46, 51.
Ruhr, the, 142.
Russian Revolution, 16, 53.

St. Petersburg, 56.
Sans culottes, 50.
Saving, 88.
Scandals, banking, 201.
Scrip, 188.
Section 7a of N. I. R. A., 215.
Securities Act, 217, 255, 270.
Semi-durable goods, 84.
Service products, 133.
Smith, Adam, 110, 138, 143.
Smoot-Hawley bill, 160.
"Social Change and the New Deal," 252.
Social Science Research Council, 196.
Socialism, 277, 283.
Socialists, 54, 187.
Sons of Liberty, 39.
Soviet Union, 199.

Soviets, 62.
Sprague, Professor, 208.
Stabilization, 160.
Stamp Act, 39.
Stamp Act Congress, 40.
Stillman, K. W., 111.
Stock market, 155, 158, 201.
Stock Exchange Act, 270.
Stockholders, 111, 113.
"Strategic Factors in Business Cycles," 84.
Super-Cabinet, 229.
Supply and demand, 116.
Supply, uncontrollable, 134.
Surplus Relief Corporation, 239, 247.
Stuarts, 26, 29.
Swope, Gerard, 215.

Taine, 20.
Tariffs, 137, 160, 165.
Taxes, 125, 276.
Tea Act of 1773, 40.
Technical change and prices, 114.
Technology, 75.
Technocracy, 191.
Technocrats, 78, 126.
Tennessee Valley Authority, 217, 256.
Terror, the, 21, 48, 64, 70.
Third Estate, 47.
Thorp, Willard, 108.
Trade and transportation workers, 99.
Trotsky, 20, 59, 62.
Tsar, 56, 142.
Tsarina, 56.
Tugwell, Rexford G., 208.
Turner, 95.

Unemployed, number of, 167, 184.
Unemployment, agricultural, 92.
Unemployment, crisis or cyclical, 89.
Unemployment insurance, 168.
Unemployment, technological, 85.
Union of Cities, 56.
United States as creditor nation, 144.
United States Chamber of Commerce, 199, 215.
Urban civilization, 103.
Urban real estate debt, 122.
Usury, 30.

Veblen, Thorstein, 192.
Velocity of credit, 206.
Violence, 13, 38, 48, 70.
Virginia, 25, 31.
Voltaire, 46.

Wage payments, 128.
Wage-earnings, 184, 250.
War, 295.
War of 1914, 140.
War debts, 177.
Warren, Professor, 208.
Warren-Pearson index, 77.
"Wealth of Nations, The," 110, 139.
Wheat, 132, 240.
White-collar workers, 99.
Wiggin, 202.
Winthrop, 42.
Working class, 53, 105.
Work sharing, 179.
Writs of Assistance, 40.

Yeoman, 25.

Zemstvos Union, 56.